SPAIN

A Musician's Journey through Time and Space

Volume I

SPAIN

A Musician's Journey through Time and Space

VOLUME I   by WALTER STARKIE

EDISLI—AT EDITIONS RENE KISTER GENEVA (SWITZERLAND)

A new age of music has been born.   Since the day Pythagoras first measured the numerical relations of the musical scale by moving a fret placed beneath a lute string, marvellous progress has been made in the art of analysing, organizing and reproducing even the most intricate musical structures.   The most recent advance has proved to be nothing short of a revolution.   When, half a century ago, at a party held in honour of Gustave Eiffel in his small apartment at the top of the Tower that bears his name, Thomas Edison demonstrated a phonograph of his invention, the first "talking machine," none of those present, neither the great French engineer nor the American inventor himself, had any inkling of the changes that queer, squeaky instrument was to bring about in the field of music.   Even today most of us fail to realize the magnitude of that upheaval.

Of all the arts music is the most abstract.   Were it not for the compelling power of rhythm, which impresses forms more or less permanently on our memory, nothing would remain of its creations.   The first musical recording machine was the human memory—imprecise and untrustworthy, but sufficiently retentive even in early times to rescue and preserve, with the aid of music, the spoken poetry of our ancestors.

Writing was invented and words ceased to vanish into thin air.   Men's thoughts were set down in writing and the literary career of humanity was launched.   Later, a system of musical notation made it possible exactly to reproduce compositions "noted" down on paper, though the interpretation of those notes left scope for a world of difference.   The *letter* lived on in the score, but the *spirit* of a great piece of music, even when perfectly realized by a master conductor or an inspired singer, died away as soon as instruments or voice fell silent, leaving behind it a haze of memories and regrets.

Those who had missed the best performances of Madame Malibran had missed them for ever, and the happy few who swore by those divine and unforgettable moments were incapable of communicating them to others.

Present-day recording techniques give lasting life to the ephemeral glory of the interpreter.   What is more, they enable him to correct and perfect his performances, to multiply and perpetuate his best moments. The work that is not a masterwork until masterfully performed can now be rendered at its best and preserved indefinitely.   This is an epoch-making event in the history of art.

Music has ceased to be a sheaf of yellowed papers read at sight by initiates, puzzled out by the profane. It stands in its entirety ready to hand, vivid and flawless, in our record libraries, just as all knowledge stands ready to hand on our bookshelves.

Hence the change that has come over our general culture.   Twentieth-century man has at his disposal not only a library enabling him to satisfy his intellectual appetites and enrich his mind, but also a "conservatory" in which the masterpieces of music may at any time be heard at their best.   In addition to that he can, if he chooses, build up what André Malraux has called a "museum without walls" containing works of painting, sculpture and architecture from all over the world in a relatively small compass thanks to photography.

The publishers of the present work feel that the time has come to combine these resources—library, concert-hall and museum—into a single instrument of exploration and discovery.   Placed in the reader's hands, it will lead him on a motionless journey through time and space to the regions of his choice.

A single box, packed with recorded music, works of art in the form of photographs, and knowledge in book form, contains the dimensions of time and space in which the traveller may move with maximum enjoyment. These three means of evocation cast their respective spells and complement each other. Whoever joins Professor Starkie aboard one of those picturesque Spanish trains here described may confidently relax and, at one and the same time, watch the passing landscape, listen to an Aragonese or Andalusian folksong sung out in unison in the neighbouring compartment, and profit by the running commentary of his travelling companion. It is this threefold communion of ideas with a country rich in colour, history and musical expression that is here proposed.

It took the wizardry of modern techniques to open the way for such a musical exploration of the world as this, inaugurated by our "Spain - A Musician's Journey through Time and Space".

Of course a flamenco is enough to conjure up a vivid picture of the Spanish soul. But Spain is more than that. Just as the open road cleaves to the landscape and the motor car penetrates into the intimacy of cities and towns, so the historical insights of Professor Starkie, the wayward line of his narrative, the choice of illustrations and the diversity of musical folklore cleave to all the forms of Spanish life. Taken together, text, music and pictures offer a panorama of Spain, seen in the perspective of the centuries, and embark the reader on a voyage of discovery to the sources of her history.

Modern man is a man who listens to the voices of the world.

Why not begin by listening to the voice of Spain, audible not only in the country's outward manifestations, but in those of its secret life as well, conveyed in a thousand interacting forms of artistic expression. If we have succeeded in effecting this synthesis, the cultured listener will find himself in possession of a new dimension of knowledge.

HERMAN GRÉGOIRE

7

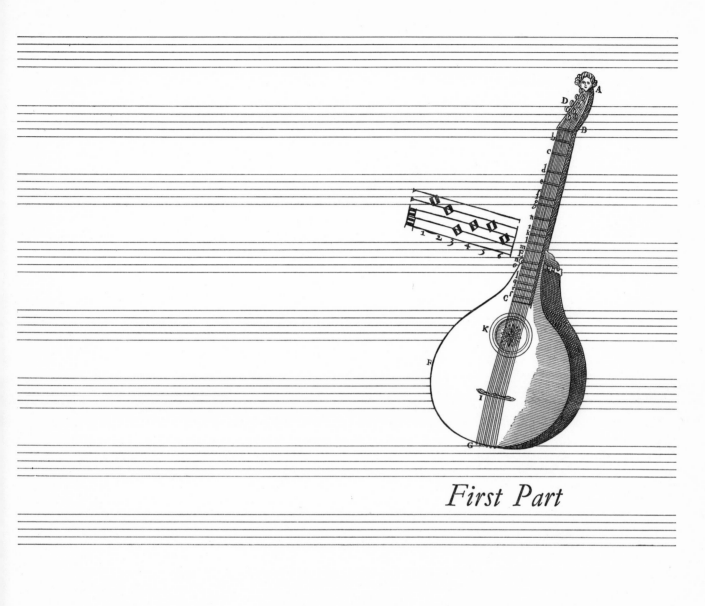

First Part

THE MUSICAL JOURNEY THROUGH TIME

Dedicated to the memory of the great Spanish composer Manuel de Falla

P R E F A C E

In the course of our musical journey through Spanish history I have at each stage invoked the aid of one of the seven great Spanish masters to act as Guide and Socratic daemon.   We start off with Saint Isidore, the first Spanish musician, and after him comes our second guide, King Alfonso X, the "Wise" and he in turn relinquishes the torch to the monarch of minstrelsy, the Archpriest of Hita, our third guide and daemon.   At the end of the fifteenth century, the age of Ferdinand and Isabel, when Spanish music becomes polyphonic, our fourth guide will be Juan del Encina, composer, poet and patriarch of the Spanish theatre.   And in the sixteenth century, during the age of Fray Luis de León and his friend the blind musician Salinas, Spanish religious music leads the world with Tomás Luis de Victoria, the rival of Palestrina.   He will be our fifth guide.   Then follows the golden age of Spanish literature in the seventeenth century, when Velasquez painted and the theatre was triumphant.   One meteoric personality and one only sums up music, poetry and the drama of that age of pageantry, Lope de Vega: Phoenix of genuises and Portent of Nature.   He shall be our sixth guide.

In the eighteenth century, when France ruled the stage and the Bourbons imposed their fashions on Spaniards and Italian *castrati* singers bewitched the court by their virtuosity, our seventh and last guide through time will be the rugged Aragonese Adam, Goya, who not only rediscovered primitive Spain but created the essential Spanish style in painting, music, drama and the dance, which has captivated the world ever since.

11

In our wandering through Spain from coast to coast we are still under the rule of the magic seven, but this time we are in quest of the seven traditional dances that symbolize the seven Spains of the coastal periphery which when combined with the central meseta of Castile and Aragon produce the Hispanic amalgam.

Following the Northern coast towards Finisterre in the West, the Basque mountaineers dance the *aurresku*, the highland yodellers of the Asturias welcome us with their stately *Danza Prima*, and in the glens of Galicia we hear the skirling of the bagpipes as the lads and lasses dance the *Muñeira*—the dance of the Miller's wife. And on the Mediterranean coast and inland, Catalonia reveals its soul in the graceful *Sardana*, but in striking contrast we watch the Aragonese villagers men and women in frenzied rivalry dancing the martial *Jota*, which, when it is transposed to the Moorish lands of Valencia adopts a discordant chant like the call of the Muezzin from the minaret. In contrast with the Moorish wailing of the Valencian *Jota* we have the Majorcan *Copeo* of the mountain or the plain with its reminiscence of Dionysiac Greek dancing.

At last we reach Andalusia in quest of our seventh dance, the primitive *Fandango* which is said to be the basis of all the rest of the dances of Spain.

"The seven styles or *râgs* of the Gypsies"
Esta gitana tiene siete duendes—"this gypsy has seven demons in her body", is a phrase we have heard applied to the dancing of the celebrated Pastora Imperio and it expresses the strange superstitious belief the gypsy has in his own demon or *duende*. The gypsy attributes a magic origin to his traditional song-styles just as the Indian does to his *râgs*, and he will say that they are seven in number and are called "the seven mysteries of the Gypsy". Among the seven he will include the four songs from *Cante Jondo*—the *caña*, *martinete*, *debla* and *seguiriya gitana* and the *saeta*, *polo* and *fandango*.

Prelude

THE BULL'S HIDE

Spain from the outset brings the prehistoric past before us, for even when we fly in an aeroplane we realize the truth of the description given of the Iberian Peninsula by the ancient geographer Strabo, two thousand years ago, when he compared the shape of the country to that of a bull's hide. After flying over the smiling green fields of England and France the tawny landscape of the central plateau of Spain makes us think of the barren surface of the moon. The actual meseta owes its present shape to the encircling mountain ranges which surround it with a kind of Chinese wall. The plateau resembles a huge brown quilt patched up here and there in red, purple, ochre and ashen grey. Brown is the colour of Castile, but it is shot with innumerable variants, and in the distance it fades away to the colour of straw. The brown earth, cork, pumice stone, the ochres and ashen greys conjure up the haunting canvasses the Cretan El Greco painted of Toledo, the brown-tinted Zurbaráns, the dusky Goyas, the earthy Zuloagas. The dry bull's hide spread over the ribs of the mountain ranges gleams like polished leather under the piercing sun and glows with intensity in the fiery sunsets which rival those of the central Asiatic plateau in majesty.

THE CENTRAL MESETA

It is a land of heroic warriors, conquistadors and ascetic mystics: Toledo crowned by its Alcázar where the Cid was one time governor: Avila a fortress of the spirit, a Castle made of a single diamond, in which there are many mansions: Saint Teresa and Saint John of the Cross, the music of Victoria: Medellín and Trujillo, the cradles of Cortés and Pizarro: the steppes of La Mancha forever haunted by the Knight of the Rueful Figure and his squire. Spain, the meeting-place of races: Toledo again with its amalgam of Christian, Jew and Moor, and its Mozarabic chant.

Spain, as Richard Ford said, is one mountain, or a jumble of mountains, all more or less connected with each other, descending in serpentizing direction throughout the Peninsula with general inclination to the West.

The country rises from the coast, directly in the North-Western provinces, but once the ascent is accomplished no real descent ever takes place—and we are on the summit of a vast elevated mass. The Pyrenees are an isthmus and a wall: they do not, as Ganivet said, prevent invasion, but they do isolate the Spaniards and allow them to preserve their independent character. Spanish history is thus a permanent war of Independence.

THE COASTAL PERIPHERY

But in Spain itself in the early nineteenth century we notice the regionalist and separatist tendencies of the coastal periphery of the country, of which Victor Hugo was fully aware when he spoke of *Les Espagnes*. The geographical form of the country with its transverse mountains caused regionalism which had been marked, even in the Middle Ages, but which did not become so apparent during the centuries when centralized Castile ruled the country. In modern Spanish literature we are struck by the marked differences that exist, for instance, between the novels of a Pyrenean writer like Pío Baroja, and a highland Cantabrian like Pereda, a Galician like Ramón del Valle Inclán and a Valencian like Blasco Ibáñez. Still more clearly do we see these differences in the folk dances and folk songs which vary even from village to village within the region. All these regions, however, North, South, East and West, have played a great part in building up the Hispanic World, for the emigrants to South America have made their *patrias chicas*, as they call them, into spiritual colonies, there, as it were, which perpetuate their ancestral memories.

TARTESSIAN SPAIN

First let us continue our journey backwards through time from Castile through the steppes of La Mancha to the Southern Coast.

Long before Castile began its crusade to unify Spain, there existed in Andalusia, before the first millennium, a powerful civilization which descended through the ancient tradition of Atlantis, the legends of Hercules and Geryon, and the myths of Plato.[1] Set at the gates of Africa, which possessed an autochthonous civilization of its own and had direct relations with Egypt and the Near East, the Cradle of the human race, Spain introduced to the Western world many of the novelties of civilization. And even today the Andalusian is conscious of possessing the oldest culture in the Mediterranean in the lands of Tartessus or Tarshish near Cádiz of the Egyptian Hercules, the fabled shore described by the Roman poet Rufus Festus Avienus in the fourth century A.D. from the sailing log given by the ancient Greek mariner a thousand years before. * Take, for example,

[1] Plato, *Timaeus*.
For the Atlantis myth see J. A. Stewart, *The Myths of Plato*, London, pp. 455-459.
* See glossary.

14

the Spanish bull of immemorial tradition which we see on Greek coins and described in the myths of Hercules: it belongs to a special autochthonous stock and has been selectively bred for centuries, thus preserving its fierceness and its habit of attacking any obstacle in its way. When the foreign traveller today sees the bullfight, the national spectacle of the country with its hosts of aficionados drawn from the humbler as well as from the wealthier classes in Seville, Ronda or in any of the small villages in Andalusia, he realizes that he has come to a land where a century and a half ago Pedro Romero, Pepe Hillo, Costillares and their followers have created, like the ten rulers of Atlantis, a caste devoted to the cult of the sacred bulls. And the chiefs of that caste do indeed remind us of the description Plato gives of sons of Poseidon on the plain of Atlantis, who, after mingling their blood with that of the bull, dressed in azure robes and, when it was dark, sat by the glowing embers of the sacrificial fires and judged and were judged in turn. The *traje de luces* of the bullfighter, the complicated ritual performed by the *mozo de estoques* (sword-handler) when he dresses his master for the sacrifice, the hierarchy consisting of the *matador*, the hero, the *banderillero* flitting on the tips of his toes like a graceful ballerina, the loutish *picador*, the Caliban of the feast, all are examples of the subtly stylized and crystallized caste system handed down from the past. And let us not think that the caste was created at the end of the eighteenth century by Pepe Hillo, who wrote his *Art of Bullfighting* using his sword as pen and dipping it in bull's blood rather than in ink: in Andalusia or El Andalús the bull has always been a totem and we find it on ancient Roman coins and in the bronzes found at Cruz de los Santos. Bull worship, as Menéndez y Pelayo tells us, existed in Spain in the remotest ages, and when the Oriental gods came with the Syrians into the Western world they found that the lands of Southern Spain already belonged to them and that their arrival was expected with longing. The bull reminds us in our journey through time that there existed in Andalusia before the first millennium a venerable civilization which descends to us through the legends of Hercules and Geryon as well as the myths of Plato.

THE PHOENICIANS AND THE GREEKS

And even if we refuse to believe in Arganthonios and the mystery of Tartessus we must accept the Phoenicians who arrived in South Spain about the same time and established their marts for the purpose of exchanging their products manufactured in the East for the gold, silver, tin, copper and bronze mined in the Tartessian sierras.

After the Phoenicians came the Greeks from the Northern shore of the Mediterranean to play out to its conclusion the mighty struggle between the Semitic and the Indo-European civilization which had started after the emergence of the Hittites in Asia Minor in the year 2000 B.C. Both the Semitic and the Arrian civilizations advanced slowly towards the West and they resembled one another in their subtle methods of penetration, but their final clash in Spanish territory is full of significance for the future history of Spain, and there is one beautiful work of art in the Prado Museum in Madrid which symbolizes the contact between Greek and Semitic civilization, namely, the *Lady of Elche*, which is a synthesis of Apollinean art and Carthaginian ornamentation. As Havelock Ellis says, she seems to have come from the hand of a sculptor who was the fellow-countryman of the captivating Spanish woman he has immortalized. How genuinely Spanish the *Lady of Elche* is we may realize by the resemblance she bears to Velasquez's *Woman with the Fan*, who, however, has grown older and more tired and is no longer beautiful. [1] That statue indeed symbolizes the part played by Spain throughout the ages, for later on the West would inherit the fruits of this effort, and the lessons taught by the Greeks would reach the rest of Spain by the indirect route of Andalusia and would continue until the sixteenth century when the arrival of the Turks in the Mediterranean would destroy the remnants of the Semitic nations. Thus the naval battle of Lepanto in 1571 would close the period which had begun when Greeks and Carthaginians came into contact on the Eastern coast of Spain. [2]

[1] H. Ellis, *The Soul of Spain*, Boston and New York, 1920, pp. 108-9.
[2] I. Olagüe, *This is Spain* (tr. by W. Starkie), London, 1954, p. 44.

THE ROMANS

After the Greeks came the Romans who, after two hundred years of struggle, finally under Julius Caesar pacified the whole country—a miracle when we remember the observations of the geographer Strabo in the first century B.C. who like modern writers rebuked the Spaniards for their individualism, saying that the Iberians possessed greater local pride than the Greeks and this prevented them from uniting together in a powerful confederation. The Romans made of *Hispania* an entity, and Livy frequently speaks of the *Hispani* in general without thinking it necessary to state whether they came from this or that tribe. Roman Spain, shortly before the dissolution of the Empire, already appeared with a precise national significance in the first Universal History, composed by a Christian, that of Paulus Orosius, a Galician disciple of Saint Augustine, who considered Spain as a province of the Empire within which Divine Providence had unified the world.

Owing to the special conditions which were then in operation, the Peninsula became a world apart from the rest of Europe and the centre of an advanced civilization not to be formed elsewhere, except in the South of France, which, owing to its close proximity, Spain absorbed in itself. Spain became so important a pawn in the Empire that she was able to impose a line of Emperors, of whom the most celebrated was Trajan, a native of Seville. Her writers such as Seneca, Lucan and Martial were the most illustrious and elegant in what was called the Silver Age of Latin: her artists, sculptors and dancers were peerless, though according to Martial the provocative dancing girls from Cádiz had an unenviable reputation among the austere members of Roman society.

THE VISIGOTHS

The Iberian Peninsula became, in fact, as Breasted says, the America of the Ancient World. After being a place of refuge, it became a land of promise, and what is more significant, when the Roman Empire was dismembered into various Germanic Kingdoms, the civilization of the Iberian Peninsula, so far from perishing, actually became strengthened, because at the time of the invasions the task of unifying the country was entrusted by the last Emperors to the Visigoths. They, moreover, were the most Romanized of the Germans, and were entirely convinced that the Roman idea of the State as arbiter of good and justice for the whole community was superior to the chaotic individualism of the other barbarian governments. And the Visigoths, though they were Arrians and hostile to the Catholicism of the Hispano-Romans, yet unified politically the whole peninsula, and a little later unified it spiritually by becoming converted to Catholicism. Thus were the ideals of a united Roman-Gothic Spain, which had been prophesied by Paulus Orosius, carried into operation in the sixth century. The achievement was mainly the work of the Saint whom Dante places in the Fourth Heaven, that of the Sun among the spirits of the great theologians. Dante says of him:

Vedi oltre fiammeggiar
l'ardente spiro d'Isidoro,

and certainly his flaming spirit illuminates the Middle Ages from beginning to end. His personality so obsessed the Spaniards from all over the country that even after death he remained as a perpetual ghostly presence in Seville, Toledo and León, and such were his miracles that he became for a time even a rival to Saint James himself of Compostella. He was called *Doctor Egregius* on account of his immense learning, and his *Etymologies*, a vast compendium of human knowledge, was one of the sources of Dante; his history of the Gothic Kings, the main authority the world possesses for the seventh century on the eve of the Moorish invasion. In succession to his brother Saint Leandro he ruled the See of Seville from 599 to 636; he trained Saint Braulio of Saragossa and Saint Ildefonso of Toledo: he created a rule for the monastic life which lasted until it was superseded by the Augustinian Rule from Italy and the Cluniac from France. But in addition to all those qualities Saint Isidore has the merit for us that he was the first great musician in Spanish History and arranged the Mozarabic Office to which Spain remained faithful through centuries of warfare and persecution, and which is still celebrated in a chapel in Toledo Cathedral.

We have selected Saint Isidore, the Egregious Doctor, as our first guide on our swift journey through Spanish music in the Middle Ages. *Sit omen tantum nomen.*

16

Chapter I

SAINT ISIDORE OF SEVILLE
THE FIRST SPANISH MUSICIAN

Although the Egregious Doctor sits enthroned in the fourth Heaven consorting with Solomon, the Angelic Doctor, the Venerable Bede and the rest of the Blest, his spirit still continues to haunt from time to time the three cities of Seville, Toledo and León, where he worked and prayed. His school at Seville continued to flourish after his death in 636 and imparted to students from all over the country the teaching of the school of Alexandria, especially in astronomy, mathematics and music. He was looked upon as the first musical theorist in Spain, for in his eyes no discipline in learning could exist without music *(sine musica nulla disciplina potest esse perfecta; nihil enim est sine illa)*. Through the Saint music became, as Saint Thomas Aquinas called it, "the first among the seven arts, and the noblest of all the sciences". And this prominence of music among the arts lasted throughout the Middle Ages. It was the only one that formed part of the mediaeval educational curriculum called the *Quadrivium*, together with arithmetic, geometry and astronomy: and without some acquaintance with its principles and practice, it was impossible to become a master of grammar, dialectic or rhetoric. Music thus from the beginning of the Christian ascendancy up to the time of the Renaissance, was regarded, not merely as the first of all the arts, but as the key to all wisdom and all knowledge, no less of earthly than of heavenly things. In those days music was the supreme art and the visual arts were considered to be mere sensual pleasures.

 THE MOZARABIC LITURGY

According to Flórez, who is our authority for the Mozarabic Rite, this ancient Spanish liturgy was introduced by the invading Visigoths, who were Arrians. It resembled the Roman liturgy, but was composed according to the model of the Graeco-Arrian, and in the early years of Visigothic domination it was slightly modified by Greek priests from Constantinople and the Byzantine Empire. Then in 633, the Spanish bishops under Saint Isidore of Seville revised the ritual with the assistance of Saints Ildefonso, Isidoro, Eugenio and Leandro, and insisted upon its adoption by all the churches. Soon afterwards, in 711, the Moors invaded Spain and the Visigoths were routed.

But although the Roman-Gothic Kingdom was destroyed and a long-drawn out period of disintegration followed, the ancient idea of Christian unity preached by Saint Isidore did not die out. It remained in the back of men's minds together with the memories of the saintly prelate whose personality, like that of Saint James the Apostle and San Millán de la Cogolla, began gradually to assume the functions of Mystical Protector.

At that time the help of the saints was sorely needed for the characteristic Iberian unsociability, as Menéndez Pidal says, had broken out everywhere like a plague, which, when strength diminishes, invades the whole body. Nobody was moved by the plight of his neighbour. There was, however, one forlorn centre of resistance which continued its staunch struggle against the Moors, namely the highlands of Asturias, but it fought on in isolation, and the Mozarab chronicler in Toledo, who writes a despairing chronicle for the year 754, omits all mention of Pelayo and his heroic band at Covadonga, either because he did not know about them or because he did not consider their guerrilla raids of significance.[1]

Nevertheless it should be remembered that the Moorish Conquerors treated the peoples who submitted to them with a good deal of tolerance and allowed them to practise their religion. Those who submitted were called *Mustarabs* (the Arabic words mean "mixed with Arabs") or Arabizants, and their liturgy soon received the name of Mozarabic. These Mozarabs continued to practise their ancient ritual which, as time went on, became corrupted owing to Moorish influences.

In spite of the tendency to disintegration which was hastened all over Europe by the rise of Feudalism, the ruined portions of the Visigothic Kingdom did not reorganise themselves on a basis of feudal vassalage, but in the form of independent kingdoms, and beside the Asturian-Neogothic Kingdom there rose the Kingdom of Pamplona in 908, the Kingdoms of Castile and Aragon in 1035 and that of Portugal in 1140. Over all these states the ancient Astur-Leonese Kingdom possessed a vague though significant imperial superiority which, as Menéndez Pidal shows, was the weak Spanish substitute of the equally weak bond of vassalage which linked up the European feudal system. These various kingdoms were gradually able to develop their own individual characteristics and spread their influence far and wide through the Mediterranean, through Africa and the Atlantic as an apprenticeship under their kings in expectation of the great days to come when they would all be reunited. The division of the Kingdoms retarded the great enterprise of the Reconquest, but in exchange it led to important expansive actions outside the Peninsula.

And just as the five Christian Kingdoms in the North of the country developed in opposition to European feudalism, so did the small *Taifa* Kingdoms among the Islamized Spaniards fight against the spirit of Islam on behalf of their separate territories.

Thus Spain, as always, was in disagreement with the two worlds that crossed one another's path on her soil.

CÓRDOBA, THE SACRED CITY OF THE MOSLEMS

Meanwhile, the Moors consolidated their power in the country and the great Abderrahman I founded the mosque in Córdoba on the site of a Visigothic church, which had itself been built on the ruins of a Roman temple dedicated to Janus. To this, he gave the name of *Zeca* or House of Purification, and he resolved that it should rival Mecca, and become the sacred city of the Western Mohammedan World. After the *Kaaba*, it would become the largest and most beautiful building of Islam in the world, with its nineteen gateways of bronze, its four thousand seven hundred lamps of perfumed oil, its roof supported by twelve hundred columns of porphyry, jasper and many-coloured marbles. But what drew the attention of the world towards the mosque

[1] R. Menéndez Pidal, *The Spaniards in their History* (tr. W. Starkie), London, 1950, p. 183.

Saint James fighting the Moors (popular Catalan colour print of the seventeenth century, after the original woodcut in the archives of the Carreras Typography.) Pueblo Español, Barcelona.

18

SANTIAGO APOSTOL PATRON DE ESPAÑA

was not its artistic splendours but the realization that the shrine contained some of the bones of the Prophet Mahomet himself. Pilgrims came from all over Europe to pray at the Holy of Holies, and in the wake of the pilgrims came architects, builders and artists, with the result that Córdoba under Abderrahman II became the most civilized city in the world, and later in the days of Abderrahman III, in the suburbs of Córdoba, amid the earthly paradise of fig-trees, almonds and pomegranates rose Medina Azahara, a palace of the Arabian Nights, whose beauty we may still recapture in the nostalgic verse and prose of Ibn Hazm's *El Collar de la Paloma*.[1] But already in the days of the second Abderrahman the moonlit patios of Córdoba had echoed to the songs of Ziryab, "The Blackbird of Sweet Song", who after being a minstrel of Harun ar Rashid, the Caliph of Bagdad, had come to live in the City of the *Zeca*. Thus Córdoba and Seville became the two great centres of Islamic culture in the Western World and there was a saying of Averroes that when a wise man died his books were sold in Córdoba; if he was a musician his instruments went to Seville.

THE DISCOVERY OF THE TOMB OF SAINT JAMES

But then on the Christian side in North Spain an extraordinary occurrence took place. In the wilds of Galicia a number of hermits and shepherds of the diocese of Iria Flavia saw night after night a big star burning low over a thickly wooded hill near the River Sar, and when they approached they saw little flickering stars among the bushes on the hill, and they heard distant music, as though choirs of angels were singing before an altar. Theodomir the bishop at once recognized the hand of God and ordered men to clear away the undergrowth. Beneath they came upon a small shrine containing the tomb which Theodomir by divine revelation recognized as that of Saint James the Son of Zebedee, whom Herod had beheaded in Jerusalem eight hundred years before.

When Alfonso II, the Chaste, King of the Neo-Gothic Kingdom of Asturias, heard the tidings he realized the full significance of the discovery. Now that Spain possessed the body of the Apostle the Christians would win the crusade, because Saint James, or Santiago as they called him, would inspire the holy war and give them faith to triumph over the Moslems who drew their strength from the relics of their Prophet in the mosque at Córdoba. Alfonso proclaimed the Apostle Patron Saint of all Spain—the Spain that was already liberated and that which still remained to be won from the Infidel. He forthwith proceeded to build a church made of stones and mud *(ex petra et luto opere parvo)*, but soon its fame grew owing to the number of miracles which took place. Alfonso II communicated the news of the discovery to Pope Leo III and to Charlemagne, the Emperor, with the result that pilgrims began to flock to Spain. Even the Moslems came to have news of the Apostle, and we find references to Compostella in Moorish authors, as for instance, in the Andalusian poet Alhaquem-al-Gazel, who accompanied a Norman delegation there in 850.

By the time of Ramiro II the idea of a Holy War in defence of Christian territories had become a reality, mainly owing to the unifying efforts of Alfonso III the Great (866-910), who, when writing the first history of the small Kingdom of Asturias, whose capital was Oviedo, calls it the history of the Goths, proclaiming by this title the uninterrupted continuity of the Gothic monarchy and declaring that the Kingdom of Pelayo, the original Asturian leader, was *Salus Hispaniae*, the salvation of Spain, and that the Spaniards would not cease to fight day and night until, in accordance with divine predestination, the Saracens were expelled root and branch.

Already by the time of Alfonso the Great, the Christians had lost their sense of inferiority in face of the Moslem enemy, and we find documents of the period calling Alfonso III *magnus imperator*, whereas before, the monarchs had been called *principes* or *reges*.[2] It was Alfonso III, too, who made Compostella the spiritual centre of North Spain by building a big Cathedral to house the relics of the Apostle, and the shrine was frequented

[1] Ibn Hazm de Córdoba, *El Collar de la Paloma* (tr. E. García Gómez), Madrid, 1952.
[2] A. Castro, *España en su Historia*, Buenos Aires, 1948, p. 109.

even by those Christians who lived among the Moors and were Mozarabs, as we know from the Moorish annalist who pays a tribute to Shant Yakob, "the Holy City of Galicia".

The Moors, however, in the tenth century had a new leader—a man of destiny who was determined to lead an *Al-Jihad* or Holy War against the Christians. This was Al-Manzor al Allah—Victor by the Grace of God. His expedition against Compostella in 997 was one of extermination, for no one could resist his troops as they advanced on the city. The city he sacked, but the tomb of the Apostle he left intact, and some chroniclers believed he was dazzled by divine splendour when he stood before the tomb of Santiago, but in any case he returned to Córdoba laden with booty, and the strongest of the Christian captives were forced to carry the bells of the Cathedral of Santiago on their shoulders. The bells were hung up reversed as lamps in the great Mosque, where they remained until 1236, when Saint Ferdinand restored them to Compostella, sending them back on the shoulders of Moorish prisoners.

The sacking of Compostella by Al-Manzor in 997 must have injured the reputation of Santiago, who had pitifully belied his title of Moor-Killer, and many of those who returned to this ruined city must have doubted in the warlike powers of their patron saint. That the Apostle himself must have realized that a good deal of scepticism was rife among his following is proved by the reappearance on the scene of our old friend Saint Isidore of Seville.

King Ferdinand I, who was more devoted to the Egregious Doctor than he was to Saint James of Compostella, was at that time occupied in preparing the solemn dedication of his new basilica in the city of León to Saint Isidore. After his defeat of King Motadid of Seville he had demanded, in addition to the usual war indemnity, that the remains of Justa, the martyred saint, should be given to him to be transferred to his capital of León, and he sent a delegation of bishops to Seville for this purpose. As the delegation was unable to find the remains of Saint Justa they took away in their stead those of Saint Isidore, the Egregious Doctor, whose learned works were in every library in Europe. At the head of King Ferdinand I's mission was the Bishop of León, Alvito, to whom Saint Isidore appeared three times saying: "I am the Doctor of the Spains and mine is the body to be removed." Saint Isidore's body, furthermore worked a number of miracles on the way back to León, curing the lame and casting out devils. Henceforth in his new sepulchre he became so celebrated by the miracles he performed in León that he seriously rivalled Saint James of Compostella. Ferdinand I, therefore, at the instance of his wife, Doña Sancha, who was such a devotee of the Saint that she called herself his spouse, built a royal Pantheon in the porch of the Saint's church after he had transferred the remains of his father King Sancho El Mayor there from Oria. And so it came about that the Royal House of Navarre, for so long the implacable enemy of León, at last recognized the suzerainty of the imperial city.

THE ORDEAL BY FIRE

Twelve years after the death of Ferdinand I, during the reign of Alfonso VI, in the heyday of the Cid Campeador, Pope Gregory VII (1020-1085) was resolved to unify the ritual throughout all the churches in the world by imposing the Roman tradition. The plain-song of the Western Church consisted of four separate schools, namely: Roman or Gregorian, Milanese or Ambrosian, Gallican or French, Mozarabic or Visigothic. Such was the prestige of the Papacy under Gregory and the spiritual power of Rome that he succeeded in superseding the other systems, and in the eleventh century a fixed ritual prevailed throughout Europe. The Church of Milan alone was permitted to retain the old Ambrosian tradition unaltered. The Gallican tradition, we should add, had already given way to that of Rome at the end of the eighth century, at the instance of the Emperor Charlemagne. In Spain, however, a bitter struggle took place, for the Spaniards clung firmly to the ritual which they had inherited from their ancestors, and which had been hallowed by Saints Isidore and Leandro of Seville and Saint Eugenio of Toledo, and they were deeply grieved that Pope Gregory should attribute the divergence of this ritual to the heretical doctrines of the Arrians or the invasions of the Moors.

SAINT JAMES. Original engraving from *La Légende Dorée* by Jacques de Voragine (1255). Saint James is represented here with his knapsack and pilgrim's staff.

According to the chronicle of Nájera it was decided to appeal to the "Judgement of God" and ordeal by fire.

A great bonfire was lit in the Plaza de Zocodover in Toledo and, in the presence of the King and Queen, the court and a great multitude—the two volumes, one of the Mozarabic and the other of the Roman ritual—were cast into the flames. Whereupon, the Mozarabic book jumped out of the fire, while the Roman remained uninjured in the midst of the flames, but Alfonso kicked the Mozarabic book into the bonfire uttering the words which henceforth became proverbial in Spain: *Allá van leyes do quieren reyes* (Where Kings wish, there the laws go).[1] Alfonso, however, limited the use of the Mozarabic rite to six parishes in Toledo, and in time it became practically extinct, except on certain festivals, when it was revived as memory.

It was, however, Cardinal Ximénez de Cisneros who revived the ritual as we know it today. When he became Archbishop of Toledo he ordered the printing of a great number of the ancient Mozarabic missals, changing the ancient Gothic characters into the ordinary Castilian letters, and he distributed them among the clergy of the six ancient parish churches of the rite. Not content with this he caused the erection of a beautiful chapel called the Chapel of Corpus Christi in the Cathedral, and he founded a college of thirteen priests for the rite, who were *Mozarabes Sodales* or *capellani*, with a head chaplain. These recited canonical hours, and said Mass daily in the Chapel of the Corpus Christi according to the Mozarabic liturgy.[2]

The first of the gramophone recordings, which will serve as musical illustrations to our journey, is an *antifona* or anthem according to the Mozarabic rite, sung after the body has been deposited near the tomb:* *Después de colocar el cadáver junto al sepulcro*. It is sung by the Antics Escolans or former students of the monastery of Montserrat. The traditional Mozarabic chant we hear today in Toledo has little to remind us of its founder Saint Isidore of Seville. Even the memory of Cardinal Ximénez de Cisneros, who revived it in the sixteenth century, has faded considerably. Pierre Aubry in the examples he gives of the chants as they appeared in the old manuscripts and as he heard them sung, shows that the chant we hear today, especially in Toledo Cathedral,

[1] W. Starkie, *Grand Inquisitor*, London, 1940, p. 376.
[2] P. Aubry, *Iter Hispanicum* in *Sammelbände der Internationalen Musikgesellschaft*, VIII, IX, 1907-1908. Fray Germán Prado, *Historia del Rito Mozárabe y Toledano*, Silos, 1928.
* First Record, *Ancient Music*, side I, No. 1.

is a heavily-moving almost syllabic setting of the words, and the grace and freedom which still existed in the days of Cardinal Ximénez at the beginning of the sixteenth century have disappeared.

Our chief source of information on the revival of the mozarabic rite is the biography of Ximénez by Eugenio de Robles, who was one of the *capellani* of the Mozarabic chapel and vicar of the Church of Saint Mark in Toledo. The principal modern authority on the Mozarabic and Toledan ritual is Fray Germán Prado of the Benedictine Monastery of Santo Domingo de Silos.

Today in the Chapel of Corpus Christi in Toledo Cathedral when I attend morning Mass according to the Mozarabic rite I feel that every object in the little chapel evokes the presence of the great Cardinal Ximénez: his Cardinal's hat still hangs from the roof in the centre, his coat of arms is stamped on the beautiful plateresque ironwork by Juan Francés, and one of the walls is adorned with a large fresco by Juan de Borgoña, representing the aged Cardinal riding at the head of his troops at the capture of Oran in 1509. As the priest says Mass according to this rite the choir chant gently in a slower rhythm than in the Gregorian, and our thoughts wander away from this tiny chapel to the lovely basilica of Santa Leocadia amid its cypress trees in the plain outside Toledo. That hermitage is known to the folk of Toledo as the Cristo de la Vega and is one of the most hallowed spots in all Spain, for in its small enclosure are buried countless memories of Visigothic Spain. It was there the Fourth Council of Toledo was held in the seventh century, under the presiding genius of Saint Isidore. It was he who ordered the first Gothic missal and breviary for the Spaniards. In Seville was the original home and sphere of influence of the Saint, but Toledo was the centre of his power, and it is the place where his memory is perpetuated today by the Mozarabic rite.

It is in León, however, in the mysterious Pantheon of the Kings, one of the most hallowed shrines in Spain, with its Romanesque wall-paintings of the twelfth century, that we feel the ghostly presence of *l'ardente spiro* of Saint Isidore, the supreme musician. It was here where the Saint is sleeping in his tomb that a solemn instance of supernatural intervention took place on the eve of the great battle of Las Navas de Tolosa in 1212. Late at night there was a mysterious knocking on the door of the church and the people in the streets heard a distant measured tread of an army marching by. The sacristan who was watching in the pantheon cried out: "Who calls?" and he heard a muffled voice answer that Fernán González and the Cid Campeador had come to summon Saint Isidore to the battle, just as Saint James had been summoned at Compostella to help the Christian hosts at Clavijo and Coimbra.

The first page of the *Liber Etymologiarum* or "Etymologies", a manuscript text of Saint Isidore (565-636), in the Royal Academy of History, Madrid. This frontispiece represents the Tree of Human Knowledge.

24

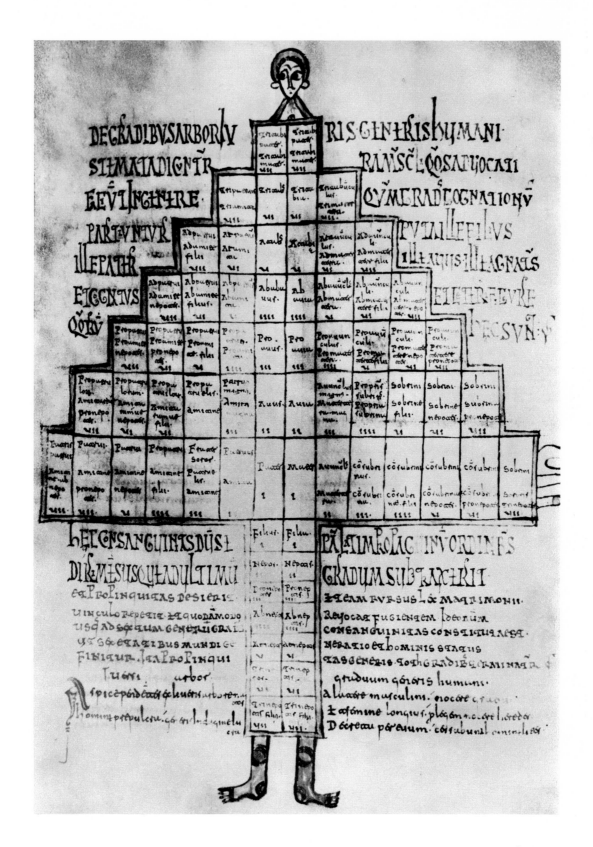

25

Charlemagne, by Albert
Dürer, in the Österr. Na-
tionalbibliothek of Vienna.
Contrary to all tradition, the
Great Emperor is represented clean-shaven instead of
" à la longue barbe fleurie ".

Chapter II

GREGORIAN CHANT,
CLUNY AND CHARLEMAGNE

Alfonso VI was by temperament and upbringing a staunch nationalist ready to defy the Pope and the German Emperor as arrogantly as his great warrior the Cid, who in the minstrel poem *Las Mocedades de Rodrigo* (The Youthful Prowess of Roderick) hurled defiance in the following words:

> May God requite thy evil, Roman Pope!
> The tribute year by year thou dost demand,
> Our good King Ferdinand shall surely pay
> In open fight tomorrow on the field.

But Alfonso's two marriages to French princesses did much to weaken the nationalistic impulses of his character, for they brought him under the influence of the great Monastery of Cluny. The great strength of the monks of Cluny was that they stood for Universal Catholicism and firmly upheld the Roman policy of centralism. Pope Gregory in his policy of reorganization of the Church resolved to employ the Cluniac monks in purging the Spanish church of its separatist traditions.

Alfonso VI felt that since God had given Spain prestige in the world through the tomb of the Apostle in Compostella, it was necessary to organize that prestige in accordance with worldly conditions, and the monks of Cluny would become admirable propagandists and enable him to strengthen his rule. In consequence, as the eleventh century advanced, the French influence made itself more and more deeply felt in Spain. Alfonso VI thus placed himself completely under the aegis of Cluny. It was Cluny that chose his second bride Constance for him: it was Saint Hugh of Cluny who prevailed upon him to submit to Cluny when he had disputes with the Papal Legate. Alfonso believed that the Monks of Cluny would resolve all the problems in heaven and on earth, but he was mistaken.[1] What had happened was that León and Castile in the eleventh century abandoned their traditional Mozarabic culture but fell under the influence of Cluny and Burgundy.

While the Spaniards with the war cry of Saint James on their lips were fighting under the Cid against the fanatical Almorávides the Dioceses throughout North Spain were being ruled by French bishops, mostly of Cluniac origin, and the crown of Alfonso VI nearly passed to a foreigner, Raymond of Burgundy.

[1] A. Castro, *op. cit.*, p. 151.

The monks of Cluny inspired the mysterious compilation called the *Codex Calixtinus* in order to boost the Pilgrimage to Santiago and give a wider significance to the cult of the Apostle. The book appeared about 1150 when the pilgrimage had become celebrated throughout the world. The miracles described in it were already known, and the story of the journey of the Apostle's body from the East was acknowledged to be the most ancient document in Galicia. The book was intended by the Cluniac propagandists to be an account of the pilgrimage written at the height of its fame, and they created the figure of Archbishop Turpin at Cluny in order to link Charlemagne with Santiago. The Emperor would thus become the first pilgrim of Saint James, and his Knights, who in the original *Chanson de Roland* had died as martyrs after a crusade, would now in the pseudo-Turpin's account die at Roncevaux on their return from the pilgrimage to Galicia.

The Codex of Pope Calixtus II has nothing of Calixtus but the name. As he was Count Guy de Bourgogne, brother of Count Raymond, Queen Urraca's husband, he was a plausible author upon whom to father the manuscript. It was the Abbot of Cluny, who in 1095, begged from Pope Urban II the pallium for Compostella, and it was Pope Calixtus II who in 1120 made Compostella into a metropolitan see.

We must now consider the deep significance of the implantation of the Gregorian rite in the history of Spanish music.

The music of the early Christian Church was not a combination of the music of Greece and Rome, nor even an adaptation of it, for Graeco-Roman music was always metric in structure, so far as it can be judged, and its rhythms and metres depended upon those of the poem, whereas plain-song, on the contrary, has only the rhythms of prose. Moreover, a typical feature of Graeco-Roman music consisted in the comparatively wide melodic leaps and in a marked fondness for the interval of the tritone or augmented fourth, while Gregorian chant moves mainly by conjunct motion and comparatively small leaps, always systematically avoiding the tritone which was regarded throughout the Middle Ages as *Diabolus in musica*, perhaps, as Cecil Gray suggests, because of its pagan associations.[1] In Greek music, according to Gevaert, we find *une beauté froide et sèche, subordination de l'élément féminin de romantisme, prédominance de l'élément objectif.* Gregorian chant is the opposite of cold and dry and is both romantic and subjective.

The liturgical chant of the Catholic Church is neither Greek nor Hebrew, nor even a combination of both, but an entirely new form of musical art corresponding to the church of Hagia Sophia at Constantinople or the mosaics of Venice and Ravenna.[2] In it we find in its most perfect form ecclesiastical monody as it was established at the end of the first millennium. It is vocal music subordinate to prayer: its rhythms are those of the spoken word, and come from the speech of classical Latin orators handed down to the Christian tunes through the *Institutiones Oratoriae* written by the Spanish-Latin philosopher Quintilian at the end of the first century and other authors.[3] The melodic principals of the ascent and descent from a centre point is essentially the musical equivalent of the curved arch and flowing semi-circular lines which constitute the dominant structural motive of Santa Sophia, and practically all Byzantine architecture, and the inner spirit that moulds the liturgical chant is similar to that which is expressed in Byzantine mosaics, mural painting or ivory carving; a curiously ethereal and timeless quality.

Everything in Gregorian chant suggests infinity, and when heard in the vast spaces of cathedrals the sound floats away in the distance and seems to become the disembodied prolongation of the majestic curves and aerial lines of the mediaeval architecture, which, we repeat, has been defined as music frozen into stone.

Among the different types of Gregorian chant we should mention the *Sequences* which were introduced in the ninth century by a monk called Notker Balbulus. These consisted in setting new music and words to the lengthy *Jubilati* or vocalises which were a feature of the Alleluia chants. These *Sequences* were often very beautiful, but they offended the priests and were banished from the liturgy by the Council of Trent, with the exception of five which were retained. One of the five is the celebrated *Dies Irae* of Thomas Celano, which is sung in the Mass for the Dead, and is, indeed, one of the most sombre and magnificent musical poems of the Middle Ages.

[1] C. Gray, *The History of Music*, London, 1928, p. 13.
[2] K. D. Hartmann, *Historia de los Estilos artísticos*, Barcelona, 1925, pp. 90-93.
[3] A. Salazar, *La Música en la Sociedad Europea*, Mexico, 1942, vol. I, p. 82. See also Armand Machabey, *Etudes de Musicologie pré-médiévale* in *Revue de Musicologie*, Paris, May, 1935.

28

Three Bishops—Detail from the altar-front of Saint Saturnine of Tabernoles—Museum of Catalan Art, Barcelona.

This altar-front belongs to a group of paintings on wood from the workshop of the Urgel Cathedral. The harmony of its lines and the perfection of its colouring make of this work one of the most effective examples of stylisation in Romanesque art.

Out of the *Sequences* developed another form called the *Trope* which is of great significance in the early history of drama as well as of music. One excellent example of the *Trope* is the *Quem quaeritis*, which is based upon the meeting of the Marys and the Angel at the tomb of Christ, as described in the Gospel of Saint Matthew (XXVIII: 1-7):

> *Quem quaeritis in sepulcro, o Christicolae?*
> *Iesum Nazarenum crucifixum, o Caelicolae.*
> *Non est hic, surrexit sicut praedixerat,*
> *Ite, nuntiate quia surrexit de sepulcro.*

> Whom do ye seek within this tomb, O Christians?
> Jesus of Nazareth, who was crucified, O heavenly dwellers.
> He is not here; for he is risen as He said;
> Go ye and announce that He has risen from the dead.

From this simple beginning the *Trope* grew and grew, gathering fresh tropes and sequences as it progressed through the centuries until eventually it became a complete music-drama in which the parts were played by priests, nuns and choristers. It was staged in the church at first, but as it evolved into a music-drama it was transferred to the grave-yard and eventually to the market-place when the parts were played by citizens of guilds, and ultimately by professional actors. Such was the origin of the liturgical dramas and the Mystery Plays which were the ancestors of the modern theatre.

When we look back on the evolution of music, which became in the West the supreme expression of mediaeval man, unless we also include architecture, which was music frozen into stone, we discover that Gregorian chant accompanied all public observances: noble and peasant, rich and poor, listened to it from the cradle to the grave. It was the music of the man praying in the cathedral, but its influences spread to life outside the church for even Spanish epic poetry was accompanied by a little chant *(tonillo de recitado)*, and minstrels and ballad singers were influenced in their performance by church singing and psalmody.

In Montserrat where the hallowed traditions of the mediaeval *Scriptorium* are carried on uninterruptedly today, some of the most important books on Gregorian chant have been published, such as *Introducció a la Palaeografía Musical Gregoriana* by Dom Gregori Maria Sunyol (1925), but what is more remarkable is that Montserrat through its choir has been in recent years re-creating in modern Spain the ancient cult of Gregorian chant, through the excellent recordings which have been made in Barcelona. Thus the world is reinvigorated spiritually by this great Roman fountain of song, which, as Cecil Gray says lyrically, is as sweet and pure and inexhaustible as the Acqua Virgo of the Eternal City itself, playing endlessly, day and night, throughout the centuries, like the fountain in the Palace of Saint Peter, before the sanctuary which is the heart and core of Christendom. The Antics Escolans of Montserrat will now sing in our recording a *Sequence* of the twelfth century *Cantantibus hodie* * preserved in the collection of Vich Cathedral, which is a characteristic example of the *Sequences* and *Tropes* in Gregorian chant.

In the next recording The Antics Escolans of Montserrat will sing the *Ave Maris Stella* ** by an anonymous composer of the thirteenth century. We should imagine this hymn chanted before the Romanesque statue of carved wood of Our Lady of Montserrat, blackened by the smoke of countless wax tapers that have been burning before her for the past nine hundred years.

* First Record, *Ancient Music*, side I, No. 2.
** First Record, *Ancient Music*, side I, No. 3.

30

Chapter III

ALFONSO THE WISE,
MINSTRELS AND TROUBADOURS

In the Middle Ages, outside the Church, there had arisen another music in the feudal castles, among the *troubadours* and *trouvères*. It was an artificial and aristocratic growth, concerned only indirectly, if at all, with the transmission of folk-song. But while the *troubadours* and *minnesinger* were singing in the castles and lisping conceits to their ladies, down among the humble folk we meet another type of performer called the *jongleur* in France, the *juglar* in Spain and the *giullare* in Italy, who was the ancestor of our modern wandering minstrels. The word was derived from the Latin *joculator* and meant, according to Menéndez Pidal, anyone whose profession it was to perform before an audience. He was not necessarily a musician; he might be a reciter of ballads, an acrobat, a juggler, a sword-swallower, a hurdy-gurdy player. His duty was to amuse and entertain people. If the troubadours were, according to our slang, "highbrows", the *juglares* were certainly "low-brows" and we can understand how deeply the former despised the latter. Their scorn resembled that which the modern trained composer feels for the popular theme-writer, or the concert violinist for the vagrant player who scrapes the strings. The troubadour, too, did not consider himself a professional entertainer: he wrote verses to his lady's eyebrows, whose inspiration spurred him on, but he would never travel the roads with a lute strung across his shoulder, hoping on his way to sing for hire.

The *jongleur*, according to the troubadour, disgraced the knight-errantry of song by his antics: he travelled with disreputable wenches who should have been publicly whipped: he was a drunkard and a base intriguer; not a word came from his mouth that was not a foul blasphemy. Yet troubadours did not disdain to employ *jongleurs* as lute players and even reciters, for we find Giraut de Borneilh travelling about with them from court to court. It was, therefore, not surprising that one should influence the other. The *jongleurs* were historically more ancient than the troubadours who only came in about the eleventh century, and in the beginnings of court poetry there was little distinction between *jongleur* and *troubadour*. From the seventh century we find the word *joculator* from which sprang the French, Spanish and Italian names and they lasted on until the fourteenth century when the word became a term of abuse and performers preferred the word menestrel or ministril. In Spain, however, the word *juglar* remained among the people, and was applied to the lonely, disreputable vagabond roaming the road and living a picaresque life.

In France and Spain in the fourteenth century writers often refer to the wandering blind minstrels who were the last singers of the epic songs. Blind men were the natural repositories of national traditions, for their memories were prodigious and undistracted by the sights of the world. They followed the rhapsodical tradition,

31

the tradition of Homer, who was represented as a blind man and who has described so graphically in the eighth book of the Odyssey the old blind minstrel, Demodokos.

The influence of those wandering minstrels upon the literature and music of Europe cannot be exaggerated. They wandered from village to village, from country to country and they were received with favours in castle or in humble cottage, in town hall or in tavern. The Arab singers wandered over the Moslem world from Persia to Andalusia. Wherever men went they would find three kinds of wanderer from whom they could glean news of the various countries; the merchant, the friar and the minstrel. The poor minstrel always went on foot; only in moments of temporary prosperity could he dispose of a horse. His simple baggage consisted of his lute or *vihuela*, his book, and two or three personal effects which could be pawned where necessary. The book was the manuscript of the epic poems or the lyrical poems which he sang, a small volume poorly ornamented. In one of the French mediaeval manuscripts we see the picture of the ancient Provençal minstrel Cercamón, or "Globe-trotter", wandering on foot with his bundle over his shoulder like the emigrants we used to see in our youth going down to the port to take the boat to America. Yet humble as the minstrels were they were welcomed by their public, high and low. No festival or banquet could be held without them. According to the mediaeval Spanish writer Don Juan Manuel, music and literature were the two most delightful pleasures of the rich man, but let us not imagine that the rich man was satisfied in those days with the mere musical or dramatic talents of his *juglar*.

The minstrel had also to be a pleasant social companion, to show skill in fishing, to be able to recite a verse message to his rich patron's fair Dulcinea. Sometimes, too, he would find himself obliged to compose a song of insult as a challenge to his patron's enemy. The *juglar* was welcomed even in the monasteries and palaces of bishops, and in England bishops as far back as the seventh century had actors and musicians in their service. In Spain the provincial Council of Toledo of 1324 denounced the bishops for admitting publicly into their palaces *juglares* and wandering women dancers called *soldaderas* to dine with them.

In spite of the minstrels the most brilliant courts of song were not in the north of Spain. It is in Moorish Spain that we get some of our most interesting descriptions of the early music, for we should remember that in the ninth and tenth centuries Córdoba was the great centre for music and the arts. The northern Christians were perpetually quarrelling with one another, and their civilization was inferior to that of the city of Emirs and Caliphs.

The earliest description of Spanish music speaks of the singing of the famous Persian musician of Córdoba, Ziryab, to whom we have already referred. Ziryab, who had been the pupil of Ishaq at the court of Harun ar Rashid, the Caliph of the Arabian Nights, left Bagdad and found a generous protector in the great Emir Abderrahman II (821-852). In Córdoba he founded a celebrated school of singing and, according to tradition, composed thousands of songs. His life was told by Al-Maqqari and Abu'l Faraj of Isphahan, who added that his songs were sung all over the Moslem world.

He divided his instruction into three courses: rhythm, melody and ornamentation. When pupils came to him asking for lessons, he would first of all test them in voice production, and one of his tests was to make them sing in a loud and prolonged "aaa...aa...aa", in order to raise their voice to the right pitch, warm it, and "submerge it in feeling". He would then test the purity and strength of the pupil's voice, its carrying power, and note whether there was any suspicion of nasal tone or difficulty in breath. When a pupil had a promising but weak voice, he was told to tie a turban tightly around his stomach, so that the voice could not find an empty or hollow cavity before issuing from the mouth. When a pupil did not open his mouth widely enough, he made him sleep with a thick piece of wood between his teeth.[1]

Ziryab caused a revolution in the teaching of songs, for whereas the majority of teachers used to sing the song straight through, and make the students imitate them, Ziryab made them first of all learn the words and the metre without the music, to mark the strong accents and the weak, and the speed of the different movements. When the pupil knew the words, he was taught the melody in its simplest form, without ornaments. Then, when he could sing it properly, he was allowed to study the grace-notes, trills and vocalises which gave the

[1] Al Maqqari, *The Breath of Fragrance of Andalusia*. English translation, vol. II, pp. 16 sq. Abu'l Faraj, *The Book of Songs*. J. Ribera, *La Música Árabe y su Influencia en la Española*, Madrid, 1927. See also R. Dozy, *Spanish Islam* (English trans. 1913), p. 261. J. Rouanet, *Revue musicale*, Paris, June, 1927. J. B. Trend, *The Music of Spanish History to 1600*. See also R. Menéndez Pidal, New York, 1926, pp. 18-21.

32

subtle expression to the song. This description of Ziryab's methods is important for those who study *Cante Jondo* or "Deep Song" in modern Andalusia. In Ziryab, too, we get a reference to what we might call the magic of music, for according to his Moslem biographers, the genie visited him in his sleep and whispered melodies in his ear. When he awoke, he called his two musical slaves, and taught them the song. Then when he had written down the words he went back to bed.[1]

Music, among the Arabs, as well as being a magic song, was related to all the intoxicants of life. Though frowned upon at first by the followers of the Prophet, it became the obligatory accompaniment to social inter-course: thus Orpheus and Dionyseus went hand in hand at those feasts of song when Ziryab "The Blackbird of Song" sang before Abderrahman as he had done before the Caliph of Bagdad. And maidens wearing saffron robes and scarves on which verses were embroidered were led before the throne by eunuchs in red tunics. All night in the palace they would sing, dance and recite poetry in a swelling orgy of light, colours and sounds. Then when the grey dawn would steal over the scene, bringing an ashy pallor to the flushed cheeks of the revellers, the musicians would become all of a sudden hushed and the Caliph would burst into tears. In the distance all would hear the calm voice of the Muezzin from the minaret calling the faithful to the morning prayer.

MINSTRELS ON THE ROAD OF SAINT JAMES

When at the beginning of the ninth century (814) the news of the discovery of the body of the Apostle at Compostela was known pilgrims began to gather there from all over the world, especially from neighbouring France, and in the wake of the French Bishops, French monks and French knights came such a throng of min-strels that the *Camino Francés* from the Rue Saint-Jacques in Paris to the "Gate of the French" at the entrance to Compostela echoed and re-echoed to the songs of the *jongleurs* and *troubadours*. And at the end of their journey, at the western entrance to the Basilica of the Apostle, the minstrels would all at once see in front of them in all its unearthly beauty the *Pórtico de la Gloria*, or Gate of Glory of Master Mateo, where Christ sits enthroned, surround-ed by angels, saints, and at his feet the Great Wayfarer Santiago. And above, seated around the throne of the Redeemer in their rainbow arch, are the twenty-four Ancients of the Apocalypse, holding their instruments and their vials of perfume. Two by two they converse quietly or wait abstractedly in the traditional manner of orchestral players for the signal from the Conductor to begin the Divine Symphony. For hundreds of years pilgrims visiting the Cathedral of Santiago used to leave, as mementoes of their visit, pieces of music, and the archives as far back as the thirteenth century were enriched by original works in mediaeval primitive polyphony, which are among the most interesting musical relics in the world.

[1] W. Starkie, *Don Gypsy*, London, 1936, pp. 65-66.

Two minstrels playing cymbals. Miniature from the *Cantigas de Santa María* (thirteenth century) in the Escorial Library.

33

Even from the *Codex Calixtinus*, or "Book of Saint James" as it was also called, which was edited by the Poitevin cleric Aymery Picaud in the twelfth century, we learn of the importance given to music at Compostela. In it we find a hymnary of the Apostle with both words, and music and the author describes how when the pilgrims came from all parts of the world, including Scotland, Ireland, Wales and England, they filled the Cathedral in "ordered phalanx", and while some played upon their native instruments and others held lighted tapers, they chanted fervent hymns.   And the author adds that the pilgrims most remarkable for their singing were the Teutons, the Greeks and the English.   They all sang the celebrated refrain of the Pilgrims' Song of Santiago:

Herru Sanctiagu,
Grot Sanctiagu,
E ultreja, esuseja,
Deus adjuva nos.

This hymn was composed by Aymery Picaud himself and has been transcribed by Canon Tafall of Santiago as follows:[1]

Dum pa-ter fa-mi-li-as ——— Rex u-ni-ver-so-rum Do-na-ret pro-vin-ci-as ———

Jus a-pos-to-lo-rum   Ja-co-bus His-pa-ni-as Lux il-lus-trar mo ——— rum

Pri-mus ex   a-pos-to-lis,   Mar-tyr Je-ro-so-ly-mis, Ja-co-bus e - gre-gi-o

Sa-cer est mar-ty-ri-o

Her-ru Sanc-ti-a-gu, Grot Sanc-ti-a-gu E ul-tre ——— ja E sus-e ——— ja!

De-us ad-ju-va nos

Even today in the Cathedral on July 25th, the Feast of Saint James, when the *botafumeiro* or gigantic censer swings exultantly through the nave shedding clouds of fragrant incense, and the massed choir sing the rousing hymn of the Apostle, we can imagine ourselves back in the twelfth century, the heyday of the Jacobean pilgrimage, when Archbishop Gelmírez ruled Galicia like a patriarchal monarch and welcomed here the greatest rulers in Christendom and their suites.

[1] Tafall, *Ultreya:* Revista Quincenal, May 15, 1920, XVII, 262. See also, Fidel Fita and Fernández-Guerra, *Recuerdos de un Viaje a Santiago de Galicia*, Madrid, 1880, p. 46.   For the music in the *Codex Calixtinus* or Book of Saint James see Dom Germán Prado, O.B.S., *Liber Sancti Jacobi Codex Calixtinus*, vol. II Música, Santiago de Compostela, 1944.

Santiago Cathedral with its wonderful archives is one of the treasure-houses for the traveller in quest of mediaeval music, and another is Montserrat, which even in the fourteenth century was thronged by pilgrims, who, as Professor Trend aptly said, left their musical visiting-cards behind them.[1] One of those melodies called *Polorum Regina* has always struck me as the most haunting pilgrim song in the world, and it must have been very popular with the Jacobeans who passed from Montserrat and Ripoll along the road through Aragon, to the West, for two hundred years later, in the second half of the sixteenth century, it was taken down in Old Castile, by Francisco Salinas, the blind professor of music in the University of Salamanca and included in his *Seven Books of Music*.[2]

Po - lo - rum re - gi - na om - ni - um nos — tra stel - la ma - tu

ti - na de - le sce - le — ra An - te par - tum Vir - go De - o

gra - vi — da

ALFONSO THE WISE AND THE CANTICLES

One of the greatest figures of the Middle Ages was Alfonso X, El Sabio, the son of Ferdinand III, the Saint, who had captured Seville from the Moors in 1248. Alfonso gathered into his court at Toledo and León the learned men of the three religions, the Christian, the Jewish and the Moslem, for he was as eager to sift the wisdom of the East as of the West, and paid as much attention to the new Roman Law as he did to the old laws and customs of Spain. He was the first European king interested in secularizing culture, which he did by expressing his vast encyclopaedic knowledge in the vulgar Romance tongue. He pointed the way to Spain's true destiny, which was to serve as a link between the two heterogeneous worlds of Christianity and Islam. Some idea of the violent opposition he had to face against his reforms still reaches us today when we read the attacks of his contemporaries calling him an impious blasphemer. Nevertheless he triumphed over his opponents and his historial works were studied by scholars all over Europe. They were translated into Catalan and Portuguese, and his oriental works were translated into French and had an influence on Dante. His astronomical tables were studied in Europe for several centuries and were read and annotated by Copernicus himself. Due to his influence the country underwent a deep cultural transformation and by his success in reconciling the forces working for innovation and those working for tradition, Spain reached one of her historical peak points.

Alfonso the Wise, in addition to his encyclopaedic books on history, law, astronomy and mathematics, made a collection of *Cantigas* which is one of the greatest monuments of mediaeval music in the world. The *Cantigas de Santa María*, which consist of four hundred and thirty poems in the Galician-Portuguese dialect, set to music, are preserved in two beautifully illuminated manuscripts in the library of the Escorial. The earlier and incomplete manuscript, which was formerly at Toledo, is now in the National Library in Madrid, and there is a further manuscript at Florence.

The *Cantigas* are popular religious songs or carols devoted to Our Lady, and giving account of her miracles, and are set to model melodies of the period. Some of them describe the adventures of pilgrims on the road to Santiago di Compostela, others embroider well-known legends familiar to us in Gautier de Coincy and the

[1] J. B. Trend, *The Performance of Music in Spain*, in Proceedings of the Musical Association, Session IV, Jan. 15, 1929.
[2] F. Salinas, *De Musica, Libri Septem*, Salamanca, 1577, p. 306.

Golden Book of Voragine, such as that of the monk who heard a bird singing in the woods and was so entranced that he stayed listening to it for three hundred years, and the story of the nun who ran away from the convent, but when she returned repentant found that Our Lady had taken her place and nobody in the convent had noticed her absence.

In one of the miniatures (page 39) two minstrels are shown playing their stringed instruments. Between them stands a table with a jar of wine upon it. One of the *juglares* is a Moor in turban, the other is a Christian. Both take part in a friendly consort of viols. Such a picture illustrates the tolerant intentions of Alfonso the Wise, who edited the minstrelsy that came from Christian and Jewish as well as Moslem sources.

In another miniature (page 37) we see the King in the centre directing his musicians. Four minstrels play instruments, two on each side of His Majesty. Behind them a group of four singers are performing. Are the players accompanying the singers separately or are they playing all together as an orchestra? Probably the instruments doubled the voices, for a century later the Archpriest of Hita tells us which are the suitable instruments for accompanying *cantigas*, and warns us that some, owing to their European character, were not suitable for accompanying Arab melodies. "Arabic music", he says sententiously "won't tolerate the bowed viol, and as for the hurdy-gurdy and guitar they are out of place in this setting." Mossen Anglés believes that the people sang, in response, the melody following each stanza, just as they did in the folk *goigs* where the Catalan *tornel* corresponded to the refrain in the French *Virelais* and the *ripresa* in the Italian *laudi*.

Misfortune dogged Alfonso's footsteps. First the death of his eldest son Fernando de la Cerda, who at thirteen years of age had been married to Blanche of Provence, the daughter of Saint Louis, at the monastery of Las Huelgas at Burgos. The death of the Infante changed the course of Spanish history. Then began dynastic troubles which plunged the country into civil war, for Don Sancho, Alfonso's second son, claiming the succession against the children of his brother Fernando, fought against his father and eventually was declared a rebel. Doña Violante, whom the King had wished at one moment to set aside, in order to marry Christina, Princess of Norway, then left him and went off to Catalonia, where she intrigued with the rest of the family against the King. Then came the rising of the nobles who resented the immense intellectual superiority of the King, and rebuked him for spending the time he should have been devoting to affairs of state, either in stargazing, chess-playing, poring over manuscripts with his Moorish and Jewish scholars, or editing the Galician poems of his contributors to the Canticles.

His palace did, in fact, resemble an international academy or a huge publisher's central office, rather than the stately residence of a King, and it must have seemed too much of a Liberty Hall to the proud barons of Castile and León, who, when they went there, found themselves surrounded by a motley crowd of intellectual-looking foreigners, all conversing on equal terms, without a trace of hierarchical distinctions or palace etiquette.

Alfonso himself, however, as the miniatures in the Canticles prove, did not spend all his time absorbed in higher studies. Like the Caliph Harun ar Rashid, he would often follow his minstrel poets, singers and players out of the palace gates into the streets and visit their haunts.

In the *Cantigas* many of the scenes in the miniatures are illustrations of the life of the minstrels, not only when they were on their best behaviour at court, but when they were drinking, gambling or consorting with their female confederates, who were called *soldaderas*. In one of the miniatures we see a tavern with a huge pigskin in the corner which resembles the one Sancho Panza saw Don Quixote slashing like a turnip, thinking it was a giant. In another miniature there is a quarrel in a gambling den and two are banging their heads together, while round the gambling table and the dice sit men and women, and at the other side two men fight together with hand and fist.

A CELEBRATED WOMAN MINSTREL

One of these *soldaderas* was the notorious María Pérez Balteira whose exploits were celebrated by eleven troubadours, including the King himself. When she stood in front of His Majesty, arrogant and beautiful, and sang her obscene songs, the King would roar with laughter at her sallies and would become more violent than any of the male gamblers.

36

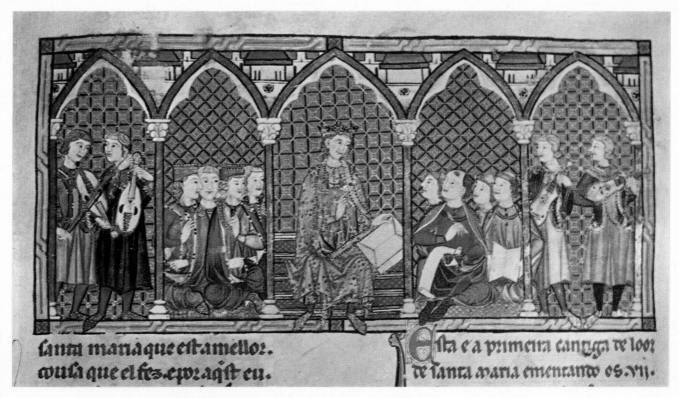

Alfonso the Wise composing his melodies amidst his court of musicians.
Miniature from the manuscript of the *Cantigas de Santa María* (thirteenth century) in the Escorial Library.

La Balteira in character was as inconsistent as Alfonso the Wise himself, for in spite of her blatant immorality, her dissipation and her gaming, she had her moments of repentance when she declared that she wished to retire into a convent, and in 1257, at the beginning of Alfonso el Sabio's reign, she bequeathed a rich estate belonging to her mother to the Cistercian monks at Sobrado, in return for a life pension. She pledged herself in the document to give service to the monastery as familiar and friend *(familiar e amiga)* and she stipulated that at her death the monks should carry her to her tomb in Sobrado in a coffin covered with three yards of crimson serge, and give her the ceremonies prescribed for familiars of the monastery. La Balteira, moreover, when in one of her religious moods, would declare that she wished to go on a pilgrimage to the Holy Land. But as the Galician singer, Pero Amigo tells us, she had qualms and was afraid to abandon her friends, nor would she set out without consulting the omens of sneezing and the flight of birds. She did, however, set out on her pilgrimage, but according to the sarcastic minstrels she went no farther than Montpellier.

Nevertheless her return to the court was celebrated in poetry and song and the veteran bard Pero da Ponte cried: "Here is our crusader pilgrim María Pérez back from overseas and so laden with indulgences and pardons that she cannot stand upright. The indulgences are precious and should have been carefully preserved, but La Balteira's trunk had no lock and the youths of the town turned everything topsy turvy and stole her indulgences, so that everyone of them she has lost."

When we next hear of her she was stationed on the Moorish border and was busily engaged in fleecing the King's archers. Later on, we hear of her on the Murcian frontier consorting with a Moorish chief whom King Alfonso was helping secretly against the King of Granada.

It is clear to us that Alfonso the Wise made use of La Balteira's sexual attractions to secure information about his Moorish enemies, and that she was a thirteenth-century Mata Hari. Whether she was a successful spy or not is immaterial, but there is no doubt that she was immensely popular among all classes in the country, and there were scores of poets who boasted they enjoyed her favours, though there was one who admitted that to win them was so difficult a task that he would prefer hanging. The King himself when writing about her love affairs did so in satirical *Cantigas de Escarnio* with many obscene allusions, but he himself was one of her most devoted admirers.

When at last she felt herself getting old she returned to her pilgrim mood and took up good works. The minstrels and troubadours found her kneeling outside a confessional in the Cathedral of Santiago in Galicia, but all she could say in repentance was: "I'm old, alas, father!" (*Soo vella, ay, capelan!*) [1]

Even the malicious gibes of the poets did not cease, for the Portuguese Fernán Velho writes that La Balteira, the repentant sinner, now that she is afraid of death, promises God that she will always keep by her side a young clerk in holy orders to protect her against the devil, and upon whom she will charitably bestow her own bed. [2] And her old and faithful lover Pero de Amboa now feels that she is irreparably lost and regrets that he has loved so old a woman, but consoles himself with the reflection that all the wealth she made in the King's palace will now be given to the young clerk in holy orders, and when the old courtesan is reduced to poverty nobody will need her services except as bawd. In the *Cancionero de Ajuda* of the thirteenth-fourteenth century there is a charming miniature representing a Galician troubadour dressed in long flowing robes, seated on a stool. In front of him stands a beautiful fair-haired girl who raises her arms and dances as she sings to the music played on a large psaltery by a *juglar*. I like to think that the miniature represents La Balteira in all her arrogant and youthful graces, when she first captivated the Wise King, and that the minstrel seated beside her is the faithful Pero de Amboa.

THE TRAGEDY OF ALFONSO THE WISE

Such was the society of minstrels and troubadours that gathered around King Alfonso the Wise when he broke away from his Academy of priests, historians, astronomers and astrologers. Among the comely poets of Provence trained in *Gay Saber* and the backbiting troubadours of Galicia with their *cantigas de escarnio* he moved as easily as he did among the priests and astronomers, and from the poems to La Balteira, we derive a more worldly impression of a King whom hitherto we have considered mainly as a figure of romance. But we remember Mariana's accusation against him of inconsistency, and in another passage the sixteenth-century historian is still more explanatory: "King Alfonso", he says, "was a great and most prudent King, if only he had learnt how to apply his wisdom to himself" (*si hubiera aprendido a saber para sí*). His greatest fault was his imperialistic craze which drove him to intrigue ceaselessly with foreign countries, in the hope of strengthening his claim to territories which he thought himself entitled to annex, owing to his universal family connections. Inside the Peninsula he laid claim first of all to Algarve, then to Navarre. Then he laid claim to Gascony which was then in the hands of the English. After some fighting the matter was settled by the marriage of Alfonso's sister Eleanor to Prince Edward, the son of the King of England, who obtained from his father the coveted province. Far more ambitious were his schemes in Germany where he became a claimant to the imperial crown as son of Beatrice of Swabia. For twenty years he nourished this vain hope and taxed Castile heavily to defray the costs of his electioneering, but in the end the Pope of the day gave his support to Rudolf of Habsburg who was elected. It was, however, the rebellion of his second son Sancho after the death of Fernando de la Cerda, that brought about the ruin of the Wise King and changed his nature from an artist and dreamer into a rancorous vindictive old man.

In a pathetic letter to Alonso Pérez de Guzmán he mentions that in all his territories only one city had remained faithful to him, Seville. "My sorrow is so great because as my fall has been from high estate it will

[1] R. Menéndez Pidal, *Poesía Juglaresca y Juglares*, Madrid, 1924, pp. 217, 231 sq. See also: R. Menéndez Pidal, *España, Eslabón entre La Cristiandad y el Islam*, Madrid, 1956. Menéndez Pidal considers that the four compositions in the *Cancionero Colocci-Brancuti* by the Compostellan Joan Vázquez refer to La Balteira.
[2] Canc. Colocci-Brancuti, No. 1504.

be seen afar. And as I was a friend of all the world, so all the world will learn of my mischance and my affliction."

After accusing his son Sancho and those who had been his friends and upon whom he had heaped benefits without number he made the following tragic declaration: "If my sons are my enemies it is only just that I should consider my enemies as my sons." The end of the letter signed by the King, reads as follows: "Written in my loyal city of Seville, in the thirtieth year of my reign, and the first of my sorrows."

All the tragedy of King Alfonso the Wise may be discovered in that letter. There was nothing left for him but to close himself up in his palace in Seville and prepare for death, and this came shortly afterwards in 1284.

Alfonso on his deathbed awoke to realize that he had all his life been living in a fool's paradise; that all his vast learning, star-gazing, astrology and philosophic speculations had lured him away from the daily problems of Spain, the Moors on the frontier, his pitiless sons and his rebellious subjects into an imaginary world of music and poetry. He had written his own life story in the canticle of the monk who lingered in the wood by the fountain, listening for three hundred years to the singing of the bird, and, he, too, had been so entranced by that magic song that for a moment he had felt as if the Queen of Heaven had carried him aloft on the wings of that songster to catch a glimpse of paradise. And the music he heard was the echo of the angels singing and awoke memories of that Divine Harmony Fray Luis de Léon would apostrophize three hundred years later in the words:

A Moorish minstrel and a Christian minstrel, both taking part in a friendly viol concert. This miniature is a good illustration of King Alfonso the Wise's intentions. He published all kinds of music, be it Christian, Jewish or Moorish. (Miniatures of the *Cantigas de Santa María* by Alfonso the Wise, seventeenth century, the Escorial Library.)

A cuyo son divino	At whose blest sound divine
Mi alma que en olvido está sumida,	My soul that in forgetfulness hath lain
Torna a cobrar el tino	With a new light doth shine
y memoria perdida	And unto memory plain
de su origen primera esclarecida	of its first splendid origin attain
Trasspasa el aire todo	up through the fields of air
Hasta llegar a la más alta esfera,	it wings, till in the highest sphere it dwells,
Y oye allí otro modo	And a new music there
De no perecedera	It hears, music that wells
Música, que es de todas la primera. [1]	Unending, and all other kinds excels. [2]

[1] F. Luis de León, *Ode to Francisco de Salinas.*
[2] Trans. by E. A. Peers.

Alfonso, like the monk in his canticle, was stricken with sadness when the bird ended its celestial song, for it had been so short-lived, but when he tried to enter his daily life again he discovered that all had changed; no one recognized him and all the world seemed out of tune, for three hundred years had passed.

There is tragic irony in the thought that the last act of this King, so renowned for his wisdom and learning, should have been to disinherit his son and heir, thus leaving behind him a legacy of chaos and civil war.

Posterity, however, has preferred to idealize the Troubadour King, and we must take him as one of the guides on our Spanish musical journey through the ages. He comes in succession to Saint Isidore of Seville who guided us at the outset towards Gregorian chant, wherein the disembodied soul of melody, freed from all shackles, soars ecstatically upwards to Heaven. Alfonso the Wise took the torch and led the way in his Canticles towards the earthly paradise of music, the *reverdie* or reawakening of nature and of joy in earthly things in the springtime of the world. For us today there still remains mysterious enchantment in the Celtic lilt of those Canticles to Our Lady, and we feel sad for Alfonso the Wise monarch, whose troubled reign reminds me of the verses of W. B. Yeats:

> A King is but a foolish dreamer
> Who wastes his blood to be another's dream.

As an example of the poetry of Alfonso the Wise we have chosen *Cantiga* No. 353*, which has been adapted by Maestro Rafael Ferrer for choir and wind quintet. It is performed by the Antics Escolans of Montserrat and the Barcelona Wind Quintet. The music subtly suggests the naive melancholy of a thirteenth-century poem written in Galician-Portuguese dialect. The four-lined refrain and the first strophe are as follows:

Quem a omagem de Uiergen	He who will do homage
et de seu Fillo onrrar,	to the image of Our Lady and her Son
d'eles sera muit onrrado	will honours receive from Them
no seu ben que non a par.	in Their glory (Paradise) which is peerless.
E de tal razon com'esta	And I shall tell you, if it pleaseth,
vos direi, se vos prouguer	a story on this subject,
miragre que fez a Uiergen	of a miracle the Virgin wrought
que sempre nosso ben quer	that we might gain the Kingdom of her Son,
perque aiamos o reyno	whence the first sin drove us,
do seu Fill', ond'a moller	a grievous sin indeed.
primeiro nos deitou fora,	
que foi malament'errar.	

* First Record, *Ancient Music*, side I, No. 4.

Chapter IV

THE GOLDEN TREASURY
OF THE MINSTRELS

The minstrel played a great part in making life agreeable by his accomplishments: he lasted longer than the troubadours because his range was greater. Mankind always needs the entertainer, and the troubadour, once the vogue of his refined song passed away, disappeared, whereas the "low-brow" minstrel still kept on wandering through the villages. The minstrel always had a touch of the devil in him, and that was why the Church pursued him, and the worthy citizen, though admiring his talents, would call him disreputable. The tradition of the Roman *Mimus*, who was *infamis* descended on the *juglar* in Spain, and from him to the wandering actor and lasted on to our day. The minstrel was considered disreputable because he played a musical instrument. But the power of playing an instrument was the minstrel's greatest safeguard, for it gave him the possibility of journeying from one country to another without ever finding himself debarred by language difficulties. After the brilliant period of minstrelsy in the thirteenth and fourteenth centuries we find the whole tradition of the wandering singer and player summed up in the *Libro de Buen Amor* (The Book of Good Love) written by the Spanish Archpriest of Hita, Juan Ruíz, which we might call the Golden Treasury of minstrelsy.[1] The Archpriest, who has been called the Rabelais of Spain, is close in poetic genius and gusto to the Father of English poetry, Geoffrey Chaucer, who was his contemporary. Certainly the Archpriest is the greatest figure in Spanish literature before Cervantes, but he deserves even more universal fame, for nobody has ever described the essence of wandering as did that portly, hirsute priest with the ferrety eyes. In his book which he meant to pass from hand to hand, we discover every type of song that could have appealed to noble, peasant, priest, scholar, musician or buffoon, in the most brilliant period of minstrelsy in the fourteenth century.

If the Canticles of Alfonso the Wise are songs chanted in the springtime of poetry and music, the minstrelsy of the Archpriest belongs to the radiant summer, and though at times the minstrel writes little poems to the Queen of Heaven in the style of his royal ancestor in song, he is a far more worldly guide for us and leads us into male and female company that would have shocked even King Alfonso. Juan Ruíz, in fact, was a village priest like Gonzalo de Berceo, but we know very little about his life from documents though a great deal through his autobiographical *Libro de Buen Amor*.

[1] Juan Ruíz, Arcipreste de Hita, *El Libro de Buen Amor*, copla 15,6. See also F. Pedrell, *Organografía antigua española*, Barcelona, 1901, p. 46. For Arab music and mediaeval Spain see J. Ribera, *La Música Andaluza medieval*, Madrid, 1925, Fasciculo b. 3, pp. 4-8.

In fact, so much do we learn about our friend the Archpriest from the autobiographical as opposed to the lyrical part of his great work that he becomes the indispensable companion of the wanderer who makes the double music journey, backward in time and forward in space.

Juan Ruíz thus becomes our third guide on the musical journey.

The Archpriest was, as he tells us, more than average tall, sturdy, thick-set, hairy, full-chested, bull-necked, black-eyed, with thick eyebrows, neat legs, small feet, sensuous lips, large ears, and expansive nostrils.

With such a companion to cheer us on our way we shall not be allowed to yawn with boredom, for he will lead us up hill down dale, and as we plod the road to Guadalajara vagabond poets and musicians of all kinds will join our band with the Archpriest prancing at our head, and he himself will become a snowball of minstrelsy, growing larger and larger as he rolls along, collecting song after song for his song-bag—Latin songs, Moorish songs, Jewish songs, French *fabliaux*, *contes* and *pastourelles*. There was nothing in life that was not grist to the Archpriest's mill; he had no personal conceit about his own work, for he would say:

Qualquier omne que lo oya, si bien trobar supiere,	Let anyone who is gifted with song
Puede mas añadir e enmendar lo que quisiere.	add and correct as best he can.

How benevolent he was in comparison to his contemporary the celebrated aristocratic poet Don Juan Manuel, the nephew of Alfonso the Wise, who was so afraid of the copyists who would re-edit his words that he corrected with his own pen his manuscript and deposited it in the monastery of Peñafiel, forbidding anyone to reproduce the book unless they copied it word for word from the monastery original!

The Archpriest's originality lies both in his style which was racy and careless and did wonders, as Fitzmaurice Kelly said, in breaking down the stiff formation of the *mester de clerecía* and in experimenting in new metres. [1] He boasts that he had left no kind unattempted, that he has written dance-songs, and serenades without number for Moorish and Jewish dancing-girls, for blind men as well as for the nocturnal wandering students and "dawn-chasers".

So bewitched are we by Doña Endrina, the fascinating widow in Guadalajara, by the wrestling Amazonian woman in the mountain passes of Segovia, by the little doxy to whom he addressed poems, that we discover the descendants for ourselves today as we pad the hoof over those roads and halt in the taverns by the way, or linger under the arcades of Alcalá de Henares. "As to my *cantares cazurros*", says Juan Ruíz, "ten books would not contain them." Now the *cantares cazurros* were roguish roundelays characteristic of the wandering minstrels and were generally then, as they are today, addressed to village doxies, and one of them has survived from the manuscript of the Archpriest entitled *trova cazurra* and beginning:

Mys ojos non verán luz	My eyes will see no light,
Pues perdido he a Cruz.	for I have lost Cruz.

Because the girl's name was Cruz a number of scholars tried to make out that the poem was an allegory and that Cruz meant the Cross of our redemption, whereas the Archpriest, who was as ribald as any of the lax clerics in Chaucer's Canterbury Tales, loved, even in the fourteenth century, to mystify his reader and with sly humour contrast the *loco amor* or worldly love with the *Buen Amor* (divine love) in a style with which we already have become familiar in the songs of the Galician minstrels who sang for the Wise King.

Cruz was evidently one of the pretty doxies who was pert to the Archpriest, and he revenged himself in the little poem. We know from various references in his book what type of girl he really admired, and he has written one immortal poem celebrating the beauty of little women which survives today in the beautiful translation of Longfellow, to the eternal discomfiture of all Junoesque ladies: [2]

[1] J. Fitzmaurice Kelly, *Some Masters of Spanish Verse*, Oxford, 1924, p. 19.
[2] This poem, translated by H. W. Longfellow, was published in *The North American Review*. Republished in *Hispanic Anthology* collected and arranged by T. Walsh, New York, 1920.

I wish to make my sermon brief, to shorten my oration,
For a never-ending sermon is my utter detestation,
I like short women, suits-at-law, without procrastination,
And am always most delighted with things of short duration.

A babbler is a laughing-stock, he's a fool who's always grinning,
But little women love so much, one falls in love with sinning.
There are women who are very tall, and yet not worth the winning,
And in the change of short for long repentance finds beginning.

To praise the little women, Love brought me in my musing,
To tell their noble qualities is quite beyond refusing,
So I'll praise the little women, and you'll find the thing amusing;
They are, I know, as cold as snow, whilst flames around diffusing.
They're cold without, whilst warm within
The flame of Love is raging
They're gay and pleasant in the street—soft, cheerful and engaging,
They're thrifty and discreet at home, the cares of life assuaging,
All this and more—try, and you'll find how true is my presaging.

In a little precious stone, what splendour meets the eyes!
In a little lump of sugar how much of sweetness lies!
So in a little woman love grows and multiplies,
You recollect the proverb says—a word unto the wise.

A peppercorn is very small, but seasons every dinner
More than all other condiments, although 'tis sprinkled thinner,
Just so a little woman is, if Love will let you win her,
There's not a joy in all the world you will not find within her.

And as within the little rose you find the richest dyes,
And in a little grain of gold much price and value lies,
As from a little balsam much odour doth arise,
So in a little woman there's a taste of paradise!

Even as a little ruby its secret worth betrays,
Colour and price and virtue, in the clearness of its rays,
Just so a little woman much excellence displays,
Beauty and grace and love and fidelity always.

The skylark and the nightingale, though small and light of wing,
Yet warble sweeter in the grove than all the birds that sing,
And so a little woman, though a very little thing,
Is sweeter far than sugar, and flowers that flower in Spring.

The magpie and the golden thrush have many a thrilling note,
Each as a gay musician doth strain his little throat,
A merry little songster in his green and yellow coat,
And such a little woman is when love doth make her doat.
There's nought can be compared to her, throughout the wide creation,
She is a paradise on earth—our greatest consolation—
So cheerful, gay and happy, so free from all vexation,
In fine she's better in the proof than in anticipating.

If as her size increases are woman's charms decreased,
Then surely it is good to be from all the great released,
Now of two evils, choose the less—said a wise man of the East,
By consequence, of woman-kind be sure to choose the least.

Such was Juan Ruíz the Archpriest and we imagine him ambling along the road with a Moorish dancing girl on each arm.   A sinner he was, but not a hypocrite, and he would have laughed hilariously at the notion that a day would come when bearded scholars would think of him as a kind of religious reformer.   "I have come into the world", he would say, "to get my eye full as well as my ear full.   When the Devil is famished he eats flies.   Today he has to tramp over hill, over dale, and he has worn out a heap of shoes dancing and gallivanting after frolicsome humankind".

Juan Ruíz was so busy getting his eye full and his ear full that he had no time for evangelizing, and the types he saw appear again and again in Spanish literature: Doña Endrina, who appears again and again in the Marquis of Santillana, Cervantes, Tirso de Molina and in many a modern heroine; Don Furón, the Archpriest's picaresque squire who is the ancestor of Sancho Panza; Trotaconventos, the ancestress of La Celestina, the bawd, and a long line of Spanish witchwives, who inspired the Archpriest to write one of the greatest poems on death in the Spanish language, for nobody knew more than he did of the fleeting happiness of a summer day.   His motto was "gather ye rosebuds while ye may", but his despairing cry:

Ay Muerte ! muerta seas, muerta e malandante !
Matásteme mi vieja : matasses a mi enante !
Enemiga de mundo, que non as semejante !

O Death! Would to God thou wert dead and doomed!
Thou hast killed our beloved crone; why didst thou spare my life?
Enemy of the entire world, none is thine equal;
Who doth not cringe in terror at thy name?

is not the mere lament by a reveller on the death of his disreputable pander, but an elegy which moves us as does Shakespeare's pathos in describing the passing of Falstaff.   Even the words Juan Ruíz uses to describe his improvizations have a special meaning current among *jongleurs* and wandering singers.   *Fablévos en juglería* (I have spoken to you as a minstrel), for instance, are words which the *juglar* used rather in the sense of the Provençal expression *or dient et content et fablent* (they say and tell and compose fables) and they sum up his rhapsodic art and epitomize all minstrelsy, for even the irregular verses devoid of the counted syllables of learned poetry were characteristic of the minstrel: so, too, were the *serranillas* or highland lyrics sung to stringed instruments by the *juglares* who threaded their way through the passes of the Sierra de Guadarrama separating the *meseta* of Segovia and Avila from that of Madrid and Toledo: characteristic too, of the minstrel performance was the adaptation of verse to music and the snatches of folk-tunes so characteristic of a wanderer who keeps his ears open in the village plazas.   Characteristic of minstrelsy again are the quotations from Arab music which the Archpriest introduces into his great burlesque struggle between Don Carnal (Lord Carnival) and Doña Cuaresma (Lady Lent).   That struggle which the Archpriest based upon the French *Fabliau de la Bataille de Karesme et de Charnage* is the climax of the *Libro de Buen Amor* written in the heyday of the minstrel tradition in the year 1330, when the first edition appeared.   Let us visualize the scene described by the minstrel to his audience in the plaza of Alcalá de Henares.

The Battle between Lent and Carnival begins with the high-sounding challenge which burly Lord Carnival sends through his emissary Sir Breakfast and Lady Luncheon to haggard Lady Lent, inviting her to joust with him in the lists on Easter Sunday before cockcrow.   Lady Lent senses that she will be defeated, so on Easter Saturday she escapes over the wall disguised as a pilgrim.   On the following morning Lord Carnival and Lord Cupid march out with all their retinue like Emperors and the whole town goes out to welcome them: the shep-

44

herds skirl on their bagpipes, the tripe-mongers play the tambourine, the boys the panpipes and a cattledrover follows them playing his citterne. Lord Carnival and Lord Cupid pass through the streets triumphantly and are received by priests and laymen, monks, nuns and ladies, and with them come a great band of musicians, playing all manner of instruments and singing a song called *Cabel el orabín* or *Calbi garabí* which according to Arabists is *Qalbî qualb àrabi* which means "my heart is that of an Arab", or in Spanish form, *Rey Don Alfonso*. This popular Moorish song was well known in the Peninsula from the time of the Archpriest in the fourteenth century down to the time of Cervantes and Lope de Vega, who refer to it, and it was quoted by Salinas in his Seven Books of Music. Salinas quotes the melody to illustrate the metre composed of a cretic and a trochee, and he adds: "The song and dance of this was frequently performed among our people and came, I think, from the Moors; for it is still sung to Arabic words." He gives the tune which in Spanish was sung to *Rey Don Alfonso*, as follows:

The description given by the Archpriest of the different instruments that celebrated the pageant of Lord Carnival and Lord Cupid is a veritable symphony, a kermesse of words exalting the art of the wandering musician, and should be inscribed in letters of gold on the main doors of the conservatoires in every country, for it betokens the great-hearted tolerance of a Falstaffian spirit, who includes all the world of music within his ken. And here for once the two antagonistic classes of musicians meet in brotherhood, the Court players in varicoloured raiment, whose profession it was to make music in banqueting halls of Kings, in the palaces of Bishops or at vigils in chapels when proud Knights watch over their arms, and their humble and despised brothers who haunt the lonely roads in the mountains and scrape their strident one-string rebecks, pick at their gritty *bandurrias* or thrum their Moorish guitars in pitiful invocation at some wayside shrine of the Virgin. The gargantuan arms of our Archpriest are large enough to enclose them all within his embrace and his cloak is vast enough to cover them with his protective warmth.

With infinite minstrel gusto he describes their instruments one by one and smacks his lips and caresses the epithets he applies to each in turn, as though he wished its notes to prolong themselves within our souls like long-drawn double notes vibrated on a Cremona violin.

As the Master of all music speaks Nature smiles, the trees bend their branches in homage, the leaves murmur, and the flowers open their many-coloured petals in wide-eyed amazement, and as the procession of golden lads and lasses advances, we hear the distant roll of countless drums of different sizes, swelling and diminishing like summer thunder, reminding me of the traditional feast of drums at Alcañiz in Holy Week.

One by one the Archpriest points to the instruments of his motley orchestra, and turning, as it were, a poetic spotlight on each as the procession passes on. First comes the sharp frolicsome twanging of the Moorish guitar, after which the Archpriest points to the big-bellied lute and the Latin guitar, and there is a hush, for the music becomes more stately, and as our Mentor explains by vivid gesture, the notes are not plucked *(punteado)* as in Moslem music but *(rasgueado)* or softly thrummed in harmonious chords. A moment later a roguish grin spreads over his ruddy cheeks, and his eyes twinkle as he points to a Moorish *rabé*, whose sour squeaky tone playing the trochaic Moorish rhythm, drowns the Christian harmony and rouses the youths and maidens to a kind of brusque fandango. The towering Minstrel Priest rattled them off one by one, allotting to each its peculiar tone foible: the triangular psaltery "like a knoll in the plains" with its twenty-three strings played with both hands; the seventy-eight-string *cañón* of Islamic India and its smaller thirty-six-string brother the *medio cañón*, with hollow parchment-covered bellies plucked like banjos; rebecks again, from Islam, but those which beggars played before the days of the *kamendjah*.

[1] J. Ruíz, *Libro de Buen Amor*, Ed. J. Cejador y Frauca, Madrid, 1913, vol. II, p. 136, note on 1229 sq.; see also J. Ribera, *Música Arabe y su Influencia, op. cit.* H. Anglis, *El Côdex musical de las Huelgas* (Musica a veus dels segles XIII-XIX, Barcelona, 1931). See also A. Salazar, *op. cit.*, vol. I.

Nearly all the instruments described by the Archpriest are pictured in the fascinating miniatures of the Escorial illuminated manuscript of the Canticles of Alfonso the Wise, but let us not forget that a century before Alfonso X, on the fifth archivolt of the portal de la Majestad of the Romanesque collegiate church of Santa María la Mayor in Toro we may see the most complete representation of the musical instruments used in the Middle Ages, more complete than that of the Gate of Glory of Santiago, for at Toro we find not only string, but also percussion, wind and reed instruments, in addition to hand-organs, panpipes, hurdy-gurdys and bells.

Recent research has shown that Juan Ruíz, the Archpriest of Hita, had technical knowledge of music, and if the suggestion made by Mossén Anglés in his edition of the manuscript of *Las Huelgas*, is correct, namely that the composer of some of the *conducti* in that collection—a certain Johannes Rodericis or Rodríguez—was our Juan Ruíz, we should be entitled to consider him a pioneer in musical composition as well as the monarch of all poet minstrels, for the following *conductus*, and the whole *codex* from which it is taken, was written during his productive years between 1330 and 1343. According to Anglés, this little work is an unique example of double *conductus* in the fourteenth century, and it will lead us gently from the world of troubadour and minstrel on a further stage of our musical journey towards the polyphonic composers.

Of Juan Ruíz, the Archpriest, we might quote the old Spanish proverb *murió el hombre mas no su nombre* (the man died but not his name). Beyond the reference to his imprisonment there are very few documentary details of his life, but how greatly he was beloved by the people of Castile can be proved by an account written fifty years after his death in 1410. A scribe sat copying a Spanish chronicle, when all of a sudden he heard a minstrel performing outside his cell in the plaza. He let his attention wander from the manuscript he was copying and copied down on a blank leaf at the end of his manuscript the programme of what the minstrel actually performed[1], thus enabling us to reconstruct the minstrel repertoire in those far off days.

But we know from the lines copied by the scribe in his gloss that when the minstrel's audience began to weary of his songs, his quips and acrobatic jumps he would utter the magic words which had awakened the thrill of expectation in the people for the past fifty years:

Agora comencemos del libro del Arcipreste.   (Let us begin from the book of the Archpriest.)

[1] R. Menéndez Pidal, *Poesía Juglaresca y Juglares*, pp. 462-467.

Chapter V

THE SONG OF THE SIBYL

Up to now on our Spanish musical journey through the Middle Ages, we have spent most of our time in Andalusia, Castile, León, Aragon and Galicia, for Saint Isidore of Seville led us from his city to imperial Toledo and from there on to his resting place in León, and he passed the torch to the Wise King, who spirited us along his royal route back to Toledo and Seville, where on his death the torch passed to our next master, the Archpriest. But there was also Alfonso el Sabio's father-in-law, the patriarchal Don Jaime El Conquistador to remind us that the Mediterranean coast had equal claims upon our musical attention and we remembered the solemn injunction given by the Wise King in his will, that his Canticles to Our Lady should be preserved in the Cathedral when he was laid to rest, and every year at the feasts of the Blessed Virgin they should be sung over his tomb both in her Cathedral in Seville and in her royal church in Murcia.

As we flit on our mediaeval time journey from Andalusia towards the Alicantine and Murcian lands, evoked for all time by the modern prose poet Gabriel Miró and his vagabond hero Sigüenza, we become still more conscious of Mozarabic influences in the lilting songs of the bronzed peasants threshing in the fields, which even recall the Byzantine chants of *Hagia Sophia*. With these haunting chants in our ears we pass on to Valencia, where the boat awaits us bound for Palma in Majorca. On the edge of the sea, towering above the port, rises the noble Cathedral of Don Jaime the Conqueror of the island in 1322, whither we shall wend our way in quest of the mysterious Song of the Sibyl, one of the great treasures of ancient Spanish music.

Though all traces of the ancient Sibyl disappeared, her prophetic spirit was transferred to the Sibylline Oracles in Greek hexameters written by Alexandrian Christians and Jews after the second century. And the Messianic prophecy, written acrostically like the Sibylline verses of Rome, with the initials forming the Greek words for Jesus Christ, Son of God, Saviour, Cross, was quoted by Saint Augustine in *De Civitate* and again appeared in the solemn Sequence of Thomas Celano:

Dies irae dies illa.
Solvet saeclum in favilla.
Teste David cum Sibylla.

And this mysterious continuity between the ancient order and the new continued to obsess the minds of men throughout the Middle Ages and the Renaissance and inspired masterpieces by Giotto, Michelangelo and Raphael.[1]

The Song of the Sibyl is performed at Palma on Christmas Eve in the Cathedral and in the churches all over the island, even in the chapels in the remotest districts. During matins, when the clock strikes midnight, after the psalmody and Lessons, a procession winds its way to the chapel of the Sacred Crib and among the clergy we see little boys dressed, some as angels and others as shepherds. Among them, one of about twelve years of age, who possesses a singing voice, is selected to represent the Sibyl. He is dressed in a long pinkish robe and head-dress of the same colour and holds an unsheathed sword with both hands pointing upwards as he marches in the procession.

After the end of the *Te Deum* a fresh procession forms led by two acolytes, holding large wax tapers, and angels, and behind them comes the *Sibiller*, as he is called, who still holds his sword point upwards. During the procession the organ plays a number of folk tunes imitating the dawn songs or *alboradas* of the bagpipe, and the choir sing *villancicos*. Then the Sibyls, accompanied by the two acolytes carrying their large wax tapers, mounts the pulpit and there is a hush of silence in the vast cathedral, for the Priests at the High Altar delay the Mass until the boy singer has performed his ancient ritual. It is a solemn moment and the congregation in their thousands are all hushed in breathless expectation of the prophecy.

Suddenly, amidst the deathlike silence the clear resonant voice of the boy chants the Prophetic Canticle of the Last Judgment:

Responsión
El ——— jorn del ju ——— di ——— ci par ——— *
rà qui hau - rà ——— fet ser - vi ——— ci. Je ——— su —
Estrofa I
crist rei ——— u - ni - ver - sal ——— homo i ver Déu e - ter - nal del
cel ——— vindrà per a jut-jar ——— i a ca - da un lo just da-rà ———

The voice of the boy, with its astonishing mixture of childlike simplicity and subtle traditional stylization, sounds as though he had inherited this Mozarabic song with its oriental liturgical flourishes through a long line of ancestors, who were in continual contact with minstrels and singers of *alatychs* from Palestine and Constantinople.

The tradition of chanting the Sibyl's prophecy was introduced by monks from Africa and the East into France, and the Benedictines of Cluny brought it into Spain in the eleventh century when they re-edited and modified Spanish Church ritual. In the fourteenth century, when Latin had fallen into disuse owing to the

[1] The prophetic books of the Sibyllina were edited with commentaries by Alexandre, Paris, 1841-1856. A later edition edited by Diels, 1891. See also Ziebinski, *La Sibylle*, Paris, 1925.
* First Record, *Ancient Music*, side I, No. 8 (version fifteenth-sixteenth century as it is sung now).

48

development of the Romance languages, the Sibylline verses were translated into Catalan at a moment when everybody was singing, in Galician-Portuguese, the celebrated thirteenth-century *Cantigas* of Alfonso El Sabio. Moreover, as Barbieri tells us in his informative note, the Catalan words of the Sibyls' Prophecy were discovered to be a paraphrase written by the notorious renegade monk Fray Anselmo Turmeda.

Anselmo de Turmeda was born in Majorca in the middle of the fourteenth century and was educated at the Universities of Lérida and Bologna. After taking orders and joining a religious order he became a Mohammedan and took the Moorish name Abdallah when he became an official in the Customs of the King of Tunis. In spite of his words mocking Christianity and the irreverent stories in his celebrated *Disputa del Ase* (which was translated from Catalan into French and German) the ex-monk Turmeda was forever homesick and dreamed of his native land as he had known it before he had become a renegade. In his *Cobles de la Divisio del Regne de Mallorques* (1348), there is constant dualism, for in spite of his external professions of Mohammedanism his emotional nature drew him irresistibly towards his beloved island of Majorca with its magic palaces, and it is one of the ironies of this renegade's destiny that his poem describing the tragic remorse of the Christian sinner on the Day of Judgment became the text of the Sibyl's Prophecy used in the churches all over his native island:[1]

Sa Sibil-la

1. El jorn del judici
   parrà qui haurà fet servici.

2. Gran foc del cel davallerà,
   Mar, fons i ríus tot cremarà
   Los peixos donaràn gran crits,
   perdent sos naturals delits.

3. Jesucrist Rei Universal,
   Homo i ver Déu eternal,
   Del cel vindrà per a jutjar
   I a cada un lo just darà.

4. Als bons dira: "Fills méus, veníu!
   Benaventurats, Poseíu.
   El reine que'sta aparellat.
   Desde qu'el mon va esse creat."

5. Als mals, dira molt agrement,
   Anau malaits en el torment.
   Anau, anau al foc etern
   Ab vostre princep de lo Infern.

6. Humil Verge! Vos que heu parit
   Jesus Infant en esta nit,
   vullan a Déus per nos pregar
   De lo Infern nos vulla guardar.

7. El jorn del judici
   Parrá qui haurà fet servici.

1. The day of the Last Judgment will come to him who has given service.
2. A great fire will fall from heaven. Seas, mountains and rivers all will burn. Even the fishes of the sea will cry out, losing their natural characteristics.
3. Jesus Christ, Universal King, Man and true God of Eternity. Will come down from heaven to judge mankind and to each will do justice.
4. To the good He will say: Come hither, beloved children. We possess the Kingdom which exists since the world was created.

[1] This version was published by F. Pedrell in *Cancionero musical popular español*, Valls, 1918, vol. I. pp. 91 ff. I heard in 1936 in Sardinia in the town of Alghero or Alguer, another version of the song of the Sibyl, which varies considerably from the Majorcan versions. The inhabitants of Alguer were colonized by Catalonia in the Middle Ages and still speak sixteenth-century Catalan. See G. Fara, *Rivista musicale italiana*, 1922, vol. XXIX, II, pp. 279-280. The song of the Sibyl was also regularly sung at Toledo in the fifteenth and sixteenth centuries by a choir-boy dressed as the Sibyl, while between each verse choir-boys fought with swords, and the choir sang a four-part setting of the words. See A. B. Barbieri, *Cancionero musical de los Siglos XV y XVI*, Madrid, 1890, p. 134. Four versions of the Prophecy were published by the Archduke Salvador of Austria in *Die Balearen*, vol. II; also by Noguera, *Memoria sobre los Cantos de la Isla de Mallorca*, Barcelona, 1893, p. 43; and by Bartolomé Torres.

5. To the wicked he will say bitterly: Go ye accursed to damnation: go ye, all of you, to eternal fire with your prince of hell.
6. Humble Virgin, thou who hast brought Jesus into the world, we beseech thee to pray to God to preserve us from hell.
7. The day of Last Judgement will come to him who has rendered service.

Such was the setting that remained in my mind when later I heard the boy in the village of Artá chanting the Sibyl's prophecy.

Responsión

El —— jorn del ju —————— di ——————— ci, par ————
——rà el qui no hau-rà fet — ser - vi ———— ci Ans del ju - di - ci
l'An - te - crist ven - dra ——————— e fe - ra —— tot lo mas - trist ——— com -
a Deu —— senti ——— qui nól ——— fe - ra mo - rir

The final strophe makes the following variation on the first syllable "Oh":

Oh ——————— hu mil Ver ——— ge! Vos qui ha-u pa - rit ———

Before saying farewell to the Sibyl I wish to note this further musical version of her song which comes from Artá, the Majorcan village of the ghostly cave which I used repeatedly to visit because it reminded me of the original grotto of the Cumaean Sibyl by Lake Avernus which the ancient world considered the entrance to the Underworld. At Artá my guide led me, torch in hand, into the vast vaulted cave which slopes downward towards the bowels of the earth, and as I descended into this Dantesque inferno I began to distinguish here and there a fantastic panorama of stalactites formed by drop after drop of water through countless centuries, and these stalactites, as though obeying the riotous imagination of a supernatural craftsman, became dragons and monsters of every imaginable shape which leered at me as I groped my way.

Chapter VI

MUSIC IN THE FIFTEENTH CENTURY

The Archpriest of Hita carried Castilian minstrelsy to its highest peak of development about 1330, but the Golden Age was of very short duration, and already poetry at Court was no longer sung but only read.   The Galician minstrels still held the field and the most eminent *juglar* of the day, Alvarez Villasandino, wrote in Galician as well as in Castilian, but he and his rival Garci Fernández de Jerena lamented that poets no longer wrote on the traditional theme of love and limited themselves to satires and *cantigas de escarnio*.

One of the main causes of the decline of court minstrelsy was the disastrous defeat of the Castilian army under Juan I at the battle of Aljubarrota on August 14, 1385, by the Portuguese.

The only poet who was able to bridge the period between the death of the Archpriest and the reign of the poet-loving King Juan II, at the outset of the fifteenth century, was Villasandino, who though by his drunkenness, his mercenary cupidity, and his skill at playing lute and rebeck, he resembled a *juglar*, was called by the courtiers of Juan II the monarch of all poets and troubadours.

Heroic poetry, which had declined in France in the second half of the fourteenth century, still lasted on in Spain, but no longer as *Cantares de Gesta*.   The fragmentary verses of the old epic form thus became the substance of what is called a popular or old ballad, which was orally transmitted from generation to generation.

When Menéndez Pidal says that the people or folk were the authors of the old ballads, he means the sum total of all the individuals who invent, remember or recite a ballad, a story or a traditional legend which is repeated from generation to generation.[1]   In the poems repeating this ballad, each performer introduces changes and variants, according to his own tastes, with the result that in the course of time it becomes rounded and polished like a stone that has been rolled along by a river flood.   Menéndez Pidal has also shown how great an influence the minstrels had on the formation of the vulgar tongue from Latin, through their constant need to make themselves intelligible to their popular admirers in the country.   These wandering musicians, he says, were the real inventors of vernacular poetry, for it was the words which conveyed the music to the people.   The *Romances Viejos* or short fragments of the long *Chansons de gestes* were sung to simple melodies which could be easily remembered by the common people.   Regarded purely as melodies, they have no great value; their interest lies in their literary and historical associations and in the manner in which they were treated by the musicians.[2]

[1] R. Menéndez Pidal, *Poesía popular y Poesía tradicional en la Literatura Española*, p. 126.
[2] J. B. Trend, *op. cit.*, p. 104.

In considering the Epic poems and the ballads and their evolution through the ages we must remember that they were sung to an instrument, and Menéndez Pidal suggests that it was possible that the irregular verse of early Spanish poetry was not really sung, but accompanied by a little chant *(tonillo de recitado)*. A chant consists of two halves. It begins, as a rule, with an "Intonation" *(initium)* leading up to the "reciting note" (tenor) on the dominant of the mode and followed by a cadence called the *Mediation (mediante)* at the end of the first half; the reciting note is then taken up again in the second half and leads to a final cadence, the "Ending" *(finalis)*. Minstrels and ballad singers were influenced in their performance by Church singing and by psalmody, for psalmody is a perfectly natural method of making oneself heard in the open air or in a large building. Let us take, for example, the most beautiful ballad of all, the song of Count Arnaldos, which has the magic spell of *La Belle Dame Sans Merci* of Keats in its haunting lines. The mariner's song from the ghostly ship carries us away into the realm of fairyland:

> *Quien hubiese tal ventura sobre las aguas del mar*
> *Como tuvo el Conde Arnaldos la mañana de San Juan.*

> Who had ever such adventure, holy priest or Virgin nun,
> As befell Count Arnaldos at the rising of the sun.

Its spell springs from its vague and fragmentary character, for it awakens the sense of mystery with its phantom ship, which will carry the Count away to adventure in far off climes. The sense of mystery is increased by the last riddle line:

> *Yo no digo mi canción sino a quien conmigo vá.*

> Would'st thou learn the great secret, in our ally thou must go.

In 1552, the celebrated lutenist Diego Pisador set it to the following tune:

In its fragmentary state it has always been considered the masterpiece of balladry ever since the sixteenth century, but the Sephardic Jews of Morocco sing a complete version telling us how Count Arnaldos boards the mysterious ship and finds there, to his amazement, his family and his retainers, who have been searching high and low for him. And thus we obtain the explanation of the first two lines of the ballad. In this way, the Jewish exiles have in their exile preserved the ancient traditions which link them to the land they so enriched by their culture. I still remember the explorer's thrill I experienced at a gathering of Gypsy tribes in the Camargue in Provence when a Jewish Gypsy from the East of Europe sang a forgotten Sephardic ballad using quaint archaic forms of speech that were current in fifteenth-century Spain.

A most welcome addition to Menéndez Pidal's monumental work on the *Romancero* is the excellent chapter on the music of the ballads written by his son Gonzalo Menéndez Pidal,[1] which supplements considerably the pioneer works by J. B. Trend and others, for he has included many musical illustrations from Tetuan, Tangier, Bucharest, Sofia, Belgrade, Constantinople, Damascus and other places. We are thus enabled to understand the significant part played by the traditional *romance* in the past five centuries from Juan del Encina to Falla and Rodrigo.

[1] R. Menéndez Pidal, *El Romancero Hispánico*, Madrid, 1950, vol. I, pp. 368-369.

An interesting anonymous engraving from the Österr.
Nationalbibliothek, Vienna, of King Ferdinand of Aragon
and Isabel the Catholic in the flower of their age.

FERDINAND OF ARAGON AND ISABEL THE CATHOLIC

In 1469 a ballad was composed, according to Barbieri, after the marriage of Ferdinand, Infante of Aragon, to Isabel the Catholic, which was celebrated at the moment when Civil War was raging, for the Catalans were in revolt against the reigning King of Aragon, John II. This is one of the most significant of the ballads from a historical point of view, for it is a contemporary musical illustration of one of the most important events in Spanish history, the union of Aragon with the Kingdom of Castile, which preceded the conquest of Granada and the discovery and colonization of America.[1]

In his opening words the anonymous author of the ballad prophetically warns both the Duke of Lorraine, Johan, Count of Barcelona, in command of the forces of that city against the King of Aragon, and Henry IV, King of Castile, of the deep historical significance of the marriage of Ferdinand in the words:

[1] J. B. Trend, *op. cit.*, p. 113.

Fuera, fuera Duque Johan,
Ques casado El Rey Fernando.
Rey Enrique de Castilla,
Porque asi profetizado,
Toma por fijo et cuñado,
Al nuestro Rey de Çiçilla.

Away, away, Duke John
King Ferdinand is wedded.
For thus as prophesied
King Henry of Castile,
Receives as son and brother-in-law,
Our King of Sicily.

Alonso de Palencia, who was the first to show the change that occurred at the death of Henry IV and the accession of Ferdinand and Isabella, compares the transformation to the sun suddenly piercing the clouds after a long storm. Modesto Lafuente, the nineteenth-century historian, says that the social anarchy of the previous period disappeared "as though by enchantment". But as Menéndez Pidal shows, this transformation did not occur with suddenness. What happened was that a period of patient reconstruction ensued in which the most important part was the restoration of justice.[1]

The melancholy King Henry IV, however, deserves to be remembered, if only for his deep love of music. Even Palencia, who all through was bitterly hostile, relents a little towards him at the end and gives him the credit for a little humanity in his treatment of the orphan son of his henchman the Marquis of Villena, who had just died. When Henry saw that the boy Don Diego was sad, he would visit him at dawn and sing to him to comfort him, accompanying himself on his lute, and the boy would lie in bed listening to the King's music. According to Castillo, the chronicler, who remained staunch to King Henry, the King's voice was sweet, and he played the lute tastefully, for he was well skilled in music and loved his instruments.[2] Not only was he a musician, but also a collector, and possessed many of the Moorish and Spanish instruments described by the Archpriest of Hita in the *Libro de Buen Amor*.

Queen Isabel inherited the King's collection of musical instruments and established in his memory in the Alcázar at Segovia a choir of forty singers. She, herself, like her half brother, was so fond of music that she carried her instrumentalists with her on her campaigns against Granada, and Bernáldez describes how in 1489, at the siege of Baza, the Moors thronged the walls to hear the music of the attacking Christian army.

The following anonymous ballad from the Royal Chapel of the Catholic Monarchs commemorates that siege:

So - bre Ba - ça es - ta - ba —— el Rey, Lu - nes, des - pués - de - yan - tar; mi -
ra —— ba las - ri - cas tien - das Qu'es - ta - ban en su re —— al

[1] R. Menéndez Pidal, *The Spaniards in their History*.
[2] E. del Castillo, *Crónicas del Rey Don Enrique IV*, segunda edición, 1878.
[3] *Cancionero de Palacio*, 1890 ed., M. H. Anglés.

54

THE ROMANCERO AND THE WAR OF GRANADA

No war save the Trojan war inspired such a wealth of ballads as the ten years' conflict (1481) which led to the final fall of the Crescent in Spain. The ballads celebrating the exploits of the Christian knights were ever answered by those devoted to the Moorish champions in continuous antistrophe. In reply to the songs of Ponce de León, Gonzalo de Córdoba or Alonso de Aguilar, we hear the refrains of the capture of Alhama, the bullfights in the Bibarrambla, the deeds of Muza and the feuds between the Zegríes and the Abencerrajes.

Reading the ballads in the *Romancero general* today we see as in a vision projected before our inner eye the succeeding events of those years and first of all we hear the refrain *Ay de mi Alhama!* (Woe is me, Alhama!) which so moved Byron that he wrote a translation, entitling it: "A very mournful Ballad on the Siege and Conquest of Alhama";

> The Moorish King rides up and down, *
> Through Granada's royal town;
> From Elvira's gates to those
> Of Bivarambla on he goes
> Woe is me, Alhama!

Diego Pisador, the lutenist and composer, set the music in the sixteenth century:

Pa - se - á — ba - seel rey mo — so Por la ciu — dad de Gra - na — da, cuan - do
le — vi - nie - ron nue - ras que Al - ha — ma e - ra Ga - na - da¡ ay, mi Al - ha - ma!

The refrain *Ay de mi Alhama!* echoes and re-echoes through our mind like a mournful dirge and prophecy of Nemesis to come. And while we read the glowing accounts of the chroniclers describing the triumphal entry of the Christian army into the Alhambra in January 1492, we hear in the distance the ballad describing the forlorn departure of Boabdil, King of Granada; *En la ciudad de Granada grandes alaridos dán*, which Walter Scott's son-in-law, the poet and lover of Spain, J. G. Lockhart has translated:

> There was crying in Granada when the sun was going down,
> Some calling on the Trinity, some calling Mahoun.
> Here passed away the Koran, there in the Cross was borne,
> And here was heard the Christian bell, and there the Moorish horn.

COLOPHON

Today as we gaze at the fifty-four scenes carved on the choir stalls of Toledo Cathedral by a German artist in 1489 under the patronage of Cardinal Mendoza, we may reconstruct in our minds the stirring incidents of that war described in the contemporary chronicles of Bernáldez, Valera, Pulgar and Palencia.

* You can hear this ballad in our first Record, *Ancient Music*, side I, No. 10, with the music of Luis de Narváez.

It is the story of chivalry becoming ceremonial display, serving as a ritual in the surrender of the Kings of vanquished cities, a kind of military etiquette reduced to impotence by the devices of the engineer and the gunner. Most of the reliefs show pieces of artillery in action. There were bombards mounted on ox-drawn carts, Italian guns made of long iron bars clamped together with iron hoops, shooting marble bullets fourteen inches in diameter; there were engines firing large globular masses composed of inflammable ingredients mixed with gunpowder, which scattered long trains of light and descending on the roofs of houses, caused extensive conflagrations.

In every one of the incidents in the Conquest of Alhama, the capture of Ronda and the siege of Moclín, the artist shows that it was the new artillery methods that enabled Ferdinand and Isabella to break down the Moorish defences. And at the same time as he shows the revolution in warfare which was to destroy chivalry, the artist revels in the final display of that chivalry in all its trappings.

But though Boabdil, as his mother Queen Aixa said, had not been man enough to defend his Kingdom of Granada, and though his followers allowed themselves to be driven out of Spain back to Africa, the Moslem descendants of these Moorish inhabitants of the Alhambra and the neighbouring Albaicín have never ceased all through successive centuries to mourn the loss of their paradise of murmuring fountains and gardens amid the green pasture land watered by the Xenil, the Darro and the Beiro and their lofty fortress with its turrets of larch or marble and cornices of shining metal "glittering like stars through the dark foliage of the orange groves" as the poets sang. Through every corner of Tetuan and Xauen today echoes the sad song of longing chanted by the Moorish minstrel as he gazes from Africa across the water at the Andalusian land of the West, fairest jewel in the crown of the Prophet...

> We have lived fair days
> In Granada, land of delight.
> Among its roses and its buds
> We have spent many a silver night.
> Alas! how cruel a destiny
> Separates us from the Andalus.

A rare engraving of Ferdinand the Catholic, King of the Spaniards and Protector of the Roman Church.
Anonymous. Österr. Nationalbibliothek Vienna.

56

Chapter VII

MUSIC AT THE COURT
OF FERDINAND AND ISABEL

Ferdinand and Isabel, as monarchs of Castile, León, and Aragon, had always been on a footing of absolute equality, as is shown by the famous proverb which came into being after the battle of Toro had consolidated their power: *Tanto monta, monta tanto Isabel como Fernando* (Isabel is the equal of Ferdinand; Ferdinand is the equal of Isabel). In the royal coat of arms, Castile occupied the right, Aragon the left, and all public proclamations, laws and coinage were to bear the joint names of the royal pair. Isabel ordered her chronicler Galíndez de Carvajal not to speak of her alone, but to employ the double expression "The King and Queen", and Hernando del Pulgar, who was wearied by the usage of this rigid formula, made fun of it by entitling an imaginary chapter of his history as follows: "On such and such a day the King and Queen gave birth to a daughter!"

Isabel, in order to win her ascendancy over Grandees like the Duke of Alba and his cousin the Marquis of Santillana, whom she made the Duke of Infantado, created a new romantic conception of *nobleza* which combined with the *courtoisie* of France and the *gentilezza* of Italy. The Queen also rejected vulgar show and gaudy ostentation that had been such a feature of her half-brother Henry IV's court in the past, and she set the fashion for all that was orderly, harmonious and severely elegant. She and her ladies wore tight bodices and long full gowns, which descended below the ankles and revealed just the tips of the square-toed shoes. It was customary to wear a veil, and over it a hoodlike covering that went under the chin, and was draped over the breast in small horizontal folds.[1]

The Queen, who was an expert needle-woman, instituted regular sewing-bees in the Palace, and she sat in the centre, surrounded by her maids of honour. While they worked, some read aloud or told anecdotes. During those palace séances a great deal of time was given up to music, for Isabella in her youth had read the celebrated *Vergel de Príncipes*, a book on education dedicated to her brother Henry IV by Ruy Sánchez de Arévalo, in which the author says that one of the excellences of the noble art of music consists in directing men, not only towards moral but also towards political virtues, which prepare them for the task of governing. Music, therefore, should be studied by Kings and Princes. "If music be the food of love, play on", was Isabel's method of attracting to her gathering of fair ladies the young scions of noble houses, and she encouraged them to join her musicians of the royal orchestra in playing the lute, the viol, or the clavecin.

[1] Walsh, *Isabella of Spain*, London, 1931, p. 364.

57

THE RISE OF POLYPHONY IN THE ISABELINE RENAISSANCE

In the fourteenth century the vogue of the wandering minstrel declined when people began to sing their own ballads inspired by fragments of the old epic poems, and life became less feudally exclusive. The triumph of the canonic principle in music and the choral polyphony of the great Flemish composers of the fifteenth century supplanted the old aristocratic art of the Provençal and Galician troubadours, and this advance coincided with the growth of commerce in the free cities and the development of the guild system. Music became more secular in tendency as the austerity of the Middle Ages disappeared.

Just as Gregorian chant corresponds to Byzantine architecture, so does the art of the Flemish composers become the musical equivalent of Gothic architecture. The Gothic style meant a "system of balanced thrusts and a logical adjustment of parts whose opposing forces neutralize each other and produce a perfect equilibrium".[1] Another and even closer analogy may be found in the art of French and Flemish tapestry, in which, as in contrapuntal music, separate threads of material are woven on a frame, in such a way as to produce a complex tissue of lines and colours. Thus the best definition that could be given of polyphonic music is that it is a tonal tapestry, or a weaving together of several voices into a definite formal design. [2]

But Gothic architecture, tapestry and polyphonic music, however, when they spread to Italy and Spain from the north became transformed by the Southern climate and temperament, and there is all the difference in the world between the shadowy brooding mysticism of a northern Gothic cathedral and the exquisite symmetry and warm harmonious colouring of an Italian Gothic cathedral.

Although the polyphonic composers such as Josquin Després (1445-1521) were Gothic in style, they belong to the Renaissance rather than the Middle Ages, and the same may be said of the German and Flemish architects who flocked to Spain during the reign of Ferdinand and Isabel. As soon as they entered the Peninsula they became obsessed by the beauty of Mudéjar decoration which had developed under the Moslems who worked for Christian masters and brought architecture, as Professor Trend appositely says, "to a delirium of lines and details". And so characteristic was this Mudéjar-German art of the reign of the Catholic Queen that it received the name of Isabeline architecture.

If we wish today as time-travellers to recapture a trace of the spirit that inspired those glorious days of national achievement, we should visit one by one the shrines where it is immortalized in stone, marble, oak and alabaster. We may, in fact, in a fascinating short journey follow the Queen herself architecturally from 1476 when she and Ferdinand in the flush of youth (she was twenty-three and Ferdinand was twenty-four) had won the battle of Toro whereby Spain became unified, to 1517 when her body was finally laid to rest beside that of her husband in the Royal Chapel in Granada.

San Juan de los Reyes, perched on the steep banks of the Tagus near the gate of Saint Martin at Toledo, is the church that was offered to God in exchange for a throne and is a hymn to Isabel's triumph carved in everlasting stone, but when it was finished at the end of the century it became the consecration of Ferdinand and Isabel's crusade which was to end the mighty drama of eight centuries called the Reconquest, and for this reason it was fitting that at the end of the Moorish War the outer walls should be hung with chains and fetters of the Christian captives (they are visible today). No building brings back so clearly the spirit of the youthful Isabel than this church with its escutcheons of Castile and Aragon upheld by lions, its initials F. Y. (Ferdinand-Ysabel) repeated again and again interlaced with fruits, flowers and grotesque beasts.

From Toledo to Burgos to the Casa del Cordón, the palace built for the Constable Pedro de Velasco, Count of Haro, by his wife to be his home on his return from the War of Granada. There Isabel and Ferdinand witnessed the great wedding festivities in honour of Prince Juan, the ill-starred heir to the throne, when he married Margaret of Austria. There too, in the same year they gave welcome to Christopher Columbus and his band of Indian chieftains from the New World, and Castile and León took America under their jurisdiction. In the Cathedral at Burgos, too, we may recapture the balance and proportion of the Isabeline Renaissance in

[1] Moon, *History of Mediaeval Architecture.*
[2] C. Gray, *op. cit.*, p. 74.

58

the decorations of the *Capilla del Condestable* created by Simón de Colonia, where Pedro de Velasco and his wife Doña Mencía de Mendoza lie sleeping, and above all in Avila, where beyond the many-towered walls, in the imposing monastery of Santo Tomás, erected by Torquemada, we discover the dim, high-vaulted church containing the white alabaster tomb of the only son of the Catholic monarchs: a supreme example of the Isabeline style by the Florentine sculptor, Domenico Fancelli. And finally we end our Isabeline journey at Granada, in the Royal Chapel by Enrique de Egas, which combines the rich, imaginative qualities of late Gothic, the elegance of the Italian Renaissance with the Mudéjar decoration.

Ferdinand and Isabel repose side by side in accordance with the wish expressed by the Queen in her testament: "that the union we have enjoyed in this world, and through the mercy of God may hope again for our souls in heaven, may be represented by our bodies in the earth." Nearby are the tombs of her daughter Queen Juana la Loca—Crazy Joan—and her husband King Philip the Fair whom the tragic Juana loved so madly that even after his death she refused to be separated from him and wandered through Spain carrying his coffin with her in the great gloomy carriage drawn by eight horses, refusing to commit it to the grave.

Anonymous engraving
of Christopher Columbus.

Within sight of these majestic tombs, whose ghostly presence haunts us even today, is the sacristy where every picture and every treasure recalls the life of Isabel and Ferdinand and their court.

Here is the ideal setting for the polyphonic music which is contained in the *Cancionero de Palacio*, the great collection of Isabeline music linking the end of the fifteenth and the beginning of the sixteenth century, which was discovered by Gregorio Cruzada Villamil in the library of the Royal Palace in Madrid and transcribed by Francisco Asenjo Barbieri.

JUAN DEL ENCINA (1469-1534)
Poet, Composer, and Patriarch of the Spanish Theatre

The *Cancionero del Palacio* or *Cancionero musical*, as it is also called, is a treasure-house of poetry and song, a hotch-potch of many varieties of music, ranging from tragic, heart-felt laments for the death of Prince Juan and of Isabel herself, to frivolous and even obscene tavern songs and carols sung by shepherds in the hills. It is of great significance in the history of Spanish music because it refutes the musicologists who have stated on insufficient evidence that Spanish music in the early sixteenth century was entirely Flemish. The Flemish influence did come to Spain, but, as we have shown, at the time when the builders introduced Gothic architecture. [1] The *Cancionero* is as Castilian in flavour as the *Libro de Buen Amor*.

The *Cancionero Musical* originally contained five hundred and fifty-one musical compositions, but owing to the loss of fifty pages the total is now only four hundred and sixty. They were composed during the last thirty years of the fifteenth and the first thirty of the sixteenth century and include court songs, ballads, *villancicos*, and popular songs. But whereas the aristocratic singers sang the melodies in three parts or more, accompanied by the harp or some other court instrument, the common people sang the *Villancicos* or popular carols, unharmonised but accompanied by the guitar.

[1] J. B. Trend, *op. cit.*, pp. 133-134. *Cancionero de Palacio*, ed. M. H. Anglés.

The very first poem set to music in the collection is by D. García Alvarez de Toledo, Count and later first Duke of Alba, a celebrated warrior who led the cavalry of Ferdinand and Isabel at the battle of Toro in 1476. He was the first of the great art patrons of the House of Alba, whose motto through the centuries was: *Nunca la pluma ha embotado la lanza* (Never has the pen blunted the lance).

The poem must have been greatly admired, for it was quoted by the celebrated Portuguese dramatist Gil Vicente in two of his Tragicomedies. In the Duke of Alba's service was Juan del Encina who contributed sixty-eight compositions to the *Cancionero*. It was in the palace of the Duke of Alba, at Alba de Tormes, that all the dramatic works of Encina received their first representation.

Juan del Encina, who is the first great figure of the Spanish theatre, was the best composer of the reign as well as poet, and as Adolfo Salazar says, was one of the first Castilian figures to show the early efforts of the Italian humanistic movement in Spain, though maintaining in his eclogues and *farsas* the tradition of the religious and popular drama of the Middle Ages.

He was born in 1469 in Salamanca and his real name was Juan de Fermoselle, son of a humble artisan. His brothers, who were musicians, were employed in work in the cathedral, and his eldest brother, Diego de Fermoselle, probably gave him his first lessons in music. Barbieri, in transcribing the *Cancionero musical*, failed to realize that Diego de Fermoselle, one of the contributors, was the brother of Juan del Encina. Another brother, too, changed his name to the Castilian one of Hermosilla.[1] Juan, it was said, changed his name to Juan del Encina, in homage to the oak of Virgil, whose Eclogues he translated.

Juan del Encina, who in early youth was a member of the Cathedral of Salamanca choir, was extraordinarily precocious, both as poet and musician, for the early works were written between his fourteenth and twenty-fifth years. His talents at first brought him to the notice of Don Gutierre de Toledo, the brother of Don Fadrique, who was *Maestrescuela* at the University of Salamanca. It was Don Gutierre and his brother, Don Fadrique, cousins of King Ferdinand of Aragon, who brought Juan del Encina to court, where he became a *cantor* in the Royal Chapel and took part in the musical and dramatic representations at court.

In those days the Queen was most anxious that her family should receive proper education. Even during the Granada campaign she never forgot the duties of matron and mother to her children, and at Santa Fé whenever she could snatch a moment from administrative duties she would hasten from headquarters to the side of her daughters to instruct them in sewing, embroidering vestments, or in illuminating missals. To her only son, Prince Juan, she was passionately attached. She called him her "angel" and she took infinite pains to train him in all the accomplishments that a wise and cultivated monarch should possess. Following the theories of her favourite book *El Vergel de Príncipes*, by Sánchez de Arévalo, who believed in the salutory effect of music upon morals, she had the prince from childhood instructed in music. The Prince in 1490 was twelve years of age and already had his own private band of players and singers under the direction of Juan de Anchieta. The prince sang part songs with four or five boys of his suite and learnt also to play the clavichord, organ, the lute, the bowel viol, and the flute. The prince had also his own drummers, sackbut players, trumpeters and tambourine players, who accompanied the dances. That information, given by Gonzalo Fernández de Oviedo in his *Libro de la Cámara*, illustrates the enthusiasm for music, dancing and plays at the Court of the Catholic Monarchs.[2] Isabel herself was personally very fond of the drama and music, and had appeared on the stage in musical entertainments, and in 1467 at a performance of the *Momos* of Gómez Manrique written for the fourteenth birthday of her brother Alfonso, she acted the part of one of the Muses and recited the Epilogue.[3]

When we examine the poems and music of the *Cancionero musical*, which is predominantly the work of Juan del Encina for he was responsible for sixty-eight of the compositions, we are struck by their secular character, which is strange, seeing that he spent all his life among clerics and became Archdeacon of Málaga, Prior of León and was at the Vatican in 1514, prior to his departure as pilgrim to the Holy Land. Many of

---

[1] A. Salazar, *op. cit.*, vol. I, pp. 316-317.
[2] Gonzalo Fernández de Oviedo, *Libro de Cámara*.
[3] J. Fitzmaurice Kelly, *New History of Spanish Literature*, London, 1929, pp. 120-121.

his poems in the *Cancionero* are dedicated to Love, Absence and Exile from the beloved; others lament in melancholy strain the vanity of human wishes, and preach the Gospel of "Gather ye rosebuds while ye may":

> Let us worries shun
> And after pleasures run;
> Troubles come apace
> Though to them we give no chase.

Others again are rustic and the poet, who is still lovesick, vows that he will give up being shepherd or cowherd and so distraught is he that he wishes to depart into exile to the wilds of Estremadura, and he addresses the poem to his friend Carillo. Others are frankly Rabelaisian and written in patois reminding us of the Archpriest of Hita. Juan del Encina, however, is an Archpriest in a minor key, without the *joie de vivre*, but gifted with the same cyclothymic temperament, and his poetry is like an April morning with alternating sunshine and showers. At times he can rise to heights of eloquence as in the noble ballad written in celebration of the capture of Granada

"Where art thou now, disconsolate King?", he cries to Boabdil. "What of thy land and people? Now is the time to forswear Mahoun and all his vile sect. Submit, good King, to our Christian law, for though thou hast lost thy Kingdom thy soul may yet be saved."

One of the most poignant of all Encina's compositions, both as regards poetry and music, is that which was inspired by the death of his generous patron, Queen Isabel, on November 26th, 1504:

Triste España sin ventura,	Luckless Spain in thy misfortune
Todos te deben llorar	All today must mourn with thee;
Despoblada d'alegría	Happiness, alas, has fled
Para nunca en ti tornar.	Never to return again.

This pathetic lament recalls the tragic funeral procession described by Petre Martyr in one of his epistles when at the end of November 1504, the body of the Queen was carried from Medina del Campo, through storms of snow and rain, to the convent of Saint Francis in the Alhambra at Granada.

Juan del Encina was a complex personality, for in him the traditional Spanish genius was in continual conflict with the humanistic spirit of the Renaissance. As Professor Valbuena Prat in some excellent critical pages says, Encina, and his Iberian contemporaries Gil Vicente and Torres Naharro, and the great Michelangelo in the Rome of the Medicis, were men of the Renaissance, who, in spite of the austere qualities of balance and proportion which they had inherited from ancient Greece and Rome, were beset within themselves by a surging tide of turbulent spiritual forces, which would eventually explode and produce the world cataclysm called the Reformation and the aesthetic revolution which artists in the Rome of the Medicis would call Baroque.

Juan del Encina's life may be explained by the three representative cities where he spent his active life: Salamanca, Rome, and Jerusalem. [1] In Salamanca, where he was born and educated, he imbibed the Spanish culture of the Renaissance as it was taught by Nebrija the great humanist, but as well we must include Encina's student adventures in the countryside on the banks of the river Tormes, between Salamanca and the castle of Alba de Tormes, the house of his future Maecenas. Encina thus may be called the "two-headed Janus of Spanish music: with one head he gazed back towards the Middle Ages; with the other he looked towards the Renaissance" whose glory he ushered in by his poems, his music and his plays.   And let us not forget that the Encina nurtured on Virgil and trained by Nebrija constantly played truant from the University classroom and wandered off into the hills with the shepherds, whose quaint turns of Leonese speech and proverbs he would reproduce later on in his *Auto del Repelón* and his Christmas and Carnival plays for the delectation of the young Infante, Don Juan, or for the Duke of Alba in his palace by the Tormes.   The Eclogues, which are also called *Autos*, are short plays, very simple in structure and action and religious in spirit, derived from the Eclogues of Virgil, but the classical themes are simplified; instead of the ancient Rome of Augustus, we discover the Castile of Ferdinand and Isabel, and Tityrus and Melibea speak in the Sayagüés patois.   Occasionally, the author introduced into his shepherd dialogues a defence of himself against his detractors.   The Carnival Eclogues, or those in honour of Saint Antruejo, the Saint of Good Cheer, recall the celebrated battle of Lord Carnival against Lady Lent of the Archpriest of Hita.   The scene takes place the night of Saint Antruejo—the end of Shrovetide, and the shepherds sing their Pantagruelian *Villancicos* in full-throated revelry:

> *Hoy comamos y bebamos*
> *y cantemos y holguemos*
> *que mañana ayunaremos.*

> Today let us eat and drink our fill
> and sing and revel to our heart's content
> for tomorrow there'll be hunger in plenty.

The later plays belonging to his second period, contain more complex situations and, as the late Professor Wickersham Crawford shows in his detailed analysis, are based upon Italian models.   The shepherds Fileno, Zambardo and Cardonio do not possess the roguish and hilarious spirits of the shepherds of the Sayago of the earlier *autos*.   They even become tragic in their loves and rebellious heroes à la Ibsen.   They belong, in fact, to the epoch of *La Celestina* (1499) when all young men were "Meliboeans" and found the relief for their love in suicide.   Here, too, the scenes remind us of the episode of the shepherdess Marcela and Crisóstomo in part I of *Don Quixote*.

In 1513, we find Encina in Rome where he was already well known, for in a Bull of Pope Alexander VI he is called a "cleric from Salamanca, bachelor, familiar of His Holiness and resident in the Roman curia".

The Rome that Juan de Encina knew about 1513 was the Rome of the Borgias and the Medici, cynical and vital, where pontifical secretaries still laughed at the *Bugiale* of Poggio and the anecdotes of Pontano and

---

[1] A. Valbuena Prat, *Literatura dramática Española*, Madrid, 1930, pp. 20-21.

Filelfo, and Pagan pageants masqueraded as religious ceremonies.   Such was the second city that influenced the art of Encina, the Rome of the Italian Renaissance, whose influences we see in the dramatic eclogues of *Plácida y Victoriano* and *Cristino y Febea*.   The former, according to his contemporary Valdés, who praises it in his *Diálogo de la Lengua*, was actually written in Rome.   There is no evidence that Encina was ever a singer in the papal choir, as some modern critics have said, and *Plácida y Victoriano* is as outrageous as many passages in the *Libro de Buen Amor*, for in one place he actually parodies the Mass for the Dead.

The Church was ever vigilant for the decorum of its ceremonies and tried to extirpate every kind of excess and evil practice, but its success was only partial.   At the beginning of the sixteenth century its watchful discipline had relaxed, especially in the matter of plays. [1]   The time spent by Encina in Rome in the early years of the sixteenth century were no less important for him musically than dramatically, for he arrived in the Eternal City at the moment when music-printing had become general.   This caused a revolution in musical taste, for people turned away from religious to secular music, and Encina, who was open to Italian as he had been to Spanish folk-influences, became fascinated by the Italian *frottole* or solo songs with refrain and accompaniment, which he adapted to the Spanish *Villancicos*.   As Professor Trend has shown, the *frottole* and many of the *Villancicos* in the *Cancionero musical* and the *Cantilenas vulgares* of the Biblioteca Columbina, though artless in style, are not really popular, but were court poetry masquerading as such.   The popular refrain was used as a contrast to the sentimentality of the stanza, while the words and music were sometimes deliberately ill-assorted to produce a comic or an ironic effect, as for instance in the cuckoo songs about cuckolds, in the use of grotesque patois, and in the songs describing the disguises which the love-sick swain puts on when he goes to serenade his lady in the street below her window.

The *villancicos* of Encina and his contemporaries which appear in the *Cancionero musical* form a link between the fifteenth century and the madrigals, which were a reaction by the cultivated poets and musicans against the *frottole* and the *villancicos* with their consecutive fifths, their refrains and rustic speech.   So great was the reaction that came in the seventeenth century against the early *villancicos* that we find the Portuguese critic João Alvarez Fronvo in 1682 declaring that Juan del Encina's *Villancico—Pues que jamás olvidaros*—was one of the only pieces of old music worthy of the attention of cultivated musicians.

Pues-que ja - más ————— ol - vi - da - ros no pue — de mi cora zón

There are delightful anonymous Christmas *Villancicos* or Carols of this period which have been recorded by the Antics Escolans of Montserrat.

The following Christmas carol, which likewise is anonymous comes from the Cancionero of Upsala.   It is entitled *Ríu, ríu, chíu, la guarda ribera*: (Rîu, rîu, chîu, the guardian of the river bank).   We give this particular one in our collection.

The words are as follows:

* *Ríu, ríu, chíu*   *mas Dios poderoso*
  la guarda ribera: *la supo defender*:
  Dios guarde del lobo   *quísola hacer*
  a nuestra cordera,   *que no pudiese pecar,*
  El lobo rabioso   *ni a un original*
  la quiso morder   *esta virgen no tuviera.*

[1] H. A. Rennert, *The Spanish Stage in the Time of Lope de Vega*, New York, 1909, p. 256.
* First Record, *Ancient Music*, side I, No. 5.

Ríu, ríu, chíu, the guardian of the river bank:
God protect our lamb from the wolf,
The mad wolf wished to bite her,
but Almighty God defended her:
He made her free from all even original sin,
that she might be the Blessed Virgin.

This characteristic *Villancico* has been adapted by Miguel Querol, the learned transcriber and editor of the *Cancionero musical* of the ducal House of Medinaceli.

As a contrast the next example of fifteenth-century music on our record is an *Alta Danza* * by Francisco de la Torre, which has been adapted for a wind quintet by Maestro Rafael Ferrer.

As a final number of fifteenth-century music we have recorded the Canción: *Virgen Bendita* ** by Pedro Escobar, which has been adapted by Miguel Querol. It is sung by the Antics Escolans of Montserrat. These anonymous Christmas carols show that there was a moral reaction in Juan del Encina and his contemporaries against the unashamed paganism and frivolity of fifteenth-century Rome. Encina turned towards the life of primitive austerity he had known at Salamanca. At forty-seven years of age he resolved to become ordained as a priest and go on a pilgrimage to Jerusalem and say his first Mass there.

In his poem *Trivagia*, which was published in 1520, he gives the account of his journey which, on the one hand, recalls the contemporary accounts of Jacobean pilgrimages, and on the other recalls the fits of remorse of the mediaeval Archpriest of Hita, which led him to visit the shrines of Our Lady the Interceder. What impressed Juan del Encina on his arrival in the Holy Land was the glaring contrast between the stark poverty and barrenness of the earth once trodden by the Redeemer and the pomp and magnificence of the Papal Court in Rome. He gives voice to his sorrowful impressions in the following lines:

The earth is sterile and most rocky,
. . . .
It surely is a cause for wonder
that such should have been the Land of Promise.

Like Cisneros, Peter Martyr and other eminent spirits of the early sixteenth century, when Spain reached the parting of the ways and was beginning the movement which would culminate in the Council of Trent, he exclaims with spontaneous faith:

O blessed land where Christ was born,
Where He suffered countless ills on our behalf,
torments and tortures and at last grim death,
at last my unworthy eyes can behold Thee.

And so three essential aspects of the Spanish Renaissance: the new spirit and racial tradition at Salamanca, the vital Roman revival and the characteristic Spanish Mediaeval reaction against the excesses of the latter, are embodied in the person and in the work of the "Patriarch of the Spanish Theatre". [1]

* First Record, *Ancient Music*, side I, No. 6.
** First Record, *Ancient Music*, side I, No. 7.
[1] A. Valbuena Prat, *op. cit.*, p. 25.

Chapter VIII

THE MYSTERY PLAY AT ELCHE

The Church put an end to pagan spectacles; but the Church itself, in the obscurity of the Middle Ages, gave origin and birth to the modern drama. At first by forming part of the liturgy, in alternating chants, dialogues and choruses, with some sort of scenic apparatus; then by amplifying and complicating these representations with the events in the life of Jesus Christ, of Our Lady, of the Saints, or of the heroes of the Old Testament. Then afterwards by permitting, within or without the churches, these embryonic dramas to be enacted in the vulgar tongue, with great apparatus, and with music, songs, and other popular pastimes, the Church greatly facilitated their growth. And when, on account of the abuses which this tolerance necessarily produced, it closed its doors to every profane element, we see the modern theatre created.[1]

Cotarelo y Mori's excellent summing up of the Spanish Church's attitude to the early theatre leads us to our next musical and dramatic experience in our journey through Spanish history.

We take leave of our patriarchal Juan del Encina in Málaga where, after his return from his pilgrimage to the Holy Land, he lived in retirement until his death in 1529, and return to the Eastern Coast, to Alicante, en route for the celebrated *Festa* or Mystery Play which takes place at the neighbouring town of Elche on the Feast of the Assumption on August 15. If we wish to prepare ourselves spiritually for the unique experience which the *Festa* can give to religious souls who are at the same time deeply sensitive to music and drama we should approach the city of Elche slowly and halt at the little pueblos in this parched, sun-drenched land of the Alicantine Riviera in which stands Elche, which has been called the "Jerusalem of the West".

Elche, nestling amidst its forest of palm trees, is a green oasis of delight in the barren land that possesses the harshness and poverty which Juan del Encina discovered in Palestine. These palm trees more than any monument evoke past history, for palms were planted here as far back as 1400 B.C. by the Phoenicians, and Pliny in his *Natural History* refers to the great profusion of palm-trees in this region in the first century A.D. These palms remind us, too, of the Carthaginians and the death here of Hamilcar Barca, the father of the Great Hannibal, and it was because of his death that Hasdrubal, his son-in-law, sacked the city. The Romans when they defeated the Carthaginians gave special privileges to the loyal city of Ilice, which were confirmed by Julius Caesar. Ilice, which is four kilometres from Elche, was a powerful Roman settlement and was privileged

[1] E. Cotarelo y Mori, *Bibliografía de las Controversias sobre la Licitud del Teatro en España*, Madrid, 1904, p. 9.

65

to coin its own money. In Visigothic times a Cathedral was built there which was recently excavated, and Greek inscriptions may be found on the mosaic floors dating from the fourth century. When the Moors invaded this region they sacked Ilice, levelled it to the ground, and built Elche among the palm trees.

As a symbol of the ancient Phoenician-Greek Elche, we have the bust of the Lady of Elche which was discovered by Dr. Campello on the morning of August 4, 1897, and immediately was regarded by the people as their dream-goddess, and they forthwith christened her the Moorish Queen. Dr. Pierre Paris, the celebrated French archaeologist, secured the image for the Louvre Museum, where it remained until the Second World War. The people of Elche, however, never ceased to mourn over their lost Moorish Queen; but in February 1941 Marshal Pétain returned the Lady of Elche to Spain in exchange for two pictures by El Greco and one by Velasquez.

The Mystery Play of Elche is the final sublimation of all the fragmentary songs and song-rituals of the people which we hear as we wander through this privileged land with its *Auroros*, its Rosaries of the dawn and ancient brotherhoods of song, whose tradition goes back to the sixteenth and seventeenth centuries. It is a mystery-play which sprang from the folk-spirit of the people, but has become modified in the evolutionary process of time as each succeeding generation transformed ritual into drama.

According to the legend which one hears in Elche, one day in the month of May, the month of Our Lady, in 1266, soon after the capture of the city from the Moors by King Jaime El Conquistador, the famous liturgical drama was found, together with an image of Our Lady in an ark, which floated to the coast of Spain. Others say it was on December 29, 1370, on a bitterly cold night that the coast-watcher Francisco Cantó picked up the ark which was floating near the seashore. According to Pedrell the ark had on it the inscription *Soy para Elche* (I am for Elche). What is certain historically is that in the mid-thirteenth century James I of Aragon conquered for Castile, in accordance with the treaty he had made with his son-in-law Saint Ferdinand, the Moorish city of Elig or Elche, but the Castilian domination did not last long, for it was incorporated in the realm of the nephew of Don Jaime El Conquistador in 1296. Furthermore, historians have also pointed out that twenty years before the city was captured by the Aragonese army of Don Jaime, it had been held by Alfonso the Wise, the son of Saint Ferdinand, who first implanted the cult of Our Lady, owing to his deep devotion to her as revealed in his *Cantigas*.

Felipe Pedrell in the study he published on the mystery of Elche in the *Internationalen Musikgesellschaft* after witnessing the performance of 1900, does not believe that the Mystery belongs either in language, structure, or significant details to the stormy years of King James the Conqueror. Rather does he believe that the *Festa* dates from a period when the ecclesiastical and lay authorities of Elche decided to abandon the tradition of performing religious plays inside the church and to erect a stage in the square outside, where the religious authorities and the city guilds could co-operate in creating one great spectacle for all the community.[1] The tradition of these open-air performances has lasted through the centuries in this region of Spain and today the yearly pageants, dances and mock battles of Moors and Christians in Alcoy, Cocentaina and other towns are remnants of the fourteenth-century rituals. In the fifteenth century there was a further evolution when the plays were transferred from the public plaza to the palace of the grandees where they became more definitely dramatic in style.

Pedrell suspected the existence of an older liturgical play and music, of which fragments were vaguely remembered by the people of Elche but never written down. For that reason he went to the performance of 1900, and then he was able to hear the whole play with the added fragments which were sung in the popular manner, handed down through oral tradition and not according to any written text.[2]

These fragments came from the original version of the play which consisted of primitive chants with Oriental or Mozarabic influences. Then came the discovery of documents relating to the Lord of Prades y

---

[1] F. Pedrell, *La Festa de Elche*, Elche, 1951. This is the Spanish translation by A.A.S. of the article published in French in *Sammelbände der Internationalen Musikgesellschaft*, Leipzig, 1900. See also J. B. Trend, *A Picture of Modern Spain*, London, 1921, pp. 213 ff. W. Starkie, *In Sara's Tents*, London, 1953. For the early Valencian sung mystery play on the Assumption see Henry Mérimée, *L'Art dramatique à Valencia*, Paris, pp. 84 ff.

[2] F. Pedrell, *op. cit.*, pp. 82-83.

Montral in the Province of Tarragona, among which was found an *auto* or play representing the death of Our Lady, another representing the episode of a Crusade to the Holy Land and some *sonus* or praises of the Virgin Mary.   The date of the letter accompanying the play is 1420 and with the latter are detailed hints of how it must be staged.

Pedrell, after studying the Lemosin text of the fourteenth-century play, came to the conclusion that it was inspired by a similar play in Provençal troubadour literature but translated into Valencian Lemosin.   Upon this primitive basis the masters of the sixteenth century grafted a magnificent polyphonic structure, inspiring themselves in the traditional cadences of folk-singing which had for centuries been current in this Mediterranean region of Spain.   In 1639, the play was revised from a literary point of view and many of the characters belonging to the primitive drama were suppressed.

Although there were originally four *Consuetas* or texts of the Mystery Play, only the fourth is extant— that arranged in 1709 by El Beneficiado Lozano—but it is significant that the natives of Elche themselves have always represented and sung annually the *Festa*, as they call it, and the melodies have been transmitted orally from father to son.   The majority of those taking part do not know how to read music, but sing in the traditional style.   Indeed we discover in the more primitive chant of the play, not only phrases and vocalizations that occur in the archaic singing of Andalusians and Gypsies in *saetas* and *Cante jondo*, but we also hear similar vocalization from the youths of Elche today when they climb the palm trees to pick dates. Perched above in the leaves of the tree, which sways perilously from side to side, they hum and chant to keep up their spirits and thus avoid thinking of the fall that threatens them.   These *trepadores* or climbers are acrobats and climb barefoot.   They walk up the tree at an inclined plane, pulling themselves up by a band of cloth which they tie round the tree.

The big Renaissance church where the Mystery takes place was burnt in the Civil War in 1937, but has been restored as it was in 1695.   It is a lofty baroque structure and makes an admirable setting for the music drama, for its wide galleries and spaces enable the spectators to witness the stage from all sides of the building. The base of the cupola is covered by a cloth representing the sky which hides the pulleys and machines used for the production.   From the dome of the church hangs a thick hempen rope covered over with blue cloth which during the performance lowers first of all a huge pomegranate containing the angel, then the golden sky-altar called the *araceli* or *ara coeli* on which are grouped the angels and cherubim.   A high wooden stage is erected in the middle of the church and each character in the play upon entering the building walks up towards the stage along a sloping platform which is called the *andador*.   The action of the play thus takes place over the whole extent of the church, on the stage, on the platform and in mid-air when the angels are poised on the *araceli*.

In the neighbouring building called the hermitage of Saint Sebastian, the actors and chorus dress before the procession makes its way into the Church, and each performer has his own chest for his robe with the name of his part inscribed on the lid.

After climbing to the top of the church tower I talked with the men whose duty it was to lower the *araceli* carrying the angels.   Before the *araceli* appears there is another structure in the form of a huge red pomegranate, the characteristic fruit of Elche, which descends from the dome and opens out, disclosing the angel who visits Our Lady in answer to her sad lament.   The *Tramoyistas* or men who work the "Pomegranate" and *araceli* have their own ritualistic tradition and lower them in rhythm with the singing.   They must use infinite care to prevent the hempen rope from swinging when they lower the *araceli*, otherwise the swaying movement would give vertigo and nausea to the priest, and the boys acting the parts of the angels.

From my point of vantage at the side I could see the *dramatis personae* make their entrance.   In accordance with ritual, as each character enters the church he is formally presented by two men dressed in black civic clothes carrying long gold staffs as their badge of office.   These two men, called *caballeros electos*, and their chief, who is called "the Standard-Bearer", patronize the performance, and they used in past centuries to defray all the expenses.   Indeed such was the rivalry between the prominent families in Elche that those elected would ruin themselves financially by the lavishness of their donations, and they were given titles in consolation. The presence of the Standard-Bearer and the *caballeros electos* is a reminder of the link existing between the leaders of the community, the Church, and the performers.   Their seats of office are set at the edge of the stage opposite to those of the local clergy.

67

It is significant too that the Elche Play is the only one in the world in which priests actually take part. By tradition Saint Peter must be a priest, and to him falls the lot of burying Our Lady. He is dressed in a yellow robe with a royal blue cloak and carries the keys. Saint John, on the other hand, is dressed in white and has luxuriant brown hair and he carries with him a copy of the Gospel. There is another priest who descends in the *araceli* and whose mission is to receive in his arms the Soul of Our Lady in the form of a diminutive statue and mount with it to Heaven. Every action of the play is performed according to traditional stylization, for there is ritual in the way the Apostles salute Our Lady, also in the way the angel kisses the palm and places it on his head before handing it to her. The organist, too, gives a touch of ritual when he plays at certain stated intervals in the play, and gives the signal to the pyrotechnicians who explode ceremonial fireworks. It is the organist alone who, owing to his many years' service in Elche, preserves in his memory the traditional music of the *Festa*, and Pedrell in his celebrated lecture in Leipzig on the play stated that the traditional singing was even more beautiful than what was printed in the *Consueta*.[1]

It must also be mentioned that whereas in most other countries folk-art was encouraged officially, the Mystery Play of Elche up to the present day has been entrusted to the limited resources of the local performers, with the result that gradually in the course of time it developed many excrescences and impurities foreign to its original character, and there was a danger that it would lose its primitive splendour. It was fortunate, therefore, that during the Government of Primo de Rivera, the celebrated Alicantine composer, Oscar Esplá in 1924 revised the whole performance, and brought some of the ancient beauties into greater prominence, as for instance the dramatic *judiada*, or struggle between the Apostles and the Jews, which was derived from the ancient play of the fourteenth century to which we referred above. The *judiada*, which is such a striking feature of the present-day performance, was omitted for over a century owing to the scandal caused by the crowd who took the side of the Apostles against the Jews.

The Mystery is divided into two parts representing in dramatic and musical form the death and burial of the Virgin Mary and her Assumption into Heaven. The first part entitled *La Vesprá* is represented after Vespers on the eve of the Feast of the Assumption (August 14): the second part, entitled the *Festa* is played on the day of the Assumption. After the moving chant of Our Lady accompanied by the two Marys as she kneels in turn before the objects that recall the principal incidents of the Passion of her Son; the Garden of Gethsemani, the Cross and the Holy Sepulchre:

Our Lady then mounts the stage and kneeling on the monumental bed sings the *Vexilla Regis*, *more hispano*, according to the directions in the *Consueta*, with the following words:

Then as the angel messenger from God descends in the pomegranate or *mangraña* he sings a long chant, which with its arabesques and grace-notes, resembles at one moment the modulations of a singer of "Deep Song" at another the *canturreo* or monotonous humming of humble artisans, which one hears in Murcia or Alicante every day, and even at times the reiterated cry of the singer recalls the *ay* with which Gypsies begin their *flamenco* song. The angel when he descends from the pomegranate hands the symbolic palm to Our Lady.

[1] F. Pedrell, *op. cit.*

As soon as the angel begins to descend out of Heaven the artillery outside fire salvos, the loud-throated bells begin to chime excitedly, the organ peals and the choir begins to sing. The words the angel chants to Our Lady are as follows:

Deu — — vos sal — — ve Ver - ge Im — pe — — ri - al

But these long monodic passages are sung in accordance with the folk tradition handed down at Elche and not according to the *Consueta* of 1709.

The two supremely important monodic fragments in the whole play, according to Pedrell, are those sung by the young boy who represents Our Lady. In the first chant, she expresses her desolate sadness:

Ay tris — — ta vi — da cor — po — — — ral O — — mon — — cru — — el...

In the second chant she sings of her great longing for her dear Son:

Gran de — — — — sig me - a · ven — — gut al cor

Del — me — — u car Fill — — —

Our Lady sings these songs kneeling on her bed and holding a lighted candle. She presents the divine palm to Saint John after repeating the ritualistic gesture of placing it on her head as the angel had done, and seeing the Apostles approaching two by two up the *andador* she addresses them, singing: *O, Apostols e germans* (Apostles and brothers). The Apostles led by Saint Peter and Saint John then intone the beautiful *ternario O, poder de alt imperi* (O Power of the mighty empire) which is a hymn of thanksgiving to the Saviour.

Our Lady says farewell to the Apostles in her song, *Ay triste vida corporal* (the first chant we have quoted) and stretches herself out on the bed. The lighted candle is placed between her hands. She disappears into the tomb and her place is taken by the statue. After the Apostles have sung their hymn of glorification of the Blessed Virgin, the gates of Heaven above open and the *Araceli* appears, and as it descends slowly we hear the hymn of the elect *Esposa e Mare de Déu* (Spouse and Mother of God).

69

The musical effect produced by the singing sky-altar floating above us is indescribable. The angels clad in blue and pink with red shoes, playing their harp, lute and guitar, seem like a sculptured group inspired by Beato Angelico which is floating gently to earth, bringing with it the ethereal harmony of the heavenly choir. The music echoes through the lofty church mingling with the harmony of the organ, and in the distance we hear the booming of the bells. The song the angels sing is *Esposa e Mare de Déu* (Spouse and Mother of God):

The second day of the Mystery is called the *Festa*, as it takes place on the day of the Assumption after Vespers. It is in contrast to the first day which is austerely religious, and gives greater emphasis to the popular side of the Festival. The Apostles (with the exception of Saint Thomas) advance up the *andador* from the church door accompanied by angels, the three Marys and the elect and they mount the stage to pray beside the body of Our Lady. Then Saint Peter takes the symbolic palm, which the angel had brought down to the Blessed Virgin from Heaven, and gives it to Saint John. Then the Apostles sing the *planctus* to which Saint John responds. At the end of the prayer and the psalm *In exitu Israel de Egypto* (in Gregorian counterpoint on plain chant) the Apostles take up the body of Our Lady, but they are interrupted by the Jews who advance singing in excited dialogue with one another:

The Jews claim the body of this woman for the God Adonay, and when the Apostles refuse, advance against them. Saint Peter unsheathes his sword and there is a general mêlée, but when they touch the tomb of Our Lady they are suddenly petrified and fall on their knees in adoration begging her to intercede with God

70

for them.   When the Apostles ask them do they truly believe that the Blessed Virgin is the Immaculate Mother of the Son of God, they answer begging to be baptized.

All this part of the Mystery Play which is called *La Judiada* is intensely dramatic, and, as we showed earlier, goes back to the primitive play.   It is significant that whereas in the *Vesprá* or first part of the play there are no notes or indications of the names of composers in the *consueta*, in the *Festa*, or second part, the names of the composers are written at the beginning of the pieces.   The three authors, according to Pedrell, were the following: Juan Ginés Pérez from Orihuela (1548) who was choirmaster in Valencia Cathedral in 1581 and in 1595 was Canon of Orihuela Cathedral.   He composed the second piece which the Apostles sing when they go to meet the three Marys and their suite.   The dramatic music of the *Judiada* and the hymn of the Jews begging for baptism was written by Antonio de Ribera who was a cantor in the Pontifical chapel in Rome from 1513 to 1523, and some of whose musical compositions are in the archives of Tarragona Cathedral.   His music, as Pedrell shows, is genuinely Spanish in style, especially in the Jewish dialogue which we have quoted.   This, with its harmonised rhythm, resembles closely the traditional song-dance, the *fandango*.   It is interesting, too, to note the close resemblance in indigenous harmonies these pieces by Antonio Ribera bear to the music-dramatist Juan del Encina, whose works were inspired by the *villancicos* and folk-music of his native province of Salamanca.   The third composer was Lluis Vich, who, according to Pedrell, lived in the second half the sixteenth century, but about whom nothing is known, except that he is mentioned as the author of the funeral song intoned by the Apostles and the Jews as they carry their tapers in the procession.   In the *Judiada* and in the following *Ternario* we get the perfect fusion between the liturgical and the folk-lore elements, and no other example of this exists in all the polyphonic works of the sixteenth century.   The three Apostles taking part in the *Ternario* enter by different doors of the church, as if to stress dramatically their individual differences—Saint James is in a brown habit and he carries the stick and wears the pilgrim's hat with the cockle shell of Compostella; Saint Mark is clad in light green and wears a purple cloak: Saint Thomas wears a green robe and a red cloak.   His entry was one of the most dramatic incidents in the play: he hastens up the *andador* in great excitement.   He is dumbfounded at the news of Our Lady's death.   He had been wandering in far-off lands, in the Indies, and had not heard the sad news, and was thus the only one of the Apostles who was not present at her deathbed.

The climax of the whole performance for the people of Elche, who fill every corner of the vast church, comes with the coronation of the Virgin Mary, which brings the work to an end.   The native of Elche, in fact, feels his conscience satisfied, provided he can just see the final coronation of Our Lady, for this he believes will make his year a fortunate one.   Similarly, there is the superstition that the actors who take part in the Mystery Play will lead charmed lives for a whole year and will not die from any accident.   There was also the custom whereby those eliminated by the sectors were named angels and were presented with yellow shoes and a sheaf of nuts as a consolation prize.   Even the red shoes worn by the angels, who descend in the *araceli*, are supposed to confer special magic privileges upon the little boys who wear them.

As the play draws nearer to its climax with the coronation the excitement of the audience grows.   Above the vast multitude the *araceli* floats in the air—pink and green and gold—a rainbow bridge linking Heaven and Earth, recalling Calderón's lovely simile of the Cross hovering above the world—a rainbow bridge of peace.   The figures of the angel minstrels kneeling at the foot of the celestial altar in the glow of the setting sun become the emanations of their own ethereal chanting and the thrumming of their guitars and harps above echo within one like a throbbing heart-beat.   In response to this celestial harmony there comes the full-throated resonance of the choir below, swelling to a great volume of sound in the Grande Fugue for four voices.   As the music soars higher and higher, so does the emotion of the people rise to the pinnacles of frenzy, until even the choir is submerged by the booming of church bells and the tumultuous murmur of the multitude.

No theatrical performance ever produced upon me so deep an impression as the liturgic drama I had just witnessed: in fact, it seemed as if I had myself just taken part in an immense drama composed of all the ritualistic spectacles I had successively seen from childhood onwards.   Inside this church-theatre on the day of the Assumption I had shared the collective religious excitement of the people of Elche in this unique play wherein no barriers divided the audience from actors, for the life, the faith, the aspirations of every one had become the theme of drama itself. Even the stray tunes and snatches of spontaneous song of husbandman and artisan in Lemosin dialect were consecrated in this liturgic play, and out of them the polyphonists of the sixteenth century had woven exquisite tapestries of sound, and by a further miracle of art they conveyed to me, too, what Goethe called, "a sense of the past and present as being one: a conception which infuses a spectral element into the present". At one moment I found myself lingering among the Jewish rabble at the gates of Jerusalem, and at another I was pitched into the mid-nineteenth and twentieth century materialism with electric bulbs and cheap tinsel. And all the time I kept wondering how the obstinate determination of the citizens of Elche had managed to prevail upon the Council of Trent in the sixteenth century to spare this one Mystery-play and allow it to be performed within a church with priests as actors. I had been profoundly moved by the open-air Passion Play at Oberammergau in Bavaria, and by *Jedermann* in the Cathedral square in Salzburg, but in neither of these had I experienced the supreme sensation of watching ritual being actually transmuted into art. I then recalled Unanumo's insistence on the fundamental harmony of opposites which we find in the Spanish character. In Spain the extremes are forever meeting, and Don Quixote chases the fire-flies of his imagination while Sancho Panza with his shrewd sense mocks him, but the shadows of the Knight followed by his squire still fall across the Spanish landscape.

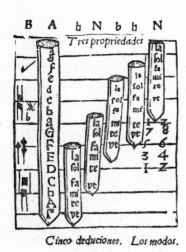

Engraving from the book: *Declaración de Instrumentos*. Juan Bermudo. Ossuna 1555. Bibl. Nationale. Réserve. Paris.

72

l Delfin de la Musica, 1538. Title page of the Treatise on the Lute by Luis de Narváez. The page represents Arion seated on a dolphin, playing the lute.

73

Cristobal de Morales (born at Seville 1500, died at Malaga 1553) was the first great musician to reveal to European art the peculiar and individual attitude of the Spanish mind. This Italian drawing is in the Royal Spanish Academy of History, Madrid.

Francisco Guerrero, Sevillan composer who has been called the "Murillo of Music". An engraving in the Royal Academy of History, Madrid.

Chapter IX

VALENCIA IN THE RENAISSANCE

Valencia, which had belonged to the Kingdom of Aragon, became merged with the United Spain on the marriage of Ferdinand and Isabella. On the death of Isabel in 1504, Ferdinand, owing to the marked hostility of his son-in-law, Philip the Fair, concluded the treaty of Blois with the King of France, Louis XII, one of the conditions of which was that he should marry Germaine de Foix, the daughter of Marie, the sister of Louis. After the death of Ferdinand in 1516, Germaine who still maintained the title of Queen, became Vicereine of Valencia, and married the Elector of Brandenburg.

All contemporary accounts pay tribute to the dramatic charm and intellectual attainments of Queen Germaine, and she transformed Valencia into a replica of an Italian city-state of the Renaissance.

At first she met with difficulties, for the Mediterranean coast was continually threatened in the early sixteenth century by the invasions of Moorish corsairs who would raid the coast and carry off men and women as slaves.

In 1519 there was an attempted invasion by corsairs at Valencia and after the danger had passed a plague broke out in the city, with the result that many of the richer citizens fled to estates in the countryside. A Franciscan preacher then denounced from the pulpit the morals of the city and so excited did the populace become that there was a massacre of suspected persons. The chaotic conditions of society in those years reflects itself in the literature written just after the Puritanical outbreak, which was even more immoral than what had been written before. The *Cancionero de Burlas* (1519) is as licentious as Aretino, and the *Thebayda*, a dramatized novel written in the style of *La Celestina* (of which two editions had already appeared at Valencia) was a poor imitation, but far more salacious than the original.[1]

Germaine de Foix, however, was a masterful woman and she soon imposed her will upon the nobles of Valencia and gave a new tone to the society there. The viceregal palace became a centre for brilliant festivities and the nobles who had scattered to their estates during the plague and the ensuing jacquerie returned to the court and gathered round the Vicereine.

No country at a particular moment of history ever influenced another more than Italy did Spain at this period of the Renaissance, but it was in Valencia that the influence was most deeply felt.

[1] J. B. Trend, *Luis Milán and the Vihuelistas*, Oxford, 1925, pp. 4-5.

The sixteenth century was the century of the lute and it occupied in the home of those days the place that the piano does today. Ever since the days of Abderrahman the Second, Caliph of Córdoba, where Ziryab had played the Oriental 'ud, the lute had enjoyed great prestige in Spain, and it was celebrated in mediaeval France and Italy by the poets. The minstrels of the time of Saint Louis, who are quoted in the *Roman de la Rose*, played *leus*, *citoles*, and *guiternes*. Dante in the thirtieth canto of the *Inferno*, describes the lute played by the Master Adamo della Ventoria, and in the *Decameron*, the lute accompanies the viol played by Queen Fiammetta. In the fourteenth century in Florence, the lute accompanied the first madrigal of the *Ars nova* and was used to guide the dance or, as it was said, *menar carrola*, which is the exact translation of the puzzling words *poner punto a la trisca* in the Archpriest of Hita's description of the lute, for *trisca* like the Italian *tresche* meant the dance. The lute in that century was used not only to accompany the voice but also to adorn it with variations and "agréments", which at a later period of vocal virtuosity were called *fioriture* and in Spain by the phrase *hacer garganta*. In the sixteenth century, according to *El Crotalón* by Cristóbal de Villalón, the lute was played both by rich players, who possessed instruments made of the finest inlaid wood, with pegs of gold, and by wandering singers, who accompanied their improvisations on uncouth roughly made instruments.

The first complete modern treatise on the lute-players of the sixteenth century comes from the pen of the Conde de Morphy, who emigrated to Paris at the time of the Revolution of 1868. In his book, which he entitled *Les Luthistes espagnols*, he takes Luis Milán as the pioneer and lawgiver of this art and follows with Narváez (Valladolid, 1538), Mudarra (Seville, 1536), Valderrábano (Valladolid, 1547), Pisador (Salamanca, 1552), Fuenllana (Seville, 1554), Venegas de Menestrosa (Alcalá, 1557) and Daza (Córdoba, 1576).

Luis Milán was a musician closely connected with the Court of Queen Germaine in Valencia for whom he translated the *Cortegiano* of Castiglione (which had already been translated by Boscán in 1534) but with important modifications. We know little about his life, except that he received a pension from King John III of Portugal at whose court he had been employed: as there were various men in Valencia at that time called Milán this is no definite proof identifying him for us. [1] At the time when his book on lute-playing appeared he was at the height of his fame as virtuoso and was a notorious Don Juan Tenorio among the impressionable ladies of the Court at Valencia and liked to call himself *El Miraflor de Milán* (the Wonderful Milán). He was renowned as a virtuoso but his reputation did not, in spite of his boasting, reach the heights achieved by Narváez in the sixteenth century. [2] Luis Milán is praised for his music but, as Juan Fernández de Heredia says, a musician should not be separated from his instrument:

> *Si la vihuela olvidays,*
> *y trobays y componeys,*
> *tomays lo que no sabeys*
> *y lo que sabeys dexays,*
> *y ansí señor os perdays.*

Luis Milán must not write verses, for his talent was to play the lute which he could do better than any living virtuoso. Milán was evidently exceedingly vain and rather a vulgar exhibitionist if we can believe the self-admiratory verses which are attributed to him:

---

[1] A. Salazar, *op. cit.*, vol. I, p. 311.
[2] *Ibid.*, vol. I, p. 386.

Maestro de todos de todo hazedor
El gran Orpheo, primero inventor
Por quien la vihuela paresce en el mundo
Si el fué el primero, no fué sin segundo,
Pues Dios es de todos, de todo hazedor.

Great Orpheus, first inventor,
thanks to whom the lute appeared in the world:
if he was the first, he was not the only one
for God is the creator of every man and every thing.

According to the Conde de Morphy, the system of tablature introduced by Luis Milán was that most generally in use until the system of Venegas de Henestrosa supplanted it. Tablature is a system which consists in telling the player where he is to place his fingers on the lute or guitar. It is a purely mechanical code of signals, whereby the player, once the instrument is in tune, has only to put his fingers down and take them up again as the signals warn him. There have been many kinds of tablature in use at different times, and tablature is still used in Spain for guitar music, as it is used at Naples for the mandoline. In the sixteenth century tablature was the most efficient form of musical notation in existence, and, as Professor Trend has shown, music preserved in lute tablature was a more accurate record of what the composer intended, and of how his composition was to sound. The lute-players who followed Luis Milán transcribed a number of madrigals and choral compositions for their instruments, and from these transcriptions can be seen which notes underwent "chromatic alteration" and where the sharps and flats were added. [1]

These facts are of great importance in musical history, for during the sixteenth century there was a gradual transition from the ancient modes to the modern major and minor scales. The transition of the older tonalities towards the firmer tonality of succeeding centuries was largely determined by the music written for the lute. [2]

Luis Milán intended his *Maestro* to be a manual of instruction with graded difficulties for those who had no knowledge of the *vihuela*. At the beginning, he gives some general definitions. He gives first of all directions for tuning the instrument. He advises the player to tune the first or highest string as high as it would go, tuning the other strings from that. The first string *(prima)* had to be adapted to the dimensions of the instrument.

Milán's instrument was the *vihuela de mano* mentioned by the Archpriest, something between a lute and a guitar. It had five double strings and one single one, which were usually tuned at intervals of a fourth, with a major third between the third and fourth strings.

When the instrument was roughly tuned or *templada*, it could be accurately tuned or *affinada* by seeing whether the unisons or octaves were in tune. "Put your finger", he says, "on the fifth part of the second string and pluck it to see whether the note is in tune with the first string."

The music starts with *fantasías* or "fancies", which are suited to the fingers of the beginner and consist of short themes developed contrapuntally, then six more elaborate *fantasías*, which in form and melody, as the author tells us, are like the Italian *pavanes* of the time:

[1] J. B. Trend, *op. cit.*, p. 39.
[2] *Ibid.*, p. 40.

The most interesting part of *El Maestro* is that devoted to vocal music.   The music is written as before in tablature in figures, not staff notation; but the voice part is distinguished from the lute part by the figures being printed in red.

In setting the Spanish ballads, Luis Milán generally used dialogue form as in the celebrated *romance Durandarte* in which the music is admirably wedded to the words, and with its striking change of key in the middle, on the words *palabras son lisonjeras*, produces a dramatic effect.   Milán says in his explanatory note that the ballad must be sung in a broad, open manner and not too fast.   The rapid instrumental passages *(redobles)* where the voice leaves off are to be taken very quickly!   In some cases, however, the singer is instructed to *hacer garganta*, which Trend explains as meaning the method of voice production affected by modern singers of *cante jondo* or *canto andaluz* in the South of Spain.

Already in Milán's music for voice and lute, we are reminded of Barnfield's beautiful sonnet, which was inspired by the wonderful art of the lutenist Dowland, the friend of Shakespeare.

> If music and sweet poetry agree,
> As they must needs, the sister and the brother,
> Then must the love be great, 'twixt thee and me,
> Because thou lov'st the one, and I the other.
> Dowland to thee is dear, whose heavenly touch
> Upon the lute doth ravish human sense:
> Spenser to me, whose deep conceit is such
> As, passing all conceit, needs no defence.
> Thou lov'st to hear the sweet melodious sound
> That Phoebus' lute, the queen of music makes:
> And in deep delight am chiefly drown'd
> Whereas himself to singing he betakes.
> One god is god of both, as poets feign,
> One Knight loves both, and both in thee remain.

It is interesting to follow, as Salazar does in his book *La Musica en la Sociedad Europea*, the evolution of the lute from its entry with the Moors into Spain until the period of its glory in the sixteenth century.   We find it represented in the manuscripts of *Los Beatos* in the tenth century and it is sculpted on an eleventh century Moorish fountain in Játiva with two holes, four strings and with its characteristic short head with the pegs bent backwards.   From the *Corpudo Laúd* or big-bellied instrument of the Archpriest of Hita with its ten strings, which is shown in the miniatures of Alfonso El Sabio's Canticles, it evolved in the fifteenth century into its final form adopting the shape of half a pear cut lengthways, but lengthening its neck considerably and arching its back.[1] Its big-bellied ancestor, however, was not altogether forgotten, for we find in the sixteenth and seventeenth century the *archilaúd* and the *tiorba* with nineteen strings and the *chitarrone* with twenty.   It is strange to note that the name *laúd* disappeared in Spain after the seventeenth century until modern times, though the instrument was given the italianized name of *vandola* or *mandola*.   That instrument, according to Bermudo, was called the Flemish *vihuela* and was originally introduced by the Flemish musicians of Philip the Fair's private Band.

[1] A. Salazar, *op. cit.*, vol. I, p. 402.

The title page of Luis Milán's celebrated book: *El Maestro* on lute playing, embodying the self-laudatory verses comparing himself to Orpheus. British Museum. London.

El grande Orpheo/ primero inuentor

Por quien la vibuela/ parece enel mundo

Si el fue primero/ no fue sin segundo

Porque es de todos/ e de todo hazedor.

79

Demōſtraciō dela vihuela de ſiete ordenes

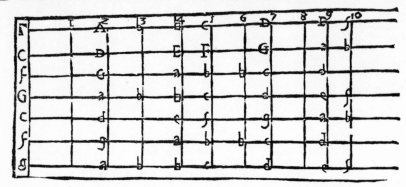

Plane of the seven orders of the lute, from the *Declaración de Instrumentos*. Juan Bermudo. Ossuna, 1555. Bibl. Nat. Réserve. Paris.

The *vihuela* was always the instrument of elegant and aristocratic society, whereas the guitar was the instrument of the people. The latter had at first only four strings, tuned with the four inner ones of the *vihuela*, and it was called Spanish guitar when it regularly began to be made with five strings. The first to add the fifth string was for a long time believed to be Vicente Espinel, the author of the picaresque novel *La Vida del Escudero Marcos de Obregón*, which Lesage rewrote as the *Histoire de Gil Blas*. It was Lope de Vega who fathered this invention on Espinel, in the following passage in his autobiographic play *La Dorotea*, where Gerarda says: "God forgive that Espinel! He has brought us those new verses, *décimas* or *espinelas*, and the five strings of the guitar, so that all the people are forgetting the noble instruments and the good old dances, what with these wild gesticulations and indecent movements of the *chaconne* which are so offensive to the decorous chastity and seemly silence of ladies." [1]

The greatest innovation which Luis Milán's treatise introduced into music was in the type of instrumental accompaniment with which he embellished his ballads and *villancicos*. For the first time, the accompaniments were written for the instrument and were not merely a substitute for the other parts in the polyphony. This idea already had been tentatively tried in the *cancionero de palacio*, but as a system it was not put into practice outside Spain until the end of the sixteenth century and the beginning of the seventeenth century by the Florentine school. [2] Luis Milán's method was to select as the foundation for his lute exercises certain melodies from the traditional *romances*, which were well known and popular. As the student knew the melody by heart he learned the accompanying harmonies more easily, and as the art developed, the instrumental accompaniment began to acquire independence, and on frequent occasions the lute alone played both the accompaniment and the melody of the piece.

After Luis Milán's *El Maestro* and in less than forty years eighty similar treatises on lute-playing appeared, and many others remained in manuscript owing to the difficulty and the high cost of printing. In 1538 (two years after *El Maestro*) *Los seys Libros del Delphin de Música*, by Luis de Narváez were printed at Valladolid. Narváez was from Granada and known abroad as Ludovicus Narvays; his motets are to be found in many foreign collections. In the prologue to his collection he says that never in Spain until his day had so inspired an art been created. This refers to the twenty-one short instrumental variations or *diferencias* and a *glosa* for two *vihuelas*, which Narváez based upon the melody of the ancient ballad of Conde Claros.

After the publication of Narváez's lute book all the following Spanish lutenists devoted themselves to the variation form. According to Trend it arose through the necessity of varying the accompaniment during the singing of a long *romance*.

[1] Lope de Vega, *La Dorotea*, Madrid, 1632, jor. I, sc. VII.
[2] R. Menéndez Pidal, *Romancero Hispánico*, Madrid, 1950, vol. I, pp. 379-380.

After Narváez, came Alonso de Mudarra, said to have been a canon of Seville, who published in 1546 a book of lute-tablature entitled *Tres Libros de Música de Cifra*, in which he includes twelve variations on the tune of *Conde Claros*. The theme is as follows:

Another very beautiful piece of music is the setting of a *romance* on the death of Absalom:

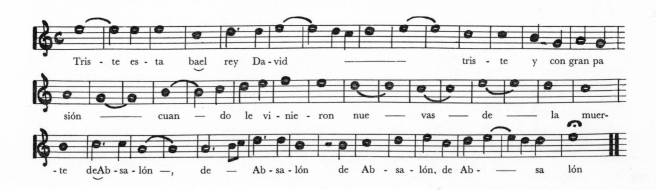

Alonso Mudarra, in addition to settings of passages from Virgil and Ovid, sonnets by Petrarch and Sannazzaro, has a setting of the *Coplas de Oro* of Jorge Manrique, one of the immortal poems of Spanish literature and one which was written just before the great historic age of the Catholic Monarchs:

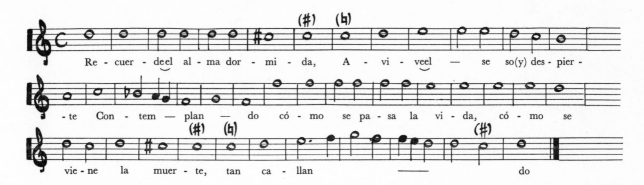

Our next number is a recording of the *romance*, *Paseábase el Rey Moro*,* by Luis de Narváez (sixteenth century), sung by Nuria Quer, and guitar accompaniment played by Eduardo Sainz de la Maza. We have already referred in the book to the setting of the same melody by Diego Pisador the lutenist. This celebrated ballad

* First Record, *Ancient Music*, side I, No. 10.

from the *Romancero* describes the sorrow of Boabdil, the Moorish King of Granada, when he heard the news of the taking of the stronghold of Alhama by the Christians at the beginning of the War of Granada. Narváez was pioneer in introducing variations or *diferencias* into Spanish music. It is interesting to note that he himself was born at Granada and must have often heard the original *romance* sung by those who had fought in the War of Granada.

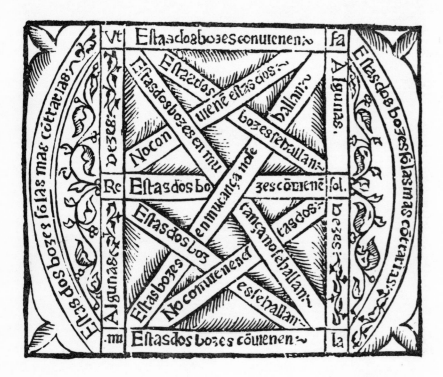

Extract from the *Declaración de Instrumentos* of Juan Bermudo. Ossuna 1555. Bibl. Nat. Réserve. Paris. It is interesting to note how the parts were printed for the singers who took part in these madrigals and villancicos. As in England, the singers sat at a table facing one another.

Chapter X

MUSIC IN THE REIGN OF CHARLES V

With the reign of Charles V we reach the full splendour of the Spanish Renaissance, which displayed itself in music no less than in the other arts. The Emperor was deeply moved by music and as a child learned how to play the clavichord, and his talent was hereditary, for both his grandparents and his mother, Queen Juana, were devoted music-lovers. Indeed, after the death of her husband, King Philip, music was the only recreation the demented Queen permitted herself, and she would sit for hours, motionless, listening to the singing and the lute-playing of Flemish musicians whom she invited to the court. For the early years of Charles it is not to Spain but to the Netherlands we must turn and the best account of those fifteen years which elapsed from his birth to his early majority in 1515 is to be found in the five hundred letters which passed between the Emperor Maximilian and his twenty-six-year-old daughter Marguerite, widow of the hapless Prince Juan, only son of Ferdinand and Isabel, who had the unenviable task of governing the duchies, counties and cities in that medley of democratic burghers and feudal lords which is included in the name of Netherlands.[1]

Marguerite, whose gay personality and dauntless courage reveal themselves in every letter she wrote, accepted the burdens imposed upon her by her father and became the Regent of the Netherlands for her nephew who, with his three sisters, was placed under her care and responsibility. Our first vision of the future Emperor comes from a contemporary description of the solemn funeral service in the church of Saint Rembrandt at Malines, for his father, on Sunday July 18, 1507. Within the church, thronged to the doors with ambassadors, bishops, nobles, princes, guilds in state costume, priests, friars and deputies, the central figure was the little boy of seven, Charles, heir to all the territories of his father, who sat in the place of honour facing the altar. At the end of High Mass when the Bishop of Arras intoned the words *Et Verbum Caro factum est*, the heralds cast their banners on the marble floor before the altar and the King-at-Arms of the Golden Fleece threw down his staff of office and cried out three times: *Le Roy est mort!* Then after a pause he raised the staff again and cried: *Vive Don Charles par la grâce de Dieu Archiduc d'Autriche, Prince des Espagnes.*

As a contrast to that colourful scene let us turn to Charles's widowed mother, Queen Juana the Mad, in Castile during that same month of July 1507.

---

[1] *Correspondance de Marguerite d'Autriche sur les Affaires des Pays-Bas*. Collected by L. Ph. C. Van der Bergh. See also A. Rodríguez Villa, *La Reina Doña Juana la Loca*, Madrid, 1892.

Ever since that gloomy night of December 20, 1506, when she exhumed the corpse of her husband from the vault in Miraflores, Juana had been wandering interminably, following the hearse drawn by eight black horses. She was clad in a long black woollen gown with sleeves that covered her hands, and after her came attendants carrying lighted torches. She insisted on travelling only by night, saying that "a widow who had lost the sun of her soul would never expose herself to the light of day". The nights were pitch dark, and the icy winds from the sierras blew across the lonely plain, and the roads were sodden after heavy rain. Behind the torch-bearers and the hearse marched a long train of nobles and prelates. Week after week, month after month the procession continued through the spring and the early summer and it was only at the end of July that her father, Ferdinand the Catholic, prevailed upon her to cease her restless wandering and to settle down at Tordesillas, where Philip's remains were laid to rest in the Monastery of Santa Clara.

Strange is it to relate that Juana la Loca, or Crazy Jane, whose living ghost had haunted the Spain of Isabel and Ferdinand, was in her living death to survive all the protagonists whose lives we have considered. She lingered in her room at Tordesillas for forty-seven years until her death in 1555.

A year after Charles's coming of age on February 23, 1516, Ferdinand the Catholic died and the Regent Cardinal Ximénez de Cisneros proclaimed Charles King, but subject to the rights of Juana, the *reina proprietaria*. After many delays the young King set out for Spain in the autumn of 1517, accompanied by his sister Eleanor and her suite, his chief adviser Chièvres, a body of Flemish and Spanish courtiers, the Castilian bishop Ruíz de la Mota, Sir Thomas Spinelly, the envoy of Henry VIII, and a fleet of forty sail.

The first serious test for Charles came when he reached Valladolid with his cavalcade and had to give audience to his subjects. Owing to his complete ignorance of the Spanish language he was unable to converse with any of the grandees, most of whom considered his inability to express himself in Spanish a deliberate insult. They were not mollified when at the interviews the Bishop of Badajoz acted as interpreter, for it seemed as if Charles had determined to behave as a foreigner in a conquered country. What really incensed the Spanish nobility, however, was the cynical behaviour of the Flemish ministers and courtiers, who began to seize all the political and even ecclesiastical posts in the country.

Queen Joan the Mad. Anonymous engraving.
Österr. Nationalbibliothek, Vienna.

While Charles was battling against opposition in Aragon especially, and the Flemings were being very effectively tricked by the astute Catalans, news arrived that the Electors had unanimously elected him King of the Romans, which meant that when the Pope crowned him, he would be Holy Roman Emperor. At once he had to abandon Spain and set out for the Empire. The Spaniards were indignant at the news of his departure, and as the King journeyed back through Castile, the wave of anger mounted to a climax when it was known that the Castilian Cortes would meet in the remote city of Santiago de Compostela.

At Santiago the King committed his final tactless blunder by appointing his Flemish confidential adviser, Adrian of Utrecht, Governor of Spain in his absence, in spite of the solemn promises he had given that no foreigner would be appointed while he was away. No sooner had the new Emperor departed than the storm broke in Toledo, where the revolt was led by a body of ancient Castilian aristocrats under Juan de Padilla.

84

Such was the unpromising start of Charles's Kingship. Few could then have prophesied that the young man of twenty who seemed incapable of initiative and was entirely under the thumb of his Flemish advisers, would, once he was firmly in the saddle, become Charles of Europe, the greatest Emperor of the West since Charlemagne.

But a new era dawned for Spain when after a long absence the Emperor held his Cortes at Valladolid in 1523. Chièvres was dead, many of the hated Flemings had disappeared and the emperor's new adviser was the Piedmontese Gattinara, who advocated a vigorous anti-French policy in Italy. Charles, however, was no longer a stranger in Spain, and every day he showed more clearly his desire to become closely acquainted with the problems of his mother country. He won favour among his subjects by his skill in jousting and especially by his attempt to learn Spanish. Cardinal Wolsey, who had met Charles in 1521 at Burgos, describes him to his royal master Henry VIII as follows: "He is very wise and well understanding his affairs, right cold and temperate in speech, with assured manners, couching his words right well and to good purpose when he doth speak."

Generally cold and grave in manner Charles nevertheless often used to laugh and was not devoid of a dry mordant sense of humour like that of a Scotsman. He was reserved but possessed also that quality of sober-mindedness which so appealed to the chronicler Hernando del Pulgar. His greatest praise was always reserved for a ruler who was a "genuine man, a hater of appearances". This quality was of paramount importance in Spain where even a poor squire of no significance would boast of his noble stock saying: "I am as noble as the King; aye and nobler, for he is half Flemish."

Such was the personality of the Emperor Charles V as the chroniclers of his reign represented him. Let us now consider his attitude to music and his relations with Flemish and Spanish musicians.

Fortunately Spain is particularly rich in musical documents of the sixteenth century, for during that period the country reached its highest degree of musical development with such great composers as Victoria, Morales Guerrero and Antonio Cabezón. In recent years the foundation of the Spanish Institute of Musicology and especially the publication by its distinguished director Mossen Higini Anglés of his two significant books on music at the Court of the Catholic monarchs, and of Charles V, have not only corrected many errors made by foreign musicologists but have given us a far clearer vision of the Spanish music of that century. One of the first and most important errors that Anglés corrected concerned the question of polyphonic music in Spain. Van der Straeten in his monumental work *La Musique aux Pays-Bas avant le XIXe Siècle* had stated that Spain only became acquainted with polyphony and began to practise it when the Flemish singers of Philip the Fair arrived in Spain in 1502 and 1506. This statement, which was repeated by other music historians such as F. A. Gervaert and A. W. Ambros, was proved patently wrong by the publication in 1890 of the *Cancionero de Palacio* by F. A. Barbieri and by the series of studies which Anglés, Santiago Kastner and other collaborators have been publishing in the past thirty years. Up to recently, too, it was erroneously held by foreign historians that Charles V had three royal chapels, one in Madrid, another in Vienna and a third in Brussels. Up to the death of Queen Isabel Spain had two chapels royal, that of the Queen for Castile, and that of the King for Aragon. When the Queen died in 1504, the royal chapel was not dissolved, but the two existing chapels became one. King Ferdinand, as Anglés shows, was even fonder of music than the Catholic Queen herself, and when she died he immediately entered in the books of his chancellory the names of the principal singers who had served the late queen, and thus kept on the unified Chapel Royal which then was exclusively composed of national musicians. The Flemish chapel of the ducal court of Burgundy, which had been attached to the house of Philip the Fair, and which he had brought with him to Spain in 1502 and 1506, did not become nationalized in Spain, either during King Philip's life or after his death. After Philip's death at Burgos on September 25, 1506, his Chapel Royal ceased to exist in Spain as a permanent institution of the royal House of Castile.

When Charles V came to Spain as King, he wished to emulate the magnificence of his father Philip's court and he brought among his suite a number of singers and instrumentalists as well as trumpets, drums and pipes. Laurent Vital, the aide-de-camp of the young King, describes the dances and festivals of folk music given by the country people for Charles on his way through the pueblos of Ribadesella, Lanés, Vicente de la Barquera until they reached Tordesillas and everywhere the village musicians alternated with the Flemish court players.

With the King was his sister Eleanor, who was celebrated not only for her charm and beauty, but also for her great skill on the clavichord, which she had learnt from the Flemish master, Bredemers. Doña Eleanor, moreover, in addition to playing the clavichord, was also proficient in the lute as well, and she was noted for her dancing and singing. She later departed to Portugal to become the bride of King Manuel. When Charles V was obliged to travel from one side of Europe to the other on his campaigns he always used to take with him his Flemish musicians from Brussels, and, as Anglés explains, this was natural, for in the first half of the sixteenth century, the Flemish composers continued to predominate in Europe and Spanish polyphonic music was hardly known beyond the frontiers of the country. We must not forget, too, that the Emperor was deeply attached to his fatherland of Flanders and to the pomp and ceremony of the House of Burgundy. He was aware that Flemish art had triumphed in Europe in the fifteenth century and that the Ducal House of Burgundy had brought lustre and refinement to court ceremonial all over Europe, and he knew that the great chapels royal of his day in Austria, Italy and Germany had been in most cases created by Flemish musicians. Surrounded as he was by politicians and counsellors from Flanders it was only natural that he should have preferred to listen to the music played by the artists of the country where he had been brought up.

When Charles V in 1518 took the title of King of Castile, we find among his court musicians a number of instrumentalists who called themselves *ministriles* or minstrels. The *ministriles* were employed in playing secular music, that is to say, chamber music during the court feasts and receptions. Those musicians, according to Anglés, had nothing to do with wandering minstrels, but were attached to the chapels royal and were employed also in playing sacred music, reinforcing the voices and in playing instrumental voluntaries during the religious services. These *ministriles* continued to take part in chapel music until the year 1572 when unexpectedly Philip II prohibited them from having access to his chapel.

To recapture the spirit of Charles V and the music of his time we should visit Valladolid, for it was there that he spent most of his time in those earlier years and the cathedral archives possesses many musical works both in print and in manuscript composed during his reign. It was in Valladolid, too, that Fray Tomás de Santa María wrote his treatise entitled *Arte de Tañer Fantasías* (The Art of Playing Fancies) which was published in 1565.

In 1525-1526, the Emperor visited Toledo to make preparations for his wedding to Princess Isabel of Portugal. The marriage took place on March 3, 1526, at Seville amid scenes of great pomp, and the Portuguese instrumentalists or *ministriles* joined their Spanish colleagues and made ensemble music, after which popular dances and folk songs were performed by the country people, but suddenly the gay music changed to funereal dirges, for news arrived of the death of the Emperor's sister, Isabel of Denmark. 1525 and 1526 were stirring years for Charles, for on February 24, 1525, on the Feast of Saint Matthias, the celebrated battle of Pavia had been fought and won by the Emperor's indomitable warrior Charles de Bourbon, the scheming Francis I was taken prisoner and the French army left ten thousand lying on the field of battle. Francis from his captivity in Madrid wrote the famous letter to his mother which said: *Madame, pour vous faire savoir, comme se porte le reste de mon infortune, de toutes choses ne m'est demeuré que l'honneur et la vie qui est saulve.* Francis whiled away his captivity writing a long poem on his defeat. He agreed with alacrity to all the terms proposed by Charles in the Treaty of Madrid of January 13, 1526, resolving in his heart to break his vows as soon as he recovered his freedom.

Charles meanwhile, who was fated always to be tricked by Francis, forgot momentarily his troubles in his happy marriage. From Seville he and Isabel had proceeded to Córdoba and Granada where they spent their honeymoon. It was on that occasion that the Emperor ordered the building of a great palace on the Alhambra hill which would proclaim to the world the victory of Christianity over the Infidel, but the palace has never been completed to this day.

So absorbed was the Emperor in his idyllic happiness with the beautiful Isabel of Portugal that the treachery of Francis I and his intrigues with Pope Clement VII came as a shock. But worse was to come. First of all came the grim tidings of the terrible defeat and death of Louis of Hungary, the husband of his sister Marie, on the field of Mohacs at the hands of the Turks, and hardly had he time to recover from that blow when he received news of Charles de Bourbon's attack on Rome and his death when climbing up a ladder at the head of his troops. The Prince of Orange took command, but the rebellious soldiers, maddened by their privations and war lust, lost all control. For eight days the eternal city was delivered over to such massacre and pillage as had never

Portrait of Charles V on horseback at the battle of Mühlberg by Titian, from the Prado Museum, Madrid.

been witnessed in human memory. Four thousand people are supposed to have been butchered in the holocaust. The Pope and some of the Cardinals escaped in the nick of time through the secret passage leading from the Vatican to the fortress of Sant' Angelo.

All Christendom was aghast at the sacking of Rome, but nobody more so than the Emperor, who, when the news came to him at Valladolid, was celebrating amid scenes of rejoicing the birth of his son Philip. Again the gay songs and paeans of joy were changed to funereal dirges and the luckles Emperor, putting on mourning, abandoned himself to despair. Yet he was not responsible for the excesses committed by the troops of Bourbon, Germans and Spaniards drawn from the dregs of society, who, moreover, had been given no pay or food and had no option but to live on what they could pillage from the Italian countryside on their march towards Rome.

All along Charles had hoped to reach terms with Clement VII by means of threats, but there is no evidence that he had given instructions to the Duke de Bourbon to march on Rome, for it was not until the city had fallen that he even knew that the latter and his army were on the march towards Rome. The eighteenth century historian Robertson, quoting Jovio and Guicciardini, waxes eloquent in his denunciations of the imperialist outrages in the eternal city. "Rome", he says, "though taken several different times by the northern nations, who overran the Empire in the fifth and sixth centuries, was never treated with so much cruelty by the barbarous and heathen Huns, Vandals, or Goths, as now by the bigoted subjects of a Catholic monarch." [1]

The following passage from the State Papers expresses in still stronger language the horror felt by all Western Europe: "They strewed on the ground the sacred body of Christ, took away the cup, and trod under foot the relics of the saints to spoil their ornaments. No church nor monastery was spared. They violated nuns, amid the cries of their mothers, burnt the most magnificent buildings, turned churches into stables, made use of crucifixes and other images as marks for their harquebusses. It is no longer Rome, but Rome's grave, (non Urbs, sed bustum Urbis). They dressed the old wooden crucifix, revered by all nations, which stood on one of the seven altars of Saint Peter's, in the uniform of a lansknecht. Saint Peter and Saint Paul, who have lain so many years buried under the altar of Saint Peter's, never suffered such indignities, even from those who made them martyrs." [2]

The Emperor was prompt to absolve himself from blame, and, in addition to putting himself and all the court into mourning, he wrote personally to all the princes with whom he was in alliance, disclaiming his having had any knowledge of Bourbon's intention. Nevertheless, as Merriman says, one cannot doubt that he intended to teach Clement VII a lesson, and, in view of the character and composition of his army, he must have been perfectly well aware that it was bound to be severe. The news was "soft-pedalled" and the blame put upon Bourbon and Frundsburg who were no longer there to defend themselves. One might admire the cool, determined restraint of the Emperor. Even after Pavia, two years before in 1525, which in some respects marks the climax of the Emperor's career, the country, through his example, received the news of the victory with utmost calm, and there was no outward joy or exultation, so now Spain, if she was horrified at the sack of Rome, made no outward sign. She was still almost a passive spectator of the deeds of her young Cæsar. [3]

We must look upon these years 1525-1528 as the happiest period in the Emperor's life, in spite of the horrors at Rome and the perpetual treasons, stratagems and spoils of his rival Francis I, which so enraged Charles that he even proposed that he and Francis should settle their differences with a duel. Once Charles had suppressed the two great rebellions at the beginning of his reign, the internal history of Spain is curiously lacking in great dramatic events. This is the greatest praise that could be given to the Emperor's constitutional and economic policy. As Merriman says, the position he had inherited was beset with difficulties, but it was a marvel that he managed as well as he did. And no less cause for wonder is the fact that Spain accepted her destiny, and with characteristic fatalism made no attempt to restrain her ruler, but urged him on to Hispanicize his originally Hapsburg point of view. And Charles as the years passed became more and more deeply absorbed by Spain until at the end he retired there to die.

[1] W. Robertson, *The History of the Reign of the Emperor Charles V*, London, 1769, vol. II, p. 286.
[2] *Letter and Papers, Foreign and Domestic, of the Reign of Henry VIII* arranged by J. S. Brewer, J. Gardner and R. H. Brodie, London, 1862-1910, 21 vols., vol. IV, No. 3200.
[3] R. B. Merriman, *The Rise of the Spanish Empire*, vol. III, p. 247.

Charles was, we repeat, at the happiest moment of his whole life, for though his marriage to Isabel of Portugal had been dictated in the first instance by policy, not affection, and, as he wrote to his brother Ferdinand, he had wedded her to get her dowry, he straightway fell deeply in love with her.

Charles was by no means a romantic hero: he had a thin, athletic body and was of medium height, with clear spacious forehead, but his eyes bulged and stared and, as people said, they looked as if they had been stuck on and did not really belong to him. The most prominent of his features was his long protruding lower jaw which caused his mouth sometimes to hang open, thus giving him almost the air of an imbecile. His complexion was pale and unhealthy, and his speech was hesitant and stammering. He worried incessantly and became at times morose and introspective, but there was an underlying sensitiveness in his nature, which made him crave for sympathy, and this he discovered in full measure in the beautiful and affectionate Isabel. She was fairhaired, slight and pale, but, as her contemporary Gómara said, "she was of the sort that men say ought to be married".[1] Sampson, the English Ambassador, told Cardinal Wolsey in 1524, two years before her marriage, that "hyrre worde and dyvyse is this *Aut Caesar aut nihil*". She was the ideal wife for Charles: she cheered him up and gave him optimism; she was the soul of loyalty, and when she appeared in public she had all the dignity of an Empress. Charles, it was said, had married her in order to leave her as regent in his place during his many absences in the Empire, but so devoted did he become to her that he regretted having to leave her side. One of the greatest bonds between the two was music, and this love which they shared in common is my justification for stressing the importance which the career and personality of Charles V possesses for those who wish to penetrate into the world of the sixteenth century, the golden age of Spanish music.

French and Flemish were his natural languages, but he was never very fluent in the former and he only began the latter when he was thirteen. His Latin was bad, his Italian worse. Of history he had a smattering, but of theology he knew next to nothing. He complained that he had been educated as if intended for a schoolmaster, but his grandfather the Emperor Maximilian never had a high opinion of his intellectual attainments, and on one occasion said that his grandson's sole redeeming feature was his love of the chase; but for that he might well have been a bastard.[2] Even eight years later when the old Emperor saw him again he gave a still more unflattering verdict, saying that Charles was as immovable as a heathen idol.[3] Charles, however, had a real taste for music, and as we said before, learnt as a boy to play the clavichord. His home life with his aunt Marguerite must have been full of music, for his beautiful sister Doña Eleanor was famed for her playing on the clavichord and sang madrigals accompanying herself on the lute. Nevertheless, in that society of cultured royal amateurs Charles as a youth remained always an enigma to his contemporaries, and all concur in calling him excessively solemn and reserved. Even the witty Peter Martyr who had tutored the young Prince Juan, the son and heir of the Catholic Monarchs, and knew Charles when he was sixteen, says: *sexdecimus est, gravitate senili* (he is only sixteen but he possesses the gravity of an old man).

When Charles arrived in Spain he had little time for music, for his mind was engrossed by other more pressing duties. The music he heard day by day was that sung and played by the Flemish musicians of his Chapel Royal from Brussels, and the only Spanish musicians were those who played secular or chamber music in the palace. When, however, he married Isabel of Portugal in 1526 a new Chapel Royal was established for her as Empress. As Anglés says, most of the ancient collections of secular music extant come from the Chapel Royal of the Queens of Spain, and he himself in his fascinating book, *Music at the Court of the Catholic Monarchs* has given much new valuable information on the performances that took place in Queen Isabel's palace circle.[4] In his following book on the court of the Emperor, Anglés maintains that it was the Empress Isabel herself who set the tone of the musical gatherings in the royal palace and that the Emperor left all decisions to her, and it was she who directed the music and indeed all the administration of her royal household. Whatever she did found favour in his eyes, and from a document discovered in Simancas, which, according to Anglés, refers to 1526, we can prove that when Isabel arrived in Spain, the royal House of Castile possessed no singers,

[1] F. López Gómara, *Annals of the Emperor Charles V*, ed. R. B. Merriman, Oxford, 1912, p. 107.
[2] Correspondance de Maximilien I et de Marguerite d'Autriche.
[3] *Letters and Papers of Henry VIII*, vol. II, p. 938.
[4] H. Anglés, *La Música en la Corte de los Reyes Católicos*, Madrid, 1941.

chapel master, or even organist, though there were trumpeters, "minstrels" and drummers (*trompetas, mines-triles y atabales*). It was Isabel who appointed chaplains, singers, selecting some from Portugal and others from Spain. Among the musicians she selected was the celebrated Antonio Cabezón, whose name appears for the first time in the document of 1526.

Thus it was the Empress who revived the musical tradition of the ancient days, not only that of Ferdinand and Isabel, but also that of Henry IV and even that of Alfonso X the Wise in the thirteenth century. Still more significant was the close bond of friendship she established through music between her native country Portugal and Spain. According to documents discovered by Anglés there had existed in the past a charming custom whereby an Infanta of Castile, when she married in Portugal, always selected among the courtiers who accompanied her in her suite a number of musicians; and if an Infanta of Portugal married a Spanish prince she always took with her to her new house some excellent Portuguese musicians, who would in Castile reflect the noblest traditions of Portuguese art.[1]

Let us in the Prado Museum, visit the room of the Titians where her portrait hangs. She is seated at a window which looks on to a landscape of mountains, reminding us of the great painter's birthplace up in the storm-capped heights of Cadore, on a spur of the Alps.

The portrait was not painted from life but from another picture by a mediocre painter, for Isabel had died on May day in 1539. Titian, however, who was a friend of the Emperor, painted for him the ghostly lady whom the latter forever saw in his dreams, and whose death had affected him so deeply. He found himself unable to face daily life and retired to the monastery of the Hieronymites outside Toledo, where he remained all alone for a long time praying and fasting. From that time, he began every morning of his life with Mass for the soul of the dead Empress, and in his chapel he would listen in rapt silence for hours to the choir singing the sacred music that she had loved, revelling in the inspired playing of the blind organist Antonio Cabezón, whose genius the Empress herself had been the first to recognize. According to a statement made by his son Hernando in the latter's will of October 30, 1598, Antonio Cabezón served at the Spanish court for forty years from 1526, the year of Isabel's marriage to Charles, to the day of his death in 1566.

Charles V was reserved and impenetrable but constant in his devotion to his friends. In his intimate life he was warm-hearted and affectionate, and after the death of his wife he could never hear her name mentioned without being moved to tears, and so unchanging was his great love for her that on his deathbed he called for her portrait and he passed away clasping her crucifix to his heart.

As we gaze today at that picture of the Empress it seems as if all her gorgeous embroidered robes, her jewels, even her hands, and her whole body were lifeless and petrified, and as if all life were concentrated in her finely moulded head and in those plaintive eyes that gaze at us from another world. Instinctively we turn away, not daring to meet that gaze which is not for us, and then suddenly we catch sight of the immense portrait on the opposite wall showing the Emperor in full armour, mounted on his dark chestnut Spanish horse and riding towards the Elbe the day of his great victory of Mühlberg on April 24th, 1547, when he smashed the army of the Elector of Saxony. Those two pictures were both painted by Titian in the same year, 1548, between January and September when he was with the Emperor at Augsburg.

That equestrian portrait, which Frizzoni considered the finest in the world, still fires our imagination, for there is no trace of the pale, scrofulous emaciated man, played upon by melancholy, hesitation and superstitious fears, and so world-weary that he was forever wishing to abdicate from his imperial position and retire to the cloister. Titian, who ennobled all his sitters with something of his own majesty, selects one supreme moment in the Emperor's life when like a Black Knight in steel armour he rode over the plains of Augsburg at daybreak with lance couched, just before the battle. In this painting the King of Spain and Emperor of the Holy Roman Empire becomes the personification of the coldness of a great general in battle and of Destiny itself approaching silent and unavoidable.

With that haunting picture in our minds we next think of the Diet of Augsburg in 1555 and the death of the Emperor's hapless mother Queen Juana at Tordesillas after her interminable widowhood and suffering of forty-nine years. Charles then resolved to carry out his abdication, and at a great assembly in Brussels of

[1] H. Anglés, *La Música en la Corte de Carlos V*, Barcelona, 1944.

90

Portrait of the Empress Isabel of Portugal painted by Titian after her death for the Emperor from another portrait by a mediocre painter. The Empress is seated at a window which looks out on a landscape of mountains, reminding us of the painter's birthplace in Cadore on a spur of the Alps.

Knights of the Golden Fleece, princes, ambassadors, nobles, bishops and accompanied by his sisters Marie Queen of Hungary, and Eleanor, Queen of France, and his son Philip he announced his intention of retiring to Spain in the following striking words: "My life has been a long voyage. Nine times have I been to Germany, six times to my Spanish realm, seven times to Italy, and the Netherlands I have visited ten times; four times have I entered France, twice have I crossed to England and again twice to Africa, and in order to accomplish all this my navies have taken me eight times across the Mediterranean and three times across the Ocean... This will be the fourth voyage to end my days in Spain." [1]

Charles spoke frankly of his failures and successes, in peace and war, and begged forgiveness for all the wrongs he had done, and assured his hearers that his constant motive had been stern duty but not thirst for power.

When it came to the moment of handing over his responsibilities to his son, the Emperor was deeply moved; tears rolled down his cheeks and the audience also wept.

When Charles departed from Brussels he selected some of his devoted friends to accompany him to Yuste. First of all Luis de Quijada, who for over thirty years had been his chamberlain and followed him in all his wars, fighting valiantly by his side. Nor did he forget the devoted Guillaume Van Male, who had written down from dictation the Emperor's Memoirs, during his long slow sailing trip up the Rhine from the Netherlands to Augsburg. He never left Charles day or night, for when the Emperor was sleepless he would read aloud to him the Books of the *Maccabees*, *Daniel* and *Esdras*, and the *Mémoires* of Commines which he called his Breviary. With him travelled also a young doctor, Henry Mathys and a distinguished Italian mechanician, Giovanni Torriano, as head clockmaker, for Charles, whose mystical broodings were obsessed by the remorseless passage of Time, liked to be forever reminded of it by the ceaseless ticking of clocks in his apartments, which he liked to mend.

On August 8, 1556, he set out from Brussels with his son Philip, who accompanied him as far as Ghent and then said farewell. It was the last time he would ever see his father. Charles travelled on with his two devoted sisters, Eleanor and Marie, who were resolved to follow him to his last retreat. From Flushing a fleet of ships took him to Laredo, and on the way an English fleet escorted him as far as the coast of Brittany. From Laredo the journey was slow and tedious, for the gout-sick, Empire-sick Emperor could only travel by easy stages. On the level ground he was carried in a horse-litter, but when he had to cross the great Sierra which divides the woods and pastures of Biscay from the parched meseta of Old Castile, he was borne by two men in a chair, and by his side rode the faithful Quijada who organized all the details of the journey.

It was at Valladolid that Charles met the General of the Hieronymites, monks of the Order of Saint Jerome, Fray Francisco de Tofiño, who was the prior of the little Monastery of Yuste. To him the Emperor had given special instructions concerning the music he wished to have in his chapel. Fray Francisco Tofiño had then searched all the monasteries of his Order to discover monks who possessed beautiful voices that they might form part of the royal choir at Yuste. By slow marches the Emperor continued his journey to the village of Tornavacas at the foot of the steep climb through the narrow pass to Vera de Plasencia, where after the peasants had cleared the path the bearers hoisted the Emperor's litter to the summit from which he could see the wonderful panorama below him. He is said to have exclaimed as he looked back at the gorge: "I shall not cross another pass, save that of death."

Today when we continue our time-journey to the ruins of the monastery of Yuste it is very difficult to visualize those last two years of seclusion, for on August 9, 1809, two hundred foragers of Marshal Soult's army climbed up and pillaged and burnt the monastery, leaving it a blackened roofless ruin. The precious archives were thus consumed, all except one volume of documents written in 1620 by Fray Luis de Santa María, which the Prior hid in some bushes when he saw the enemy arriving. This book the Prior lent to Richard Ford when the latter visited the ruined monastery before the publication of his celebrated Handbook for Travellers in Spain (1845). Antonio Ponz and Richard Ford were impressed by the restricted surroundings chosen for his last retreat by the greatest ruler in the world whose boast was that the sun could not set on all his territories. [2]

[1] C. Hare, *A Great Emperor*, London, 1917, pp. 264-265.
[2] A. Ponz, *Viaje de España*, Madrid, 1784, new edition Madrid, 1947, vol. VII, carta VI, pp. 631-635. R. Ford, *Handbook for Travellers in Spain*, London, 1845, vol. I, p. 553.

He only built four rooms, each with large fire-places, for he was a gouty and phlegmatic Fleming.

His life at Yuste however, has been, as Wyndham Lewis says, grotesquely deformed by novelists. Richard Ford comes near the truth when he says that Charles lived there half like a monk, half like a retired gentleman: although strictly attentive to his religious duties he amused himself with his flowers, rides, mechanical experiments and the visits of his young son, Don Juan of Austria. His was no morbid unsocial misanthropy, but a genuine weariness of the world and a wish to be at rest. He sedulously avoided all allusions to politics; neither was he in his dotage, although enfeebled in health from gout; his ambition and passions were subdued, but not his relish for intellectual and innocent recreations. He did not lose touch with outside affairs, but received many visitors who gave him accurate information about war and politics all over Europe. Many rumours spread from Yuste to the outside world that Charles might even leave his retreat and lead an army for the defence of Navarre, but if Charles ever said anything to encourage such ideas it must have been, as Quijada reported, "from mere policy". [1]

Much of Charles's time every day was spent listening to music. Although a music-lover he was the frankest of critics and his biographer, Fray Prudencio de Sandoval, describing his life at Yuste says that on many occasions the monks heard him moving behind the door which led from his apartments to the high altar. They saw him beating time and heard him singing with the choir; and if any singer chanced to make a mistake he would mutter: "*O hideputa bermejo!* Whoreson rogue! he went wrong there*", or some such expression.

One day a maestro de Capilla came from Saville, a friend of Fray Prudencio, called Francisco Guerrero, bringing with him a book of Motets and Masses which he had composed. The Emperor gave orders for one of the Masses to be sung. When it was over he sent for his confessor and said to him: "*O hideputa*, he is a clever thief this Guerrero; he has stolen this passage from so-and-so and that one from someone else." The singers were amazed, for they had not noticed the plagiarism until it was pointed out to them afterwards.

The Emperor was always dressed in deep mourning for his wife and the hangings of his bedroom were black, but he had also brought with him from Flanders sets of beautiful tapestry worked with allegorical figures, landscapes and flowers, which he hung on the walls of the other rooms. His bedroom on the first floor adjoined the church, and through the window he could see the high altar from his bed, and by opening it he could hear Mass, and listen to the singing of the choir. Titian, his favourite painter, whose portrait of the Empress was always nearby, was a continued reminder of the ancient happy days, and he had brought to Yuste not only the master's portraits of himself at all ages but also those of his son Philip, of his daughters Mary and Juana. The famous Saint Jerome by the Venetian master was the altar-piece of his private oratory, and the magnificent picture of the Trinity he placed over the high-altar of the church.

After his music and his pictures came his library with its collections on science, history and religion. Guillaume Van Male still devoted himself to reading aloud the favourite works such as the *Consolations* of Boethius, the *War in Germany* written by Avila under the Empress's direction, the *Meditations* on Saint Augustine and especially the *Mémoires* of Commines and the *Cortegiano* of Castiglione, which delighted him. A passage led from his room to the garden and to his favourite walk, which was on the western terrace at sunset, whence he could gaze at the panorama of mountain and plain. Nearby was a short alley of cypress trees leading to the chestnut forest and beyond, at a little distance, to the hermitage of Belén where he would go every day to meditate. He was very fond of birds and loved to observe their ways as he walked in the small convent garden where he grew rare plants, including the Indian Pink which he had brought back from the shores of Tunis. It was as a result of a chill he caught when lingering one evening at sunset on the western terrace that his final illness came upon him and on September 21st, 1558, he breathed his last.

[1] R. B. Merriman, *op. cit.*, vol. III, pp. 399 ff. Fr. Prudencio de Sandoval, *Historia de la Vida y Hechos del Emperador Carlos I.* Quoted by R. Mitjana, *Francisco Guerrero*, Madrid, 1922, pp. 12-13. Male, *Lettres sur la Vie intérieure de Charles V.* D. B. Wyndham Lewis, ch. VIII and epilogue. This is an excellent summing up of Charles the Emperor as man.

Chapter XI

PHILIP II
The Maecenas of Spanish Music

Philip II, although in his youth he did not receive so solid a musical education as his father, for his talents were not as precocious as those of the latter, nevertheless up to the age of twelve years when his mother the Empress died, lived in an atmosphere of music. As a small child he and his sisters Doña Maria and Doña Juana were given lessons in the clavichord by the celebrated player Francisco de Soto and lessons in the lute by Santiago Pérez; they were also taught to dance the pavane and the *gallarda* by Diego de Hernández. From the documents we learn that Don Felipe was considered an excellent dancer in palace circles, but no mention is made in any of the letters of his skill as player of the lute or clavichord. Although the Emperor Charles V by nature and temperament was profoundly inclined towards music and later in life looked upon it above all as an aid to prayer, he gave but little encouragement to Spanish singers, instrumentalists, composers or printers of music. Philip, though not a performer like his father, gave continual encouragement all his life to sacred music, and endowed schools of music, defrayed the cost of music publications and displayed unfailing generosity to musicians, writers and artists of all kinds. Charles V, as Anglés says, was a born artist and would seem to have been destined to be the ideal prototype of the musical Maecenas of Spanish composers. Nevertheless from the documents we discover that the true Maecenas was Philip II and, historically speaking he and his ancestor Alfonso X, the Wise, were the two Spanish Kings who gave the greatest stimulus to both religious and secular music in their country. Unfortunately, as Anglés adds, no biography up to date has appeared doing full justice to the Prudent King, as he was called by his subjects. Many have described him as an exacting and ascetic monarch, or else a silent, cold and calculating task-master, insensible to the refinements of art and incapable of human affection. English and French historians love to stress the colossal "failure" of Philip II, and Hume stated that Philip in exchange for the greatest heritage that Christendom had ever seen, with the apparently assured prospect of universal domination which opened before him at his birth... "closed his eyes upon dominions distracted and ruined beyond all recovery, a bankrupt State, a dwindled prestige, a defeated cause".[1]

[1] M. A. S. Hume, *Philip II.*

Other more romantic historians concentrate upon the Escorial of Philip II:

> The ultimate word of Castile... a grey rectangle on the bleak Sierra. Behind, upon three sides, the immense mountains. Below, the rock and clay that join Madrid to Avila. Four storeys of granite... It is the masterwork of Philip II. And Philip is a masterwork of Spain. The Spanish will to forge a unity from the warring elements of its life won no darker victory than his. He was the grandson of the Most Catholic Kings. He was the heir of their impossible purpose. His Empire spanned the world. Never has there been its like. Portugal, Holland, Franche-Comté, Austria, the Americas were bulwarks of his house. He strove to make of this delirious chaos a unitary world to bespeak Christ... Philip lived in the scaffolding of a Dream. The Dream was good, for it was to create and rule a unitary world. But the scaffolding was warfare, intrigue, laborious documentation. For peace he went to war; for light he plowed the dark. He spent his years and his people and at the end he felt death. [1]

To the defence of King Philip come the Catholic Champions, foremost among whom was William Thomas Walsh who after his striking biography of Isabel the Catholic produced his more controversial work on Philip II, which was the first definitely to challenge the whole Anglo-Saxon conception of Spanish history and break a lance for the most calumniated of Kings. The seven hundred and seventy pages of Walsh's work on Philip II are the answer to the following forceful paragraph with which the eminent historian and Hispanist Professor Merriman sums up his survey of the reign of the Emperor Charles V.

> Spain's inherited religious role—her most sacred duty as she conceded it to be—committed her in advance to that very policy of persecution and intolerance which the more fortunate and enlightened nations to the north of her were gradually to abandon in the succeeding years. She was landed in a sort of a strait-jacket of unbending mediaevalism, from which honourable escape seemed utterly impossible; she was almost obliged to be an anachronism. Against freedom, both national and ecclesiastical, she had been forced to take her stand. Verily she was the child of fate.

Against the accusation that Spain is an anachronism Walsh thunders:

> It is false to say that "Spain hated to look forward: she loved to look back". She was never conscious of "looking back" when she looked at Christ in His Church Catholic. It is you who look back to pagan times when there was no Christ on the Cross to reproach the sins of your age; it is the Spanish Catholic who looks ahead to the future, for Christ is eternal and only the eternal can be truly called the future. [2]

In his early twenties Philip, according to documents, was a normal young man, very keen on sport, and already an enthusiastic patron of the arts, who treated painters and musicians as friends rather than with the condescension of a royal Maecenas. [3] Even after Philip's death, in 1600, the painter Gaspar Gutierre de los Ríos wrote of Philip's *mucha humanidad y suavidad* with painters and sculptors.

During his regency Philip showed himself an able administrator and he became very popular with the Spanish people. His marriage to his cousin the Infanta of Portugal, however, only lasted one year and eight months, for she died, leaving a delicate baby, Don Carlos, behind her. But Philip resolved to marry again. The opportunity was not long delayed. In 1553, the delicate young English King Edward VI died, and Charles wrote from Brussels suggesting that Philip should take Queen Mary Tudor for his wife. In his reply Philip said to his father at the end of his letter: "All I have left to say about the English affair is that I am rejoiced to hear that my aunt has come to the throne of the Kingdom, as well out of natural feeling, as because of the advantage mentioned by Your Majesty where France and the Low Countries are concerned." The more Philip thought about the proposed match, the more it appealed to him, for he imagined himself as King of England by the side of Mary, hailed by the Catholic majority of Englishmen as the saviour of their country.

[1] W. Frank, *Virgin Spain*, London, 1917, p. 139.
[2] W. T. Walsh, *Philip II*, pp. 715-717.
[3] The magnificent collection of Van der Weyden, Hieronymus Bosch, Breughel, Titian, Tintoretto, Veronese gathered by Philip II are today the heart of the Escorial and Prado Museums.

PHILIP II'S JOURNEY TO ENGLAND

Although King Philip II in later life looked upon England as a penance which would remain until the end of his days, for in that country was the harbour and breeding-place of all his worst enemies, in his youth the island appealed to him as to most Spaniards of those days as the home of romance and chivalry. England, not France, was the realm of King Arthur and his Knights of the Round Table. The island supplied the enchanting if nebulous background for the adventures of Amadis of Wales and Palmerin of England, and Spanish chroniclers loved to give rein to their imagination when they described its people.

Thus Gutierre Díaz de Gámez (1379-1450), the squire of Don Pedro Niño, in his *Victorial* has an interesting passage summing up the national character of the English and of the French:

The English, he says, are very different to the people of other nations with whom they live at variance. There are many reasons for this: first of all because such happens to be the nature of their ancestors; secondly because they live in a country which is rich in produce and in metals; thirdly because there are many living in a comparatively small space, that is to say, the population is very large, even though the island is extensive. They say that in that country mortality is low and that their harvest is rarely bad. Besides, they are encircled by the sea, and for this reason they do not fear anyone.

As for the French, they are a noble nation; they are wise and learned and expert in all things that relate to good-breeding, courtesy and elegance. They make a brave show in their clothes... They love to please and honour greatly all foreigners; they know, too, how to praise and they greatly celebrate high deeds. They are not malicious; they forget their worries, and they are courteous and gracious in their speech: they are very gay, love pleasure and go in quest of it. Both sexes are much given to love and pride themselves on it, and such qualities exist in them by nature, for the climate of their country depends upon a star called Venus.[1]

Philip himself when he landed at Southampton was like a prince out of romance, with his pale skin, flaxen hair and beard, clad in his suit of black velvet and silver, wearing his dark cap with its golden chains and gallant plume. As he rode through the town on his Andalusian pony which had been sent to him by his bride, he looked like a king, and he was one, for the Emperor had made him King of Milan, so that he might meet Mary Tudor on equal terms. His suite were delighted with their reception, for the stately English manor houses set in the midst of wooded parks again reminded them of the romances of chivalry, and at Winchester they were shown the table of the Knights of King Arthur, and they saw English ladies riding on horseback unaccompanied, and managing their horses as though they had been men. After praying in the beautiful Cathedral at Winchester where a *Te Deum* was sung in his honour, he proceeded to the Queen's palace where, after changing into doublet and hose of white kid, embroidered with gold, and accompanied by the Duke of Alba, the Duke of Feria and his retinue, he met his bride.

Mary, who was twelve years older than Philip, was a short slender woman of thirty-eight, dressed in a black velvet gown with a petticoat of frosted silver, and a jewelled girdle and collar. Her head was encased in the characteristic Tudor toque decked with pearls. Her hair was reddish, her complexion pink and white. The portrait by Antonio Moro, which hangs in the Prado Museum, shows her as she appeared that day to Philip: a slightly faded little lady who, in spite of her gorgeous dress and her shy smile, bore traces in her careworn face of the sufferings through which she had passed in the years that followed the death of her mother, Catherine of Aragon. Mary at once fell in love with Philip, and he on his side behaved towards her with exquisite tact and courtesy, in spite of the report written by the Venetian Ambassador that he hated his wife. Cardinal Pole, the Pope's legate, probably was nearer the truth when he reported to the Holy Father that Philip could not be more devoted to Mary if he were her son. There was, from the first, an intellectual bond between the two, for Mary's education was equal to that of Philip's. She had been carefully brought up by her mother, Catherine, whom Erasmus had called "a literary miracle", and from her ninth to her fourteenth year her tutor had been the great Spanish humanist Luis Vives, who had held a chair at Oxford, founded by Wolsey. Vives had written a Latin manual for her and dedicated to her the "mottoes" and prayers in Latin, which she memorized. But those days with Vives remained a dream of an idyllic past which had ended abruptly when he was expelled in 1529 for refusing to approve of her father's divorce from her mother.

[1] *Crónica de Don Pedro Niño, Conde de Buelna*, ed. Eugenio de Llaguna Amirolo, Madrid, 1782, chap. XVIII and XXX.

The other great bond between Philip and Mary was music, and here Mary possessed a certain superiority over Philip, for she like her sister Elizabeth was an excellent player of the virginals. Mary inherited this talent from her mother, who had played the instrument and had brought her Spanish musicians with her when she had set out for England to celebrate her marriage with the delicate Prince Arthur of Wales. In the years of persecution, the virginals became for Catherine, as they did for her daughter Mary afterwards, the one consolation in moments of affliction. From the Articles of the Treaty of Marriage between Philip and Mary which Santiago Kastner examined in the London Public Record Office, we know that there was a proviso stating that the Prince had to be served by Englishmen exclusively.[1] Nevertheless, Philip brought all his court musicians from Spain, in order to show off the excellence of his chapel royal, and with them travelled his favourite organist and composer the blind Antonio de Cabezón. The King was very proud of Cabezón and had taken him with him on his state visite to the Netherlands and many cities in Italy in 1548. Although Kastner did not find in the archives any description of the musical festivals held at the marriage of Philip and Mary, he discovered in Simancas a letter of the Spanish Ambassador in London in 1554, Don Juan de Figueroa, addressed to the Emperor, describing how Queen Mary's minstrels came and played for the King.[2]

🐚 MUSIC AT THE ENGLISH COURT IN THE SIXTEENTH CENTURY

Music in the reigns of Mary and Elizabeth reflected the brilliance of the age and its condition has been well stated by Hullah: "In the sixteenth century we not only sang and played as much and as well as our neighbours but we sang and played our own music. It is no exaggeration to say that the English hold and are recognised as holding a very high place among the composers of the period. Tallis, Farnaby and Byrd in the Service of high Mass and Anthems; Motley, Ward and Wilbye in the Madrigal; Bull in performance as well as in composition, Dowland, the friend of Shakespeare, in song and part-song, and last, and not least, Orlando Gibbons." These are all names that can challenge comparison with Victoria, Morales and Cabezón in Spain and Palestrina, Orlando di Lasso and Luca Marenzio in Italy.

Thomas Morley, one of the best musicians of the period, in his delightful and amusing book called *A Plaine and Easy Introduction to Practical Music*, published in 1597, says:

"According to custom, after supper parts were handed round by the hostess. Philomathes has to make many excuses as to his vocal inability, and finally has to confess that he cannot sing at all. At this the rest of the company 'wonder' and some whisper to their neighbours how was he brought up."

There are no contemporary accounts of Mary's playing of the virginals, but there is a delightful incident concerning her sister Elizabeth's playing, which deserves mention here, for many a time did she play for Philip after that fateful day in April 1555, when Mary invited her to Hampton Court and lodged her in the apartment just vacated by the Duke of Alba.

Elizabeth had been put in the Tower by her sister after the Wyatt plot, though on the latter's succession, she had gone to mass and opened a chapel in her own house, saying to Mary that she wished to return to the faith of her fathers.[3] Mary, however, distrusted her younger sister and wished to send her to Spain under the care of Philip's aunt Mary, Queen of Hungary, but Philip refused, for he thought that a much better plan would be to marry her off to the Duke of Savoy.

When Elizabeth arrived at Hampton Court on April 17, 1554, she was still under an armed guard and the Queen would not see her, but according to French accounts, she sent a message to her to dress up in her richest robes for the King's coming.[4]

The contrast between the two sisters was indeed striking. Mary, in her thirty-eighth year; short, very thin, prematurely gray, her looks marred by anxiety; Elizabeth just on twenty, full of the bloom of

---

[1] G. Kastner, *Contribución al Estudio de la Música Española y Portuguesa*, Lisboa, 1941, p. 81.
[2] *Ibid.*, pp. 82-83.
[3] W. T. Walsh, *op. cit.*, p. 158.
[4] J. E. Neale, *Queen Elizabeth*, London, 1934, p. 87.

98

life; moderately tall with fine figure, reddish gold hair, olive complexion, green eyes and shapely hands.

The old world and the new: such were the two daughters of Henry VIII.

Philip was impressed by Elizabeth, and it is said that not only did he force a reconciliation between the two sisters, but he was present at the scene, hidden behind an arras. Elizabeth's skill on the virginals, to which we referred, on one occasion led Sir James Melville, the Ambassador from Mary Queen of Scots, into an awkward position. He describes the incident in his *Memoirs*:

> The same day after dinner, my Lord of Hunsden drew me up to a quiet gallery that I might hear the Queen play upon the virginals. After I had hearkened awhile, I took by the tapestry that hung by the door of the chamber, and seeing her back was toward the door, I entered within the chamber and stood a pretty space, hearing her play excellently well; but she left off immediately, so soon as she turned her about and saw me. She appeared to be surprised to see me, and came forward, seeming to strike me with her hand, alleging she was not used to play before men, but when she was solitary, to shun melancholy.[1] She asked me how I came to be there? I answered: "As I was walking with my Lord Hunsden, as we passed by the chamber door, I heard such a melody as ravished me, whereby I was drawn in, ere I knew how; excusing my fault of shamelessness as being brought up in the Court of France, where such freedom was allowed; declaring myself willing to endure what kind of punishment her Majesty should please to inflict upon me for so great offence. Then she sat down upon a cushion and I upon my knees by her; but with her own hands she gave me a cushion to lay under my knees; which at first I refused, but she compelled me to take it. She enquired whether my Queen or she played best. In that I found myself obliged to give her the praise."

Engraving of Philip II, Prince of Spain, son of the Emperor Charles V. Österr. Nationalbibliothek, Vienna.

Melville was Ambassador from Mary Stuart in 1564, and it is possible that Queen Elizabeth herself quietly arranged the little comedy herself, for the Ambassador tells us that before the stolen interview she had asked him many questions abouts his Queen. How was she dressed? What was the colour of her hair? Which of the two was fairer? Which was higher in stature? Then she asked what kind of exercises she used. "I answered", said the Ambassador, "that when I received my despatch, the Queen was lately come from the Highland hunting, that when her more serious affairs permitted, she recreated herself in playing upon the lute and virginals." She asked if she played well. Melville, being a very wise man, as well as a diplomat replied: "Reasonably for a Queen."[2]

[1] Early writers use the name virginal, spinet and harpsichord loosely to describe any keyboard instrument in which the strings are plucked. The name virginal has no connexion with Queen Elizabeth, for it was used before she was born. It may possibly have some connection with the popularity of the instrument among young ladies whereas the lute was the instrument mostly played by men. But the name is most likely derived from the Latin word *Virgula* meaning a little stick—referring to the *Jacks* that, incidentally, are described in Shakespeare's sonnet quoted on page 207. The *Jacks* pluck the strings. Grove's *Dictionary of Music and Musicians*, 5th ed., 1952, vol. IX, pp. 22-23.

[2] A. H. Henderson, *Old English Keyboard Music in Proceedings of the Musical Association*, 29 March, 1938.

ANTONIO DE CABEZÓN, THE "SPANISH BACH", AND HIS INFLUENCE

The visit of Antonio de Cabezón and the court singers to England in 1564 has given rise to a number of erroneous statements by foreign writers imperfectly acquainted with Spanish music, as for instance that made by W. N. Grattan-Flood, who alleged that Antonio de Cabezón imitated the instrumental style of Tallis as the result of his visit to England, where he heard the latter's works.

Santiago Kastner has corrected these misstatements, and by comparing the works of the two great masters he shows that there is no similarity between the two either in construction or in technique.

In any case, we must remember that Tallis wrote for the virginals, which require the special kind of musical ornamentation used by the English master, and also the *sfumato* quality of keyboard technique, neither of which have anything in common with the musical texture of Cabezón's music, which was written specially for the clavichord and the organ, two instruments distinct in tone quality to the virginals. Kastner compares the *Felix Namque* Variations (1562) of Tallis in the *Fitzwilliam Virginal Book* with the *Diferencias* of Cabezón, who returned to Spain in 1555, and maintains that the Variation form which had been, as we have seen, an ancient tradition among Spanish lute players, was actually introduced to England for the first time by Antonio de Cabezón and his brother. Furthermore, after examining the works of the Tudor composers Tye, Taverner and others, especially those composed on liturgical themes for the organ, he is of the opinion that they are inferior to those by the great blind composer of Philip II, based likewise on liturgical themes, and to those by other Spanish composers whom Venegas de Henestrosa included in his celebrated *Libro de Cifra Nueva*. That work was published in 1557, but the music had been collected ten years previously, that is to say before Antonio de Cabezón set out with Philip and his suite for England in 1554.[1] And to those examples included by Venegas he would add those published in their works by Tomás de Santa María and Juan Bermudo. It is interesting to note in both Spanish and English composers of that period the identical tendency to evoke and interpret through music the religious text to which the liturgical melody refers. Also the music of both countries reflects the same note of gentle melancholy, the same humanistic yearning, but whereas the character of the English music is more natural and human, the Spanish is more inclined towards mysticism. And just as the religious poets and mystics glossed in their poems the Biblical quotations, so did the Keybord Players in England and Spain comment in their music on the melodies from the liturgy. The compositions of Tallis for the organ are still closely linked with the Motet and similar vocal forms and there are but few technical devices derived from the organ or the keyboard instruments. Tallis limits himself to vocal imitation and does not, like his Spanish contemporaries, vary his music with glosses, gracenotes and ornamentation, and his counterpoint had not like that of the others yet acquired an intrumental character. Kastner, too, is of the opinion that the English organ technique of the sixteenth century was not as richly expressive as the Spanish, which was more advanced, for whereas Tallis still belonged to the former Gothic period in music, Cabezón had become entirely absorbed by the Renaissance. Against those who held that the early organ music of the sixteenth century had a historical rather than a musical interest, because instrumental style and the organ itself were too rudimentary to allow even so great a composer as Tallis to approach here the standard he reached in his choral works, Kastner maintains that such criticism may, perhaps, be levelled at English organ and instrumental music of that time but not at Spanish organ and instrumental music of the first half of the sixteenth century, which was not by any means rudimentary.

All English musicologists have been puzzled by the abrupt transition between Tallis and Byrd, for the latter who was born in 1542, "was bred up to musicke under Tallis", according to his contemporary Anthony Wood, and became one of the little choir boys of the English Chapel Royal. So close were the relations between Tallis and Byrd that they published together the *Cantiones sacrae* in 1575. Kastner in this connexion makes the interesting suggestion that Byrd came into direct contact with Cabezón when he was about twelve years old,

---

[1] These works of Antonio de Cabezón may be studied in the excellent critical edition of the *Libro de Cifra Nueva* of Venegas de Henestrosa, which forms the second part of Mossen Anglés's book *La Música en la Corte de Carlos V*.

and being wonderfully precocious like the young Bach, Händel or Mozart, listened with rapt attention to the Virginalistic variations of the blind Cabezón, and inspired by him, raised the variation form in England to its greatest heights.   We may also believe that Tallis must have spoken to his pupil Byrd of the art of Antonio and Juan de Cabezón, for there are many similarities between the art of Cabezón and that of Byrd, and years later that of the other Virginalists, such as John Bull (1562-1625) and Peter Philips (1550/1560-1628) who carried on the technical devices of Byrd.

Esther Nadal de Janés has played for our recording *Diferencias* (Variations) for harpsichord; *Diferencias sobre el Canto del Caballero* by Antonio de Cabezón.*

Cabezón the blind organist, clavichordist and composer of Charles V and Philip II, whom Pedrell called "the Spanish Bach", considerably enriched the resources and repertoire of the clavichord owing to his deep knowledge of the lute and harp.   At Valladolid, where the court habitually resided in 1526 and the following years, he consorted with Tomás de Santa María and, as Kastener points out, it was there that he first met the vihuelist Luis de Narváez.   We note in Cabezón Flemish influences, owing to the close relations between the Spanish chapel of Empress Isabel and the Flemish chapel of Charles V.   Cabezón like Bach came of a family of musicians: his brother, Juan de Cabezón, accompanied him in the royal suite to England and elsewhere abroad: his son, Hernando (1541-1602), succeeded him in his post and became one of the favourite musicians of Philip II and Philip III.   Antonio de Cabezón's biography has been published by Santiago Kastner (Barcelona, 1952).

 SHAKESPEARE AND MUSIC

How oft, when thou, my music, music play'st
Upon that blessed wood whose motion sounds
With thy sweet fingers, when thou gently swayst
the wing concord that mine ear confounds
do I envy those Jacks that nimble leap
to kiss the tender inward of thy hand

Shakespeare. Sonnet CXXVIII.

England at this time was on the threshold of her most glorious period of poetry and music, reflecting the youthful vitality of the Elizabethan era.   Music ceased to be exclusively religious and entered all phases of life.   In the *Book of Ayres*, for example, there is a reference to the folksong called "Come o'er the Burn, Bessy" quoted by Shakespeare, containing an allegorical second stanza comparing Bessy to mankind, who is bidden to cross over the confines of the ancient world where she has been held captive.   Shakespeare is full of references to music, and from his plays we see how thoroughly English life in the sixteenth century was saturated with music. With the exception of Othello, who "does not greatly care to hear music", most of the characters praise it.   The magic isle of Prospero is full of "sounds and sweet airs that give delight and hurt not"; Desdemona sings of her sorrows; and Ophelia of her passion; Jaques in the forest of Arden can "suck melancholy out of a song as a weasel sucks eggs"; Sir Andrew Aguecheek "plays his viol-de-gamboys better than any man in Illyria".   Silvia is celebrated in the loveliest of serenades: Lorenzo courts Jessica in the most famous musical passage in Shakespeare.   Even the clowns have their snatches of broken melody, and the sheep-shearers by the sea coast of Bohemia are "three-men, song-men all, and very good ones but they are most of them means and bases: but one puritan amongst them and he sings psalms to hornpipes".

There is very little about painting and sculpture in Shakespeare, for music was the art that was the centre of his affections.   One of the greatest modern authorities, Dr. E. H. Fellowes, who published so much of the

* First Record, *Ancient Music*, side I, No. 11.

music of Shakespeare's day, gives in his book on the English Madrigal a charming description of a Tudor manor called Hengrave Hall, describing the routine of a great Elizabethan household:

"The day began about 6.30 and the morning was occupied by the men in field sports and by the women in reading and embroidery.   The dinner hour was usually about twelve and the afternoon was spent in the garden or bowling green or tennis court, if the house were rich enough to possess one.   Supper took place about 5.30 and then the company spent the time playing chess, backgammon, cards, dice, singing of madrigals, supporting the voice with a 'consort of viols' or listening to the playing of the 'musicyons' in their gallery overlooking the hall.   Much time was also spent by both sexes in playing the virginals and the lute as well as in singing songs.   The lute was played by the ladies as well as by men at this time, and Hengrave Hall, being a rich household, had always a master of Music, such as Master John Wilbye, the most renowned composer of his day, who was house-hold musician to the Kytsons at Hengrave Hall from 1593 until 1626.   His lovely madrigal, *Lady*, *when I behold*, forever evokes memories of the music of that golden age."

BERRUGUETE, PALESTRINA AND THE COUNTER-REFORMATION

In Spain, in the second half of the sixteenth century, Shakespeare's great contemporary Lope de Vega, describes in his plays, and especially in his scenic novel and autobiographic work, *La Dorotea*, a similar society to the Shakespearean which was music-loving and sang madrigals as well as folk songs and ballads, upon which the "Monster of Nature", as he was called by his contemporaries, would often base his dramas.   In Lope de Vega, however, we find fewer references to music than in Shakespeare, but far more to painting and sculpture. Lope grew up in the period when people still remembered the majestic figures of Alonso de Berruguete, whose austere and massive personality gives us a clue to the difference between the Spanish society of Philip II's reign under the shadow of the great movement of the Counter-Reformation and the age of Elizabethan England.

To understand the spirit personified by Berruguete we must continue our time-journey to Valladolid where he had sculpted figures which, his friend Cristóbal de Villalón said, "lacked only the breath of life to speak".   Berruguete (1486-1561), by his life, covers the whole period we have been considering since the Catholic Monarchs and the Granada War and, what his contemporaries called his *fogosidad* or passionate vitality expressed the essential individuality of Spanish Catholicism.   He truly possessed the *terribilità* or fury of Michelangelo, but not the Italian's imagination or sense of beauty.   His works are allegories describing the crusading drive of Spain against Infidels, heretics and pagans.   He was weaned on the classicism of Rome, for he spent ten years there as a youth and came under the influence of Michelangelo, and he entered into a competition for a bronze copy of the *Laocoon*, which had recently been unearthed, and made a wax model; but the prize was awarded by Raphael, who acted as judge, to Jacopo Sansovino.

It is important to note how the Spanish artists, whether in poetry, painting, sculpture, architecture or music, came into close contact with their celebrated Italian contemporaries at the moment of the Council of Trent, when Palestrina cast away his rich musical inheritance of the Netherlands, stripped himself of all his material possessions, as it were, and became a kind of musical Saint Francis, preaching the absolute impersonality of the greatest religious art.   For just as the priest officiating at the altar ceases temporarily to be an individual and becomes a mere passive vessel or instrument of the divine rite, so the fitness of music to the celebration of the divine rite depends largely on the extent to which the composer has been able to submerge his individuality and become an impersonal agent.   And it is because no composer is more successful than Palestrina in fulfilling this condition and in achieving this state of artistic humility that he must, as Cecil Gray says, be considered the greatest of all religious musicians, with the possible exception of the anonymous creators of Gregorian chant. [1]

Cecil Gray in his illuminating study of the church music of the sixteenth century compares the difference between the old and the new music to that between a trackless mediaeval forest with its gnarled and moss-grown

[1] C. Gray, *op. cit.*, pp. 77-79.

tree trunks and its thick tangled network of spreading branches through which no light can penetrate, and a cultivated park with neatly trimmed hedgerows, well-kept paths, smooth lawns and terraces and swans floating serenely and majestically on ornamental lakes. In his more mature work Palestrina deliberately and systematically avoided the modal asperities of the older music and inclined towards modern tonality and towards a more vertical, harmonic style of writing. The same kind of transformation, we might add, took place about the same time in French literature, when the rich, exuberant, vivid and picturesque idiom of Rabelais and Montaigne gave place to the elegant, refined and somewhat colourless language of Malherbe and Descartes. [1]

The Palestrina style, however sublime in the works of the great master, was a pernicious model for the disciples who followed, and led to the impoverishment and decadence of contrapuntal art. It contained the seeds of death, for it deprived polyphony of the strength and energy necessary to resist the continual assaults of homophony at the end of the sixteenth century.

It was at this moment that Spain, whose artistic genius had been quickened by the close contact existing between the two countries throughout the Renaissance, produced three composers, Cristóbal Morales, Francisco Guerrero, and greatest of all, Tomás Luis de Victoria, who not only rivalled Palestrina but embodied in music the spirit of the Counter-Reformation, which was predominantly Spanish in character and origin. As Miguel de Unamuno said: "Was there not something akin to cultural hegemony in the Counter-Reformation of which Spain was the champion, and which actually began with the sack of Rome in 1527 by the Spaniards, a providential chastisement of the city of the pagan Popes and the pagan Renaissance."

Up to recent days, it was usual to regard the Spanish school of church composers in the sixteenth century as a part, or at least an offshoot of the Roman school, and differences were vaguely ascribed to the greater influence of the Flemish school upon Spain in the reign of Philip the Fair and the Emperor Charles V. But, we repeat, the researches of musicologists such as Pedrell and Mossen Anglés have shown that in spite of the close political and artistic relations between Spain and the Netherlands in the sixteenth century, there did exist a native Spanish school possessing clearly defined characteristics stretching back to the Middle Ages.

And here we may stress the analogy existing between styles of architectural construction and styles of musical composition, which is more valuable an illustration in Spain than in other countries, for the three styles of the later Middle Ages, Romanesque, Mudéjar and Gothic can be paralleled in Spanish music. Just as the polyphonic composers of the North, the English and the Flemish, discovered a new technique and new forms, so did the composers who supported their tone structure by voices moving contrapuntally, and as the architects searched for decorational devices in flowers and stylized them, so did the composers of Masses seek their inspiration, not only in the melodies of the Church, but also in popular songs of the day. [2] The French used such tunes as the celebrated *L'Homme armé* and *Mille Regrets*: the English Tye and Taverner wrote Masses on the tune of *Western Wind*: the Spaniards Morales and Guerrero wrote Masses on the songs *Tristezas me matan* and *Dormendo un Giorno*.

CRISTÓBAL DE MORALES (1500-1553)

In Cristóbal Morales, a native of Seville, who was educated in Rome where the Flemish school was the dominant influence, we find unmistakable Spanish characteristics. Like Herrera, the architect of Philip II's Escorial, he was a master of proportion, and his melodic line possessed a flexible beauty. Although he owed much to the Flemish, especially to Josquin des Prés, he was, as an expert critic has said, "the first great musician to reveal to European art the peculiar and individual attitude of the Spanish mind". [3]

He was essentially Andalusian in character and tradition and so proud of his native city, Seville, that he always added the latinized *hispalensis* after his name. His pride finds full justification when we remember that

[1] *Ibid.*, p. 79.
[2] J. B. Trend, *op. cit.*, p. 134.
[3] R. Mitjana, *Estudio sobre Algunos Músicos Españoles del Siglo XVI*, Madrid.

our first guide on our musical time-journey through Spain was Saint Isidore of Seville, whose tradition lasted through the centuries even to the fifteenth when the city rivalled Salamanca as a centre of musical studies. Moreover, the first and second printed Spanish music books appeared in 1494 and 1496 at Seville, which was called even then "the chief city of the world", according to the printer's boast on the title page of the 1494 book.[1] Morales grew up in an atmosphere of music, for he was a pupil of Pedro Fernández de Castilleja, the successor to the composer Pedro Escobar, whose music was bought for the *Biblioteca Columbina*, by the son of Christopher Columbus.   Castilleja was called "the master of the Spanish masters" (*maestro de los maestros de España*) by Guerrero, who was chapelmaster of Seville Cathedral for thirty-five years.   As a little boy, Morales was one of the *seises* or choristers in the Cathedral, who in addition to singing were required then, as they are still today, to perform on the occasion of the feast of Corpus Christi, their ceremonious dance in front of the high altar. Morales, if we judge by the lengthy Latin dedications to his two Books of Masses in 1544, which are written in Ciceronian prose, must have been an excellent student of classics.   In one of his dedications he claims that from an early age he had devoted himself to the so-called liberal arts, which were called *Trivium* and *Quadrivium*.

According to Mitjana, Morales was supposed with some probability to have sung at the marriage of the Duke of Calabria to Queen Germaine de Foix, the Vicereine of Valencia, and there he met the Neapolitan musicians of the Duke's suite.   Also when the Emperor Charles V was married to Isabel of Portugal at Seville, Morales sang in the choir which welcomed the King with an outburst of song when he entered the precincts of the Cathedral by the Puerta de Perdón, leading to the Courtyard of the Orange-trees.   The Emperor, as we have shown, never travelled without his choir of Flemish singers and his chapelmaster, who at that date was Gombert.   It is interesting to note that as a result of that meeting Morales became a friend of the Flemish composer, and several of Gombert's compositions may still be seen in the choirbooks of the Cathedral, besides those of Morales and his master, Castilleja.[2]   It was in the year of the Emperor's visit that the choir school of Seville was established by the Archbishop Alonso Manrique and Fernando Contreras, the celebrated preacher.

After holding the post of *Maestro de Capilla* of Avila Cathedral during the years 1526 to 1530, Morales's next important appointment was in 1535 when he was admitted as a singer in the papal choir.   The pontifical choir had included Spanish choristers over a hundred years before the days of Morales, and the Spanish Popes, Calixtus III and his Borgian nephew, Alexander IV had especially favoured them.   So important indeed, did Spanish influence become in Rome that the nationalistic Julius II tried to end their dominating position in 1512 when Ferdinand the Catholic manipulated Italian politics through his diplomatic agents.   Clement VII, relied still more upon them.[3]   There was a great deal of national rivalry and jealousy between the Spaniards and the Italians, because Spanish singers were greatly in demand in Rome for the Choir of the Sistine Chapel, owing to the great expressiveness of their singing.[4]   One author of the sixteenth century, describing the various styles of singing employed by different races, says: *Les Anglais jubilent, les Français chantent, les Italiens ou bien bêlent comme des chèvres ou bien aboient comme des chiens, les Allemands hurlent comme des loups et les Espagnols pleurent parce qu'ils sont amis du bémol*.   This description is interesting both as a reference to the moving timbre of Spanish voices and as an illustration of the Spanish fondness for *música ficta* or chromatic music.

Morales, thus, when he arrived in Rome, found himself surrounded in his intimate circle by Spanish musicians such as Núñez Calasanz, Escobedo, and Ordóñez, who were intensely nationalistic in their outlook. It was fortunate that his appointment coincided with the accession of Pope Paul III, who was a great lover of music and enlarged the Papal choir from twenty-four to thirty-three, raised its pay and imposed new regulations. In later days historians used to refer to the days of Paul III as the golden age of music in Rome.

The earliest known work of Morales is a six-part cantata *Jubilemus Omnis Terra*, written for the peace celebrations in 1538 at Nice, when the Emperor met Francis I, and in the presence of Pope Paul III concluded a truce.   The Emperor and the King brought their own singers, who joined with the Roman choir in the Cantata by Morales.   The work is constructed upon a plan often used by the composer in his motets.   Five of the voices

[1] R. Stevenson, Article on *Morales* in Grove's Dictionary, 5th ed., London, 1954.
[2] J. B. Trend, *op. cit.*, p. 145.
[3] R. Stevenson, *op. cit.*, vol. X, p. 878.
[4] F. Pedrell, *T. L. Victoria*, Valencia, 19, p. 127.

sing the Latin text in counterpoint while the sixth voice sings the one word *gaudeamus*, again and again to the same six notes. This device was characteristic of Flemish composers and had been used by Gombert.

From the anonymous history of the Emperor and from references given in the excellent bibliography of Sánchez Alonso we learn details of the meeting between the two inveterate enemies. The Pope was determined to use all the resources of music and pomp as well as the art of diplomacy. He spent three hundred *baiocchi* out of his private purse on velvet gowns for the twenty singers who accompanied him to Nice, and he prevailed upon Morales to produce a work whose sumptuous six-part harmony would reflect the solemn grandeur of the occasion when the two rival monarchs of Christendom would meet before his throne. The famous triple interview resulted in temporarily despoiling the Duke of Savoy, two thirds of whose estates were occupied by Francis, and almost all the rest by the Emperor. The truce was prolonged for ten years, but the fundamental problem of Milan was not touched. One month later the two rivals met again at Aigues-Mortes: they exhausted themselves in protestations of affection, they dined and wined together, and even shared the same bed, and for two years the veneer of friendship remained, for Charles in 1539 was entertained by Francis in Paris and was received with greater pomp than was reserved for the host himself. [1]

All this splendour is reflected in the two movements of the Cantata with its underlying *ostinato* figure like a *leit motif* and its five-voice discourse on the virtues of the Pope, the Emperor and the King. This composition, like so many other ancient works, survived because it was transcribed by Enriquez de Valderrábano in 1547 for two lutes and by Fuenllana for one lute in 1554.

In 1539, Morales wrote another six-part cantata *Gaude et laetare Ferrariensis Civitas*, which was sung at Ferrara in honour of Ippolito II d'Este's elevation to a cardinalate. Ippolito d'Este, the builder of the Villa d'Este at Tivoli, with the most beautiful gardens in the world, was resolved to maintain the tradition of art and pageantry in the court of Isabella d'Este, the fairest and most perfect flower of womanhood in the Renaissance. Here again Morales followed his device and made the five voices deliver the formal address of welcome, while the sixth—the second treble—repeats the words: "I will magnify thy name for ever and ever." [2]

In Rome the papal choir used, from time to time, to perform in the Sistine Chapel during the years when Michelangelo was covering its walls with paintings, but on most occasions they sang in the Pauline Chapel and in the churches outside the Vatican. Formerly, Morales was thought to be a falsetto, as were many Spanish singers in the choir, but recent evidence seems to show that he was a baritone. [3] During the second five years of his stay in Rome Morales produced a great number of works, and from documents we know that he lost an ever-increasing amount of days from his choir duties on account of ill-health. In 1543, we find him in Genoa awaiting the arrival of the Emperor Charles V, and it was said that he was trying to change his service from Pope to Emperor as a result of quarrels with Spanish members of the choir, which led to his being fined two hundred *baiocchi* for misconduct. In 1542, he published at Venice his Magnificats, and in 1544, two volumes of Masses. Also in 1543 he began to publish his three volumes of Motets. Although during his Roman period Morales had entered into close contact with great patrons such as the Pope, the Emperor, and Cosimo de' Medici, he was disappointed in his petitions, for neither the Pope nor Cosimo took him under their protection and junior members of the choir, such as Arcadelt, who had not distinguished themselves in the composition of sacred music, were given preferment. For this reason he returned to Spain and was appointed *Maestro de Capilla* in the Cathedral of Toledo, the see of the Primacy of Spain, at the very large salary of forty-three thousand five hundred *maravedis*, which was paid to him because of the great reputation he had gained by the publication of the Masses. [4] Morales would seem to have been thriftless in his personal economy, though it must be remembered that out of his salary he had to pay for the board and lodging of his choirboys. From account books of the time, it appears that he fell into debt and this may explain the reason why he only held the post for two years and accepted odd engagements, including that of private chapelmaster to the Duke

[1] R. B. Merriman, *op. cit.*, vol. III, p. 267.
[2] This "occasional Cantata" and that of 1538 were discovered by Mitjana in the university library of Upsala in a book entitled *Il Primo Libro di Motetti a Sei Voci*, Venezia, 1549.
[3] R. Stevenson, *op. cit.*, p. 879, who quotes from the *Liber Punctorum* or day-by-day record of the choir's activities.
[4] *Ibid.*, p. 880.

of Arcos.   In 1551 he was appointed *Maestro de Capilla* to the Cathedral of Malaga, where he spent the last two years of his life in still greater financial difficulties, illhealth and unhappiness than at Toledo.   From the contemporary documents it appears that he was unable to impose discipline upon his choristers and had to call in the help of the ecclesiastical authorities to curb their insubordination.   In May 1553, according to one of the documents, he was reprimanded at a chapel meeting because his choristers had misbehaved during a procession, and he himself was obliged to pay a fine of a day's pay, and the singers were denied three day's pay.   So desperate were his financial worries that he asked for leave of absence for travel and tried to get re-elected to his old post at Toledo, but there he had enemies like the *Maestrescuela*, who voted against his re-election.

As a proof of the growing international fame of Morales it is interesting to note that while he was writing to the Toledo Chapter begging to be reinstated as chapelmaster, in France, François Rabelais was writing his *Gargantua*, and in one of the scenes he describes a beautiful garden in which he imagined that he heard Morales and other joyful singers making sweet music *(Morales et autres joyeux musiciens... mignonnement chantants)*.

The best contemporary account of the music of Morales comes from the sixteenth-century critic Juan Bermudo, who called him "the light of Spain in music", and surprisingly adds that Morales was a "foreign composer", because, as he explains, "though his music possesses the charm and pleasing sound of Spanish music, yet it does not lack the profundity, the technical skill and the artifice of foreign music". [1]

The reputation of Morales increased by leaps and bounds after his death, and during the following thirty years his compositions appeared every year in France, Spain, Germany, Italy or the Netherlands.   His fame even spread as far as Mexico, where his music was performed in 1559 at the solemn commemorative service for Charles V, and Cervantes de Salazar in his *Túmulo imperial*, 1560, said that on the great occasion the music of Morales "gave great contentment to the audience".   The earliest printed polyphony copied for use in the New World was by Morales—the Masses of 1544. [2]

In the eighteenth century, Morales was considered by Adami in 1711 the most important composer of the papal chapel between Joaquin des Prés and Palestrina.   He added that the motet of Morales entitled *Lamentabatur Jacob* was the most precious work in the entire Sistine Chapel archives, calling it "a marvel of art". And Fornari in 1749, when discussing the significance of the famous *Missa Papae Marcelli*, praised Morales as the composer who first showed the right way to set words intelligibly in a contrapuntal fabric.   Padre Martini praised Morales not only for his technical mastery in counterpoint, but also for his imaginative use of his resources.

Stevenson in his excellent critical article in Grove's dictionary discounts much of what Eslava and Pedrell (who was more interested in Victoria than in Morales) said and concentrates upon the criticisms of Bermudo, and he expresses regret that today Morales is more praised for the plangent expressiveness of the great motets *Emendemus in melius* and *Lamentabatur Jacob*, which show only one phase of his genius than for his canonic feats in such a work as the *Ave Maria Stella*, which show the complete style of the master.

The motet, which gave greater possibilities to the composer for artistic invention and ingenuity than the more restricted *conductus*, became the favourite form from the thirteenth century onwards.   From the fifteenth century it was applied to every choral part of worship.   It was essentially the embroidering of a borrowed theme of words-and-music with one, two, or three other sets of words-and-music.   It was, in fact, closely connected with the expansion of a liturgical text which is called a trope.   By the end of the fifteenth century the motet reached its final form of a short composition for unaccompanied voices, written in contrapuntal style upon a Latin Text, which is usually liturgical or quasi-liturgical in character.   During the century 1500-1600 all the great polyphonic composers wrote motets...

O Magnum Mysterium, which we have recorded,* is one of the most beautiful of the motets of Morales and shows a different phase of the master's genius to the more familiar motets which we have mentioned.   It is sung by the Antics Escolans of Montserrat.

[1] J. Bermudo, *Declaración de Instrumentos*, Bk. V. Osuna, 1555.
[2] R. Stevenson, *op. cit.*, p. 88.
* First Record, *Ancient Music*, side I, No. 12

FRANCISCO GUERRERO (1527-1599)

The expressiveness, which was one of the characteristics of Cristóbal Morales, according to his contemporaries, becomes the most distinctive trait of the younger Sevillian composer Francisco Guerrero, who was the son of a painter, Gonzalo Sánchez Guerrero. He, too, was a pupil of the same master, Fernández Castilleja, but as he says himself, he learnt much from his study of the works of Morales, "who led me far enough on the right road of composition to enter for any post of *maestro de capilla*". Guerrero, after being appointed in 1545 to the Cathedral at Jaén became cantor at Seville and after the retirement on half-pay of Castilleja became the director of the choir school there. In 1556, he visited Lisbon to present his first book of masses to King Sebastian, and in 1557 he sent his music to the Emperor Charles V in his retirement at Yuste. The Emperor, as we have already seen, was a keen but brutally frank critic, and his coarse dictum doubting Guerrero's originality as composer has often been quoted, but whether the Emperor's criticism was justified has never been proved.

In 1570, Guerrero was a judge of a competition at Cordoba and he and his singers accompanied the archbishop to Santander to receive Princess Anne, daughter of the Emperor Maximilian II, who was betrothed to Philip II. In 1574, we find Guerrero in Rome where he seems to have lived on half-pay from the chapter of Seville for a number of years. He was of adventurous as well as of religious disposition, and became a pilgrim to the Holy Land like his musical forerunner Juan del Encina. His account of his pilgrimage, which he entitled *El Viaje de Jerusalem que Hizo Francisco Guerrero, Racionero y Maestro de Capilla de la Santa Iglesia de Sevilla*, became so popular that ten editions were printed in the course of the seventeenth and eighteenth centuries. In the prologue to this work, he gives his autobiography which we can supplement by the account given by the father-in-law of Velasquez, Pacheco, in his *Libro de Descripción de Verdaderos retratos de Ilustres y Memorables Varones* (1559). [1] The highest tribute to the music of Guerrero came from his contemporary Vicente Espinel, the author of the *picaresque* novel *Marcos de Obregón*, who praises him for his *Villancicos* or folk songs and his madrigals, and speaks of his artifice and his "sprightly counterpoint" (*gallardo contrapunto*). Cerone, on the other hand, praises him for his "grave and devotional music which is so well written for voices".

Guerrero had not the strength and austerity of his predecessor Morales, but he was a lovable character, with a sunny Andalusian disposition and his elegiac religious music is, as Cecil Gray says, the feminine counterpart to that of Morales, with the gentle melancholy of his fellow-countryman, the painter, Murillo. When we listen to his beautiful madrigals we understand the significance of a form of composition that made its appearance in Italy at the beginning of the sixteenth century, derived from pastoral songs, which were popular in the fourteenth century, and were revived and perfected as an art-form in the sixteenth by the famous composers Luca Marenzio, Monteverdi and Gesualdo, Prince of Venosa. In the madrigals of the Roman or Southern school, the polyphonic element tends to dominate, whereas in those of the Northern or Venetian school, the character is more harmonic. In the madrigals of Willaert, Carlo Gasualdo, Prince of Venosa (a magnificent figure of the Renaissance whose lonely position apart from his contemporaries in music resembles that of El Greco in painting) and Luca Marenzio, the Neapolitan, we find chromatic progressions which foreshadow Wagner and Debussy.

Morales and Guerrero followed the path traced out by Marenzio and gave to the madrigal art-form a wistful serenity which still charms the ear. Guerrero's setting of the famous madrigal by Gutierre de Cetina, *Ojos claros*, *serenos* and *Prado verde y florido* (wrongly attributed to Navarro) are characteristic of his genius. Many of them were published in his *Villanescas Espirituales*. The tradition of the madrigal was carried on by Guerrero's successors Juan Navarro, the author of the sparkling madrigals *La Monja* and *Susana*, and Ginés de Morata. These madrigals survived owing to the arrangements made for the lute by Fuenllana, Daza and others, and the lovely *Prado verde y florido* was first published by the Conde de Morphy from the lute version of Daza. What is of extreme interest to us in our Spanish Time-Journey is the use Guerrero makes of the Mozarabic liturgy in his settings of the Mass, such as *Rex Virginum amata*, *Deus Mariae Decus*, and in the Kyries of the Masses *De Beata*

---

[1] The most complete modern biography of Guerrero is by R. Mitjana: F. Guerrero, *Estudio crítico biográfico*, Madrid, 1922.

Virgine, for again we are reminded of the flaming spirit of Spain's first musician, the Sevillian Saint Isidore. The Antics Escolans of Montserrat sing our recording of *Esclarecida Madre* * by Guerrero, a charming example of a "religious madrigal", a Spanish type to which we have become familiar through the successors of Juan del Encina, Juan Vázquez, Diego Garzón and others.   R. Mitjana in his *Encyclopédie de la Musique* has made the interesting observation that the original of *Esclarecida Madre* appears in the manuscript of the Medinaceli *Cancionero* under the profane title of *Esclarecida Juana*.

We also include in this record another piece from the celebrated *Cancionero* of Medinaceli sung likewise by the Escolans of Montserrat *En el Campo me metí***, a *Villancico* by Ginés de Morata, adapted by Maestro Miguel Querol Gavalda.   The latter lived from 1926 to 1936 in the Monastery of Montserrat, studying music and philosophy, and was a member of the Chapel of the celebrated Abbey.

Since 1952 he has acted as Vice-Director of the Spanish Institute of Musicology.   He has published the *Cancionero musical de la Casa de Medinaceli* in two volumes, a magnificent anthology of Spanish madrigal composers of the sixteenth century, including also works of sacred music by Morales, Cabezón, Gombert, etc.

En el Campo me metí by Morata possesses a delightful freshness and lyricism.

* First Record, *Ancient Music*, side II, No. 1.
** First Record, *Ancient Music*, side I, No. 9.

An interesting drawing by Titian of Philip II.   It is in the Castle of Chantilly.

🎵 TOMAS LUIS DE VICTORIA (1540-1611)

Avila rises from the solemn immensity of the Castilian meseta like a fortress of the spirit. When the wanderer today gazes at the city from the plain, it becomes, with its walls, turrets and bastions, an epitome of the Spanish Middle Ages.   It personifies the spirit of Castile in its ceaseless struggle for the Western Christian world against the Infidel from the East.   Even the Cathedral crowning the city becomes an impregnable citadel of the soul and the peasant whom the wanderer sees digging the hard ground at the base of the walls murmurs between his teeth the characteristic proverb of the city *Cantos y Santos* (Stones and Saints).   Today in Avila the wanderer sees nothing but stones and saints, for Avila, poised on the summit of a rugged mountain with its granite structures rising in tiers above the ashen plain, is "Avila of the Saints", the inner castle of the soul of Saint Teresa with its seven mansions.   To mount its narrow streets towards the fortified Cathedral means to tread the Saint's Way of Perfection up which she travelled in search of freedom of the soul.   But Avila, the wall-girt city, has a double name and significance, for before Saint Teresa and Saint John of the Cross made it Avila of the Saints, it assumed great significance in the mind of the Spaniards through its name *Avila de los Caballeros* —Avila of the Knights, a name which perpetuates the grim drama enacted there in July 1465, when King Henry IV of Castile and León was dethroned in effigy by the Archbishop of Toledo and the Knights of Santiago, Calatrava and Alcántara, and the young Prince Alfonso, brother of Isabel of Castile, was proclaimed King of Avila, a prophetic moment foreshadowing the future destiny of Spain under the Catholic Monarchs.

In Tomás Luis de Victoria, who was born in Avila in 1540, the Spanish characteristics we noted in the Sevillian Morales and in Guerrero are still more marked, and it was said that his music had been "generated from Moorish blood", but there is no truth in that statement, for Victoria was a Castilian by birth, a Roman by education, and one of the greatest representatives of the Flemish-Roman school of polyphonic church music.

He was essentially a Spaniard from Castile and his genius is dramatic and reminds us of the polychrome statues of his contemporary, the sculptor, Alonso de Berruguete.   As one of his latest biographers says, it is a striking coincidence and may be regarded as a symbol of the close connection of the Spanish music of the sixteenth century with Spanish religion that Avila, the birthplace of Saint Teresa, the most striking embodiment of the Spanish religious spirit, was also the birthplace of Victoria, the noblest representative of Spanish music. [1]   The mystico-ascetical spirit peculiar to Spain is in both, and it is the expression of this spirit in Victoria's music that justifies us in rebutting the absurd view held by critics in the past who labelled him "the ape of Palestrina". Victoria is as unmistakably and inimitably Spanish—Castilian, even—as a portrait by El Greco, a polychrome statue by Berruguete, a *plática* between Sancho and Don Quixote or a dusty road in La Mancha. [2]

He is the greatest figure in Spanish music, and as we listen to one of his masses or his motets our thoughts turn to El Greco, whose later pictures with their unearthly light and conflicting rhythms seem the embodiment of musical harmonies, and we remember the biography written by the patriarchal Manuel Cossío, the apostle of El Greco in the modern world, who described how the Cretan painter, as he painted his visions in his palace by the Tagus would call the musicians to play to him as they used to do in the days of his youth when he sat at the foot of Titian.   In no other religious music do we find such religious exaltation as in Victoria's which carries us aloft into the swirling cloud harmonies of El Greco's picture, but we never lose sight of the austere walled fortress of Avila, and we remember the words the composer wrote as the preface to his book of Hymns in 1581: "Many evil and depraved men abuse music as an excitant in order to plunge into earthly delights, instead of raising themselves by means of it to the contemplation of God and divine things...   The art of song should be entirely devoted to the aim and end for which it was originally intended, namely to the praise and glory of God."

No two human personalities could be in greater antithesis to one another than Victoria and Palestrina in spite of the radiance and God-intoxication of their music: whereas Palestrina was an Italian layman of the Counter-Reformation whose lyrical nature and gift of spontaneous melody reflected the suave, undulating lines

[1] J. R. Milne, article on *Victoria* in Grove's Dictionary, 1945 ed., vol. VIII, pp. 766-767.
[2] J. B. Trend, *op. cit.*, p. 160.

of the Roman landscape, Victoria was ascetic Castilian priest, born in the austere town of Avila of the Saints. For him the external world did not exist and he repeated continually the lines of Saint Bernard:

Quisquis amat Christum, mundum non diligit istum, sed quasi fetores spernit illius amores. (Whoever loves Christ loves not this world, but shuns its loves as he would a noisome stench.)

Saint Teresa in her *Book of the Foundations* mentions Victoria's brother, Agustín, as one who had helped in her work for her religious houses.

In Rome, where Victoria went in 1565 to pursue his ecclesiastical studies, he entered the German College which had been founded by Saint Ignatius de Loyóla in 1552 to combat Lutheranism. Victoria's life fluctuated between that of a priest and that of a musician. Having a natural genius for composition, he devoted himself to writing Church music, but would not compose secular works even as a relaxation. In 1569, he gave up his training for the priesthood and became chapel-master and organist at the church of Santa Maria di Montserrato, the church in Rome of the Spaniards from Aragon, but he returned in 1571 to the Collegio Germanico as an assistant teacher and he succeeded Palestrina as *maestro di cappella* at the Roman Seminary. In the following year, he produced a book of motets which opens with one of his most famous, known as *O quam gloriosum*, which was wrongly attributed by Pedrell to Morales, though Victoria includes it among his own works in his edition of 1583. Particularly moving are his motets for Holy Week, especially *Vere Languores nostros*, and the *Tenebrae*. These works, with their deep pathos and sincerity, are essentially Spanish, but their simplicity reminds us of the motets of Palestrina written in 1563 and 1569. But though Victoria's general style was based upon that first fully developed by Palestrina, Palestrina in his turn was partly influenced by Victoria in his later adoption of what he himself described as a more ardently passionate style *(usus sum genere aliquanto alacriori)* for his motet from the canticles published in 1584. [1]

In his collections of Canticles, Magnificats and Marian antiphons which appeared in 1581, and in his Hymns for all the year, which were published in the same year, Victoria declares in the dedications to the Pope Pius V's nephew and to Pope Gregory XIII that his whole ambition was to employ music solely as instrument to raise the mind gently to the contemplation of divine truth. He describes himself as driven by a sort of natural instinct *(naturali quodam furor instinctu)* to the cultivation of sacred music. In 1583, Victoria who now signed himself as *reverendus dominus, presbyter Abulensis*, dedicated his book of masses to Philip II and in the preface declared after reviewing his own career as a composer that he was now weary and wished to withdraw into retirement, where he might devote himself to divine contemplation befitting a priest. The book of masses he presented, therefore, to the King as the final fruits of his talent *(postremum hunc ingenii partum)*.

Although Victoria said farewell to music in 1583, we find in 1585 his celebrated *Officium hebdomadae sacrae*, which contains the chief music for Palm Sunday and Holy Week. This collection contains some of the most beautiful music of the composer, such as the Communion motet, *O Domine Jesu Christe*, the *Tantum ergo* for the mass of Holy Thursday based on the Spanish popular tune, the *Pange Lingua* and especially the *Vere Languores*, which is sung at the adoration of the cross, and the *Vexilla Regis* written *more Hispano*, upon an ancient Spanish melody.

In 1592, in Rome, he published his second book of masses dedicated to the Prince Cardinal Albert, sixth son of the Empress María, who had been Archbishop of Toledo, but had been allowed to resign his church functions and marry and become lay Viceroy of Portugal for the King of Spain. Among the seven masses contained in this book we would mention the magnificent *O Magnum Mysterium*, in which the composer adopts in the *Gloria* and *Credo* the *parlando* homophonic style of text declamation which makes a dramatic contrast to the beautiful themes of the Christmas motet after which the mass is named.

In 1600, Victoria, who was now enjoying royal patronage, published a further book of masses, motets, magnificats and psalms which he dedicated to Philip III. These works were intended for performance in the chapel of the *Descalzas reales* in Madrid, to which he was chaplain. It was in 1600, too, that he published a beautiful setting of the hymn *Ave Maris Stella* in which the melody is given complete in every verse to the soprano.

In 1603, the Empress María died and Victoria as a tribute to her memory composed, and in 1605 published at Madrid, what most critics regard as "the crown of all his works"—the *Officium Defunctorum sex Vocibus in Obitu*

---

[1] J. R. Milne, *op. cit.*, p. 768.

et Obsequiis Sacrae Imperatricis. This Requiem was his own swan song, for it was written with the presentiment of death, and it is instructive to note how Victoria and, two centuries later, Mozart ended their lives of intense artistic creation with an office for the dead.

One of the greatest musical experiences of my life was to have heard those two wonderful swan songs on the same day. Both works separately have a great message for humanity: that of the sixteenth-century master gives us the sublime voice of the universal church, for Victoria in that work builds upon the Gregorian melodies and as an individual fuses his genius with that of collective humanity in passionate prayer. Before each part of his Mass, the Introit, Gradual, Offertory, Sanctus, Benedictus, Agnus, Communion, motet and response he introduces a theme chanted by one voice, which serves as the *motif* for polyphonic development. The theme gives us the melody, the rhythm, the colour and the tonality of each little section. Thus Victoria, the contemporary and spiritual brother of Saint Teresa of Avila, builds his tone edifice like a Gothic Cathedral, and our thoughts and emotions lose themselves in the vast shadowy expanses of the nave, whereas Mozart in his wistful music transports us to a Hellenic temple under a sunlit sky, giving us here and there swift visions of cupolas and rococo adornments falling in ruins, and sounding the dismal knell of a world in dissolution. Both composers, the Spaniard and the Austrian, welcome Death the deliverer and turn their fading eyes towards God.

The mass of Victoria has a far deeper message, for as we listen to its solemn harmonies we are transported in time back to the dying sixteenth century and we find ourselves standing with El Greco among the mourners at the burial of the Count of Orgaz. So silent are those mourners, so rapt in expectation, that even the flames of their torches are motionless and unflickering. Even their delicate fingers are stretched out in passionate expectancy for they are all poised on the edge of the world, listening... Far above their heads through the clouds here and there shadowy figures appear, emanations of the divine light and music: yet those souls of the elect, instead of floating serenely in the ethereal radiance, seem on the contrary to reflect in some mysterious way the passionate melancholy of the solemn figures below gathered around the tomb of the Count of Orgaz. They are not at peace in their heavenly mansions, but wait in agonized suspense for the Last Judgment...

Cecil Gray in summing up the musical qualities of the three Spanish Church composers of the sixteenth century says that Morales with his continual *memento, homo, quia pulvis es,* resembles Zurbarán's sombre paintings of monks praying surrounded by skulls and other macabre reminders of human mortality; Guerrero whose music is the feminine counterpart to that of Morales he compares to the wistful Madonnas of Murillo; and Victoria with his solemn harmonies he compares to El Greco, who in his great picture painted in 1584, illustrated the mood dominant in the minds of Spaniards at the end of the sixteenth century when the death on the scaffold of Mary Queen of Scots led to the tragic Spanish Armada; the shattering of Spanish hopes and the fleet scattered on the high seas; the Sack of Cadiz by Essex, the favourite of the Virgin Queen, and lastly, the lingering death of the Prudent King in his monastic tomb of the Escorial.

Victoria is represented in our record by his magnificent and celebrated motet *O vos omnes* * sung by the Escolanía and the choir of Montserrat under the direction of Dom Ireneo Segarra. The motet has been adapted by Dom David Pujol.

꣑ THE SPANISH COUNTER-REFORMATION AND MUSIC

During the whole of the period called the Counter-Reformation, which began with the Council of Trent (1548-1560), religious and artistic sentiments, customs and even the dress which men wore were predominantly Spanish, and Victoria was the musical embodiment of the Catholic Revival, which marked a great reaction against the harmony of the Neoplatonists. The Council of Trent produced the Counter-Reformation and the return to austerity and renunciation. An overmastering feeling of melancholy descended upon musicians, painters, sculptors, writers such as Victoria, El Greco and Cervantes. Saint Ignatius in his crusade had

* First Record, *Ancient Music*, side II, No. 2.

finally vanquished Erasmus, hence the *Tenebrae* and the *Requiem* of Victoria, *the Burial of the Count of Orgaz* and *Don Quixote*. The melancholy was not Spanish only but European, for we find the same musico-mystic meditation in Victoria's contemporaries in England, the Catholic Tallis and Byrd, who wrote music for both communions, the Roman and the Anglican. We find it in France in the essays of Montaigne, and in the fashionable cult of melancholy in England in the years around 1600, which finds complete expression in Shakespeare's Hamlet.

In studying the history of music it is instructive to note that just as music was the art best fitted to interpret the ideals of the early Catholic Church, so it was the art that expressed most completely the Catholic reaction against the pagan humanism of the Renaissance, and Baroque art, whether sacred or secular, was the art-expression of the spirit of the Counter-Reformation.

The Counter-Reformation, we repeat, was largely a Spanish movement, and Saint Ignatius de Loyola, the founder of the Society of Jesus, who played so dominant a role in the movement, was a Spaniard. The two greatest mystics, Saint Teresa and Saint John of the Cross were Spaniards and Spanish theologians, and Spanish Cardinals played the leading parts at the Council of Trent. Góngora in literature, El Greco in painting and Churriguera in architecture are the most complete examples of identical baroque tendencies.[1] Likewise the whole spirit of Southern Baroque music was predominantly Spanish, but Spain produced no great composer of her own after the death of Victoria. The Baroque ideals passed to Naples, which in those centuries was a mere province of Spain, ruled from Madrid by a Viceroy and dominated by Spanish cultural influences. Naples, however, through Alessandro Scarlatti and his son Domenico, would in the seventeenth century carry on the torch, and Alessandro may be looked upon as a forerunner of Mozart. His son Domenico Scarlatti would show the transition from the Baroque to the Rococo age and by his residence in Spain would become a great forerunner of modern Spanish music. His music and that of his disciple Padre Soler would lead to the harpsichord concerto of Manuel de Falla.

Great changes took place between the sixteenth and the seventeenth centuries. Whereas the music of the Gothic age was architectural and vocal, that of the Baroque era was pictorial and instrumental, and shortly before 1600 Italy produced the *basso continuo* which enabled virtuosi to appear. The great task of the musicians of the seventeenth and succeeding centuries was to extend the "tone corpus" into an infinity of tone. The new-born orchestra did not observe the limitations imposed by the human voice, but treated it as a voice to be combined with others. Melody and embellishment now in the seventeenth century combine to produce motive and this leads to the rebirth of counterpoint, and the fugal style of Frescobaldi leads to the culminating figure of J.-S. Bach.

Abandoning the vocal masses without accompaniment, the Baroque movement produced the orchestrally-conceived oratorios of Carissimi, the Dramatic Cantata and the Operas of Monteverdi. Then arise the sonata-like forms of suite, symphony and concerto grosso. Music through Corelli, Händel and Bach becomes the ruling art of the West.

[1] C. Gray, *op. cit.*, pp. 142-143. The adjective "Baroque", like "Gothic" in the eighteenth century and "Impressionistic" in the nineteenth, was originally a term of reproach and was applied to the least worthy aspects of seventeenth-century art instead of being applied to all the art products of a particular period, which possess clearly recognizable stylistic qualities in common.

The Entombment of Christ, a polychrome sculpture by Juan de Juni (1507-1577). Museum of Valladolid. This group was intended for the Chapel of Don Antonio de Guevara, Bishop of Mondoñedo and chronicler of Charles V. Its composition, which is related to theatrical art by the dramatic expression and attitudes of the figures and their realistic painting, is truly representative of the Spanish baroque style. It is the masterpiece of Juan de Juni.

Chapter XII

MUSIC AND THE THEATRE
in the seventeenth century
IN ITALY AND SPAIN

MUSIC, THE CINDERELLA OF THE ARTS IN THE RENAISSANCE

People often wonder why Spain's golden age in literature, painting and sculpture, which gave to mankind the masterpieces of Cervantes, Lope de Vega, Tirso de Molina, Calderón, Velasquez, Montañés and Zurbarán did not produce a composer worthy to be the successor to Victoria.

Why was it that the great movement of the Counter-Reformation, created by the Spanish clerics, whose ideals were embodied in the solemn music of Victoria, Morales and Guerrero, did not in Spain itself stimulate music in the same way as it stimulated the Spanish drama of the golden age?

The explanation lies in the nature of the Renaissance itself. Cecil Gray, always one of the most suggestive, as well as provocative of musicologists, even goes so far as to assert that there was no adequate parallel in music to the great stylistic transformation which took place in literature, architecture, sculpture and painting, during the century and a half that elapsed between the fall of Constantinople in 1453, from which the Renaissance was generally supposed to date, and the commencement of the seventeenth century, which marked its close.[1] Neither intellectual curiosity, nor lust for knowledge, nor desire for personal glory could be satisfied to any great extent by the art of music. The cult of antiquity, which influenced the styles of all the other arts, could not find expression in music, because no examples of Greek or Roman music which could serve as models were known to exist. But apart from those purely practical considerations there were other deeper reasons why the Renaissance could not find full expression in music.

Western European music was, to a greater extent than any other art, the direct creation of Christianity, and indissolubly bound up with the expression of Christian values. If the ideals of pagan antiquity were to be expressed in music it would have been necessary for composers to abandon the entire traditional legacy they had inherited from their predecessors, on account of the associations that music had acquired during centuries

[1] C. Gray, *op. cit.*, p. 117.

115

of service on behalf of the Church and its ritual.[1]   The course of development followed by the different arts in the Renaissance was the exact opposite to what had occurred at the beginning of the Christian era.   Then it had been music that had taken the leading part among the arts, while the plastic arts and especially the art of sculpture had been relegated to a position of secondary importance and forced to adapt themselves to the primitive expression of Christian values.   Now in the Renaissance the positions were reversed, and whereas the Renaissance spirit began to show itself in sculpture as early as the thirteenth century, it did not appear in music until the seventeenth century, and even when it did enter it impoverished music and reduced it to a mere decorative embellishment of words instead of being supreme as it had been in the early days of Christianity.

✤ THE MASKED IMPROVIZED PLAY OF THE COMMEDIA DELL'ARTE

When we compare the Renaissance literary comedy of the Plautus model with the farcical plays of the *commedia dell'Arte*, we find that, whereas in the former, expression was crystallized by the author in accordance with the literary tenets of the time, in the latter plays much was left to the spontaneous efforts of the individual actors and their *lazzi* or stunts.   The chief characteristic distinguishing literary *(commedia sostenuta)* from popular comedy was the abolition of written dialogue in the latter.   The author in the *commedia dell'Arte* only sketched out the scene of the play which the actor had to fill in by his own inspiration   We have no certain information as to when the true *commedia dell'Arte* first appeared in Italy, but there is no doubt that it was flourishing in the second half of the sixteenth century; and even in 1570 we find its actors in France delighting the court of Charles IX by their sallies.[2]

In the *commedia dell'Arte*, where improvization and surprise were the *raison d'être* of the piece, there were no prologues, for they would have taken away all the excitement from the public if they knew what the result of the plot would be.   Andrea Perrucci, an actor who wrote at the end of the seventeenth century a book on stage-improvizing, shows that the effect aimed at by the dramatist was to awaken surprise by every means, and to embroil the intrigue in the most intricate fashion.   Then at the end must come the unravelling.

The lost children must be found by their parents; the young heroine must marry the hero; the villain must be shown up, in order that the public may go home contented with their evening's amusement.   The whole play, in fact, corresponded to the humorous and the exciting film stories that are watched by crowds in our picture-houses.

The author duly wrote down the play in its broad division of acts and scenes, and left the dialogue and the interpretation to the actors.   It was altogether a play for actors, and we might say that the actors created it, for the skeleton as written by the author gave a feeble idea of the action.   In addition, each actor was provided with a *zibaldone* or repertory book in which were written all the conceits and witticisms proper to his own part. As each actor always performed the same part he gradually accumulated a big mass of "quips and cranks and wanton wiles" called *concetti* and *lazzi* to add to his *zibaldone*, whether he was Pantalone (Pantaloon), Arlecchino (Harlequin), or Pulcinella (Punch).

What attracted the public in the *commedia dell'Arte* was not so much the network of intrigue as the traditional characters with their masks, for the mask which covered the face of the actor made him into a marionette and a symbol of a region.   The characters were the silly, doddering, lovesick old man, called Pantalone— "the lean and slippered Pantaloon" of Shakespeare, who personified the Venetian merchant: then the pedantic Doctor Graziano, who was professor in the University of Bologna; and there were the lover and his fair lady; but most important of all were the two servants, one stupid and one clever, who in the North of Italy were called Harlequin and Brighella.   In Naples and the Campania he was called Pulcinella, the ancestor of Punchinello,

[1] C. Gray, *op. cit.*, p. 118.
[2] W. Starkie, *The Commedia dell'Arte and the Roman Comedy* in Proceedings of the Royal Academy, Dublin, April 1924.

Polichinelle and our Mr. Punch.   The plot of the play revolved around the character of the silly old man and the two lovers, but it was always the clever servant who rescued his master from his difficulties so that all might end happily.

Another character who assumed great importance in those plays was the bragging captain, who was a descendant of the celebrated *Miles gloriosus* of Plautus and the Thraso of Terence.   He was always boasting of his valour, his charm and riches, while in reality he was an ugly lout and in addition, a coward.   He was always in

A comic sixteenth-century engraving of three of the personages of the commedia dell'Arte.   Harlequin wearing his black mask asserts that the best way to charm his mistress is to become a dog-faced musician; Corneto the Zany agrees to strum his lute though he has not learnt to read a note; as for the "lean and slipper'd Pantalon" he will follow his part in falsetto.

Harlequin.   Zany Corneto.   Il Segnor Pantalon.

O la belle chanson, Pantalon chantons bien,
Si voulez esgayer vostre maistresse belle,
C'est le moyen certain pour en fin iouïr d'elle,
Qu'estre museau de chien, dy-ie musicien.

Accordons nous tous trois, si bien & proprement
Que puissions l'endormir au doux son de ma lire,
Encor que comme vous ie n'aye apris à lire,
Ie ne laisseray pas de iouër brauement.

Courage (mes amis) ie chante le dessus,
De ce plaisant trio, composé pour madame,
La douceur de ma voix luy penetrera l'ame:
Mes passages ne sont ni tortus ni bossus.   J.

love and ever ready to pick a quarrel with his rivals. In conversation he always used the most fantastic and high-sounding metaphors.

Owing to Spanish domination in Italy in those centuries, it was always held that the Captain satirized the Spanish soldiery in Naples. But it was necessary for the actor to be very cautious in representing the bragging captain, for the Spanish conquerors would not allow themselves to be caricatured as other nations did: they were willing to laugh at his boasts, but they would not allow a character, even on the stage, to represent a soldier's cowardice.

The costumes and the masks of the characters were stylized. The Pantaloon wore red hose, red doublet and red cloak like a Venetian merchant, and on his head a red cap with a point, which was a caricature of the Doge's horn, and on his face he wore a black mask with long hooked nose.

The Doctor Graziano from Bologna, the centre of learning, was dressed as a lawyer, doctor or university professor in black cloak, black hose, with leather purse and belt and a black cap. Harlequin, whose name came originally from the French Hellequin, who was leader of a band of devils, was originally a stupid clown and was a foil to his clever clown companion Brighella, and both of them originated in Bergamo in North Italy. In France, Harlequin became the wily Scapin of Molière and the prototype of clever servant and confidant; in Spain he fused with the *gracioso* or *donaire*, who descended from the *bobo* or simpleton of the plays of Encina. But Harlequin in his striped costume, which derived its origin from the *Mimus centunculus* of Latin comedy, finds his counterpart in the South of Italy in Naples where Pulcinella symbolizes the gaiety and immortal spirit of drollery of Maccus, the clown of the Atellan farces of antiquity. Pulcinella, the clown, as Croce says, personifies the people of Naples, and his stylized costume consists of a white shirt, baggy breeches and a white cap, though when he emigrated to France in the seventeenth century, he dressed in doublet and breeches of yellow and red.[1]

Such was the Italian *commedia dell'Arte*, which invaded Spain after France in the second half of the sixteenth century, and influenced not only the full-length plays of Lope de Vega in technique, but also the *entremeses*, *sainetes* and one-act farces which were regularly played as curtain-raisers between the *jornadas* or acts of the full-length plays. Furthermore, even in full-length plays and the music plays of the *opera buffa*, which were introduced into Spain from Southern Italy in the seventeenth century, we can note the influences of the traditional improvized play, both as regards acting technique and construction.

🟰 THE SPANISH COMEDIA

To Bartolomé Torres Naharro and Lope de Rueda belong the signal honour of having been the "first inventors" of the comedia in Spain: Torres Naharro was the first Spaniard to write comedias in the manner in which they were afterwards taken up and brought to the highest development of artistic form by Lope de Vega. His comedias are in verse, while Lope de Rueda's are in prose.[2] This information was given by Rueda's contemporary Timoneda who was the first to couple the names of both dramatists as founders of the Spanish drama.[3] Lope de Rueda's historic importance lies in the fact that it was he who invented the *paso*, a dramatic interlude portraying a simple episode such as a quarrel between man and wife over the price of olives not yet planted, or an invitation to dinner from a penniless student. Rueda's career as actor-dramatist is of great historic interest, because Cervantes saw him in the flesh when he stood as a boy of ten or twelve in the square of Valladolid, watching delightedly the crude horseplay of those farces played by the author and his actors. He never forgot those farces of Rueda and over fifty years later, in the prologue to the volume of his plays (1615), he gives us a reminiscent picture of the strolling players.

[1] B. Croce, *Pulcinella e le Relazioni della Commedia dell'Arte e la Commedia popolare romana*, in Saggi sulla Letteratura del Seicento, Bari, 1911, ch. IV.
[2] H. A. Rennert, *The Spanish Stage in the Time of Lope de Vega*, New York, 1909, p. 13.
[3] He published the works of his friend Lope de Rueda at Valencia in 1567.

118

Madrid became the capital of the country in 1560 and it was found necessary to establish a permanent place where the players might perform. Then in 1565 a number of citizens of Madrid, who had founded a charitable fraternity called the *Cofradía de la Sagrada Pasión* to feed and clothe the poor and equip a hospital for women suffering from fever, obtained the privilege of providing a place for representing all plays given in Madrid, and resolved to devote the funds thus raised for the benefit of their charity. Two years later in 1567, another fraternity was founded called the *Cofradía de Nuestra Señora de la Soledad*. The two brotherhoods purchased for the representation of plays a number of *Corrales* or yards of houses in the neighbourhood of the *Puerta del Sol*, including one in the Calle del Principe, which was called *Corral de la Pacheca*, as it had belonged to a certain Doña Isabel Pacheco. In those yards, which resembled the inn-yards in England where plays were performed, the stage was set at the back, and the larger portion of the audience watched the performance standing in the courtyard, while the windows of the principal building and of the surrounding houses served as boxes for the well-to-do spectators.[1]

Such were the stage conditions when the actors of the *commedia dell'Arte* arrived in Madrid in 1574, under the celebrated actor, Alberto Nazeri de Ganassa, who was said to have invented the character of the second clown or zany, called Harlequin. He had been in France since 1571, where he and his company had been received with acclamation. In Madrid he presented his plays mostly in pantomime, it appears, but he succeeded in the same year in obtaining the privilege to erect a theatre in the *Corral de la Pacheca* where the stage, raised seats and *patio* were exposed to the inclemency of the weather, so that if it rained no performance could be given. With the help of two carpenters and using the boards and canvas of the *Corral de la Pacheca*, Ganassa built the theatre with a roof covering the stage and the sides of the *patio* and over the latter he stretched an awning to shade the spectators from the sun. The *patio* or pit of the theatre was patronized by the rabble—the *Vulgo* or *gente de bronce*, who viewed the play standing. On account of the infernal clamour and din they made, they were called *mosqueteros*. The same conditions obtained in France and England and the boisterous rabble stood, as did the "groundlings", in the pit of the inn-yards of London. According to Pellicer, Ganassa and his Italian company, who were called *I Gelosi*, in addition to pantomime, performed Italian plays in which the characters were called Harlequin, Pantaloon and the Doctor, and he brought his actors to Seville in 1575 where they appeared in the *Corral de Don Juan*, which had been used as a theatre as early as Madrid.

So great were the crowds that thronged the *Corrales* in Madrid on Sundays and feast-days, when plays were performed, that the two *Cofradías* resolved to erect their own permanent theatres, and the first one in the Calle de la Cruz was opened in 1579 and the second in the Calle del Principe in 1582. We should note, incidentally, that in 1576, three years before the building of the *Corral de la Cruz*, in Madrid, the first genuine London playhouse, the *Theatre*, was built by James Burbage, one of the Earl of Leicester's players, and in 1582 another theatre called the *Curtain* was erected, close to the former in Finsbury fields. The *Corral de la Cruz* and *Corral del Príncipe* after 1584 were the only public theatres in Madrid and, as Rennert says, their glory in the annals of modern drama is surpassed only by the *Globe* and *Blackfriars* in London.[2]

It is a remarkable coincidence that the dramatic careers of the two great authors of the English and Spanish drama began about the same time, for Lope de Vega, who was born in 1562, began to write for the public stage about 1585. Shakespeare, who was born in 1564, came to London in 1586(?) and became attached to one of the theatres. Each rose to the topmost pinnacle of the dramatic art of his country, but whereas Shakespeare completely outshone all his English contemporaries, Lope de Vega was the first of a team of dramatists, which included serious rivals for pre-eminence, such as Tirso de Molina and Calderón. Lope de Vega had his own patron, the Duke of Sessa, just as Shakespeare had his Earl of Southampton, but neither dramatist ever received any help or encouragement from his monarch. There is no proof that Elizabeth or James I ever gave personal patronage to Shakespeare, nor did Philip III or Philip IV ever bestow any favour upon Lope, though Cristóbal Pérez Pastor discovered in 1908 a document showing that the young wife of Philip IV once paid him one hundred and fifty ducats for one of his comedias.

---

[1] Pellicer, *Tratado histórico sobre el Origen u Progresos de la Comedia y del Histrionismo en España*, Madrid, 1804, vol. I, p. 22.
[2] Rennert, *op. cit.*, p. 34.

It is strange that neither poet seems to have attached much importance to the fame he had won in the field of drama, while each was extremely proud of his other poetical compositions. Shakespeare polished the verse of his *Venus and Adonis*, and his *Rape of Lucrece*, and Lope de Vega trimmed his *Hermosura de Angélica* and his sonnets, while both mysteriously neglected the works which have since become the treasures of mankind. Lope de Vega, it is true, wrote so vast a number of plays that he could never have hoped to revise them all, but Shakespeare never worried about the fate of his plays, once they were in print, and as Collier says: "He never corrected a line of them after they were in type." [1]

Lope wrote in 1604 of his plays: "If anyone should cavil about my comedias and think that I wrote them for fame, undeceive him and tell him that I wrote them for money." Shakespeare after his retirement from the theatre in 1611 went to live at Stratford, and though he visited London on frequent occasions never revised or corrected his plays, but allowed them to go through the world regardless of their fate, and mangled and deformed copies of some of his greatest works were circulated for many years until the appearance of the folio of 1623, thus justifying the couplet of Pope on Shakespeare:

> For gain, not glory, wing'd his roving flight,
> And grew immortal in his own despite.

MUSIC AND DANCING IN THE SPANISH THEATRE

At the time of Lope de Rueda, in the middle of the sixteenth century, the music accompanying the plays acted in public squares, was, as we have seen, provided by one or two persons who sang an old ballad without the accompaniment of the guitar, behind a woollen blanket, which served as a curtain and separated the dressing-room *(Vestuario)* from the stage. According to Cervantes, it was Pedro Navarro of Toledo who brought the musicians upon the public stage. Here they sang before and after the performance of the farce, or between the acts of a comedia. Even in 1593, we find music consisting of a viol and guitars as the indispensable accompaniment to a play, and this at a later date was increased to two or three violins and an oboe. Most of the actresses, however, were dancers and most players were hired both to act and dance, and in the seventeenth century more musicians were engaged.

It is important to note that in Spain from the earliest times music and dancing were closely linked with drama. [2] As early as the beginning of the Christian era Spanish women were celebrated as dancers, and as Ticknor observes, "dancing has been to Spain what music has been to Italy, a passion with the whole population". As Cervantes says:

> *No ay muger Española que no salga*
> *del vientre de su madre bayladora.*

> There never yet has been a Spanish woman
> Who was not born into this world a dancer. [3]

Spanish dancers were famous among the ancient Romans, and Juvenal and Martial speak with relish of the provocative women dancers of Cádiz.

Martial's words are:

> *Nec de Gadibus improbis puellae*
> *Vibrabunt sine fine prurientes*
> *Lascivos docili tremore lumbos.*

[1] J. Payne Collin, *Memoires of Actors*, London, pp. 66-67.
[2] H. Rennert, *op. cit.*, pp. 67 ff.
[3] Cervantes, *La Gran Sultana*, jrn. III (*Ocho Comedias*, Madrid, 1615).

120

From the King and Queen down everybody danced, and it was said of the sombre, religious Philip III that he danced very well, and that it was the thing he did best and enjoyed most.[1]   Dancing in Spain was in accordance with religion, for music was a part of all religious festivals and no *auto sacramental* could be celebrated without music and dancing.   The festival dances could be elaborate affairs, for in 1579 a certain Jusepe de las Cuevas produced a dance, representing the battle of Rodrigo de Narvaez with the Moor Abindarraez, at the festival of Corpus Christi, and in 1590 we hear of eight ducats being paid to Leanor Rija, a mulatto, to appear on a car at Corpus Christi, in Seville, and dance, sing and play the guitar, timbrel and tambourine together with four women and two men.[2]

In 1609 the City of Madrid paid for a dance at the Corpus festival the sum of 1550 reals to Andreas de Nápesa.   The dance was called a *danza de cascabel*, which meant that it was one that could be danced by the people through the streets.   The *danza de cascabel* was, in fact, a popular dance for the masses, but it would have been considered undignified for masters to take part in such a performance.   For princes and people of high reputation, there was always the *danza de cuenta*, a more stately dance.[3]

There was a distinction drawn between the words *danzas* and *bailes* : *danzas* are measured and grave movements in which the arms are not used but the feet only, whereas *bailes* allow freer gestures of the arms and feet at the same time.[4]   The *bailes*, as they were called, were always accompanied by words or by singing, and each had its own particular melody to which later variants were sung.   These dances were frequently very indecent or *deshonestos*, and the authorities would often intervene and suppress them.   They were however as inseparable from the comedia as the interludes and *entremeses*, and often each act or *jornada* would end with a *baile*. It is interesting to compare with this the custom of the Elizabethan stage where plays began with a prologue and ended with a "jig", which was described as a "dramatic performance in rhyme, every part of which was sung by the performers and was exhibited as an afterpiece".[5]

Of all the stage dances or *bailes* the most notorious in the seventeenth century was the *Zarabanda*, which, to judge by the evil reputation it had in those days, must have been a very different kind of dance to the slow stately Sarabands of Corelli and Bach with their ornamental repeats in extempore.   Some say the word originally came from the Persian *Ser-band*, others say the dance was invented in the middle of the sixteenth century by a dancer called *Zarabanda*, who came from Seville or Guayaquil, after whom it was named.   According to Rennert, the earliest authentic date for it is contained in the *Cancionero Classense* which was copied by Alonço de Nabarete of Pisa in Madrid, in 1589, where it is described as follows:

> *La Çarabanda esta presa*
> *que dello mucho me pesa*
> *que merece ser condesa*
> *y también emperadora :*
> *"A la perra mora!   A la matadora!"*

> The *Zarabanda* is my obsession
> Of that I am certain:
> It deserves to be a countess
> And even an empress:
> Off with the *perra mora* and *la matadora!* [6]

The *Zarabanda*, the *Perra Mora* and *La Matadora*, according to this reference were three characteristic *bailes* well known in the sixteenth century, and they consisted of about a hundred verses with refrains and

[1] Julio Monreal, *Cuadros Viejos*, Madrid, 1878 (chap. on *Los Bailes de Antaño*).
[2] J. Sanchez Arjona, *Anales del Teatro de Sevilla*, Sevilla, 1898, p. 7.
[3] Cervantes, *Don Quixote*, ed. Clemencín, vol. VI, p. 273.
[4] González de Salas, *Nueva Idea de la Tragedia antigua*, Madrid, 1778, p. 171.
[5] A. W. Ward, *History of English Dramatic Literature*, vol. I, p. 476.
[6] H. Rennert, *op. cit.*, p. 70.

ritornelli and were danced by two men and a *gracioso* or clown.   Even Lope de Vega did not disdain to compose them, for we find one *baile* of his entitled "Knight of Olmedo", printed at the end of part VII of his *Comedias*, at Barcelona in 1617.   It consists mainly of snatches from the old popular ballads.

The *Zarabanda*'s bad reputation is referred to by Cervantes in his interlude *La Cueva de Salamanca* where the barber says that it and other *bailes* were invented by the devils in hell.   All authorities in Spain, in fact, agree that it was "pestiferous" and some refer not only to its indecent writhings and contortions, but also to the obscene words that were sung to its rhythms.[1]   What is most strange is that this dance, which all agreed to be immoral, should have been danced at the festival of Corpus Christi in Seville in 1593, when the *autos sacramentales* were represented by the company of the celebrated actor Jerónimo Velasquez.   Many remonstrances were made against the dance, according to Cotarelo y Mori, but the *Zarabanda* was followed by other dances such as the *Chacona* and the *Escarramán*, which were likewise condemned by the clergy, and we find a Catalan Jesuit P. Juan Ferrer saying that many people in Barcelona were so scandalized at the lewdness of the *Chacona* and the *Escarramán*, which were sung and danced on the stage, that they left the theatre to avoid seeing and hearing them.   Nevertheless, in spite of the clerical opposition to such dances, we find Cervantes and Lope de Vega, who were great admirers of popular dances, introducing them into their works.   The former introduces a *Chacona* in his exemplary novel *The Illustrious Kitchen-Maid*, which is danced by muleteers and Galician girls to the following refrain:

> *El baile de la chacona*
> *encierra la vida bona.*
>
> The chacona is a treasure
> Makes of life a real pleasure.

In the third stanza, he links it with the notorious *Zarabanda* and *La Perra Mora*, making fun in truly outrageous Lopesque fashion of the priesthood to which he later belonged, and denouncing the prudes:

> *Que de veces ha intentado*
> *Aquesta noble señora*
> *en la alegre Zarabanda*
> *el pésame y perra mora*
> *entrarse por los esquicios*
> *de las casas religiosas, etc.*
>
> Oft that noble dame Chacona
> With the Saraband allied,
> Has put our carking cares to rout
> And the black bitch has defied.
> Oft Chacona makes its entry
> Through the chinks of convent cell,
> And that tranquil virtue flutters
> Which in sacred haunt should dwell.

According to Cotarelo y Mori the *Chacona* in Spain was a brilliant and showy dance *(airosa y vistosa)* with castanets, accompanied by various instruments and full of gaiety and *joie de vivre* with its refrain:

> *Assí vida, vida bona,*
> *Vida vámonos a chacona.*
>
> Such is life, bonny life
> let us all dance the chacona.

---

[1] Alonso Lopez Pinciano, *Filosofía Antigua Poética*, Madrid.

Some of the other ancient dances introduced by Cervantes into his interlude *El Rufián Biudo* are: the *escarramán*, the *turdión*, the *pavana*, the *canario*, the *Rey Don Alonso*, the *Pésame dello*, the *zambapalo* and the *gallarda*.

Lope de Vega in his great scenic novel of five acts, *La Dorotea*, which he had begun in his fiery youthful years, when he was in love with the beautiful young actress Elena Osorio, and finished in 1632, three years before his death, writes in a tone of melancholy reminiscence of those old dances, and like Horace mourns the passing of the years. Alas, he cries, the old dances are being forgotten by the people and we have no more the provocative gestures and lascivious movements of the *chaconas* which so grievously offended the chastity and silent decorum of the ladies. Where, alas, are the *Alemana* and the *Pié de Gibao* which used year in year out to cheer our mirthful parties?[1] As for the *gallarda*, which Lope mentions, it was one of the stately Spanish dances like the *pavana*, and it is celebrated by his contemporary and cross-grained rival Góngora in one of his ballads as follows:

> *Que quiere doña María*
> *Ver bailar a doña Juana*
> *Una Gallarda española*
> *Que no ha danza más gallarda.*

> Lady Mary wishes to see
> Lady Joan dance a Spanish *Gallarda*,
> For there's no dance in the world
> So grave and stately as the *Gallarda*.

But in spite of the enthusiasm of Cervantes, Lope de Vega and Góngora for the ancient dances, the clerics had the last word and the Jesuit historian Mariana, like the great churchman Cardinal Segura, Archbishop of Seville in our days, fulminates against the evils of immoral dances, and devotes a whole chapter (XII) to the *Zarabanda*. He denounces the song and dance, saying that it was danced in one of the most illustrious cities of Spain in the procession and festival of Corpus Christi, making a mockery of Our Lord at the very time when He should have been honoured. And worse still, in the same city, in various convents of nuns during the same festival that dance was performed with such obscene movements that those possessing any sense of decency had to cover up their eyes for shame.[2] Padre Mariana, who believed in its Spanish origin, ascribed its invention directly to the devil. The same low opinion of the Saraband was held in Italy, for Marini in his poem *L'Adone* (1623) says:

> *Chiama questo suo gioco empio e profano*
> *Sarabanda, e Ciaccona, il nuovo Ispano.*

> (The new Spaniard calls his impious and profane pleasure
> the Saraband and Chacona.
> This is an allusion to the supposed American origin of the dance.)[3]

In spite of its sinister reputation in Spain and Italy at the end of the sixteenth century, the Saraband became exalted in status in France, for it was introduced into the French court in 1588 and later on we find Richelieu wearing green velvet knee-breeches, with bells on his feet and castanets in his hands, dancing it in a ballet before Anne of Austria.

In England the Saraband did not become fashionable until well into the seventeenth century, but like many court dances of the Baroque epoch, it was used as a musical form in addition to its function as a dance. But in England a characteristic rapid Saraband in 3/4 time became fashionable and we find them in the suites

[1] Lope de Vega, *La Dorotea*, Madrid, 1632, jorn. I, sc. VII, fol. 40.
[2] Mariana, *Contra los Juegos públicos*, in Bibl. Arch. Esp., vol. XXXI, p. 433.
[3] Grove's Dictionary of Music, V ed., 1954. Articles on "Saraband" by W. B. Squire.

of Matthew Locke for four viols and in Purcell's sonatas of three parts. In the course of the seventeenth century the Saraband became an English country dance, for we find it in Playford's *Dancing Master* of 1651.[1]

In Spain, in the seventeenth century when plays became more elaborate in staging and pageantry, the dances developed into what were called *Danzas habladas*, or dances composed of many persons who were dressed up to represent any episodes in history. These dances were performed at the festival of Corpus Christi and the expenses were defrayed by the various guilds. Thus in Spain as in Italy the drama after emancipating itself from the control of the Church drew its support from the *gremios* or guilds, such as that of the tavern-keepers, the glove-makers, the cobblers, as the case might be, who employed the services of the *autor* (author, manager and producer) of the company to produce the play.

Our recording * includes a *Canario* by Gaspar Sanz adapted by Germán Lago and played under his direction by the Orquesta Ibérica of Madrid. Gaspar Sanz was a celebrated seventeenth-century Spanish guitarist, born at Calanda in Aragon, the town famed for its dancing. He took his degrees in philosophy and theology at Salamanca and proceeded to Naples where he terminated his studies. In 1674 he published at Saragossa a book of tablature, a precious anthology for guitarists, which not only instructs in the Spanish guitar but also gives variations in French, Italian, English as well as Spanish styles of guitar-playing. The book, which was re-edited several times, is a treatise on the harp and the organ as well as the guitar.

Gaspar Sanz's playing aroused the enthusiasm of his contemporaries: one of his panegyrists said: "Some charm us, but Gaspar Sanz disturbs us." In the introduction to his treatise he invokes the authority of Saint Augustine. He also pays a tribute to the writer and musician Vicente Espinel, crediting him with having added the fifth string to the guitar. Gaspar Sanz's treatise is of great interest for the dance-music it contains of the time of Lope de Vega and Calderón.

The *Canario* was an ancient dance, probably originally from Spain. It was an animated dance in 3/8, 6/8 or 3/4, in ternary measure and resembled the *giga*. It had graceful *zapateo* or footwork and was often included in ballets of operas by Lully and others.

Pellicer mentions it in his *Tratado historico* among the ancient dances *(bailes antiguos)* along with the *Turdion*, the *Pavana*, the *Madame Orliens* and the *Pié de Gibao* etc.

⟆⟑ LOPE DE VEGA, PORTENT OF NATURE (1562-1635)

The Spanish conquests in Italy from the days of Alfonso V of Aragon to the great captain increased the tendency among the foremost writers in Spain to despise their own national poetry, music and drama, calling them rude and uncouth, and turn to conquered Italy for inspiration. Once again, we have an illustration of the saying: *Graecia capta ferum victorem cepit*. Torres Naharro, Lope de Rueda, Timoneda, and their followers devoted their energies to imitating Italian comedies and novels: Spanish musicians imitated the madrigals of Luca Marenzio and Monteverdi, or the melodramas of Peri, and in lyric poetry, as Lope de Vega said, the native genius of Spain had disappeared, owing to the craze for imitating the Italian muse.

Then in 1579, like a bolt from the blue, came a play by the Sevillian dramatist, Juan de la Cueva, called *La Muerte del Rey Don Sancho*, based upon the most famous of epic stories, the Siege of Zamora. There was a sensation in the theatre when the actors declaimed the lines of the ancient ballad, which every member of the audience had known by heart since childhood. It was thus possible for the public, through its memories

[1] *Ibid.*, p. 418.
* First Record, *Ancient Music*, side II, No. 5.

Adoration of the Shepherds : little known masterpiece by Domenikos Theotokopoulos, known as El Greco (1541-1614). For a long time it belonged to a convent at Toledo, but in 1955 it was acquired by the Prado Museum.

of the Romancero, to collaborate intimately with the actors on the stage, and this imparted to the characters in the play a vitality which had not existed previously in the theatre.

After that experiment it became clear that what Spain needed was a truly national poet who would revitalize the whole art of the drama. It was then that Lope de Vega, that "portent of nature" and "Phoenix of Geniuses" as he was called, appeared in the theatre.

Of Lope it may be said that he created the Spanish national theatre and built up an entire dramatic history of the country from chronicles and ballads, interweaving ballad phrases with his verses in such a way that the original cannot be separated from the new. This he could do all the more easily because the best Castilian ballads cut short the narrative, leaving only the dialogue. From his earliest years, Lope's imagination was attuned to the traditional ballads which were venerated by the people as the records of the nation's history rather than enjoyed as poetry. Lope, however, was able to breathe into those legends of past heroes the magic of his genius and transform them into drama. And what is still more remarkable is that Lope's vast erudition acquired later, and his enormous reputation among men of letters, did not in the slightest degree diminish his vivid and intensive feeling for traditional poetry. His heart was always open to the artless simplicity of folk-songs, for they awoke in him deeper harmonies.

Menéndez Pidal, with rare acumen, points out how deeply suggestive was the technique employed by Lope de Vega in these plays based on traditional themes. He made use not only of the traditional narrative elements, but also of the short refrains that were sung by the people and, in this way, he was able to convey dramatic emotion by subtle means here and there throughout the play.[1]

In one play, entitled *Las Almenas de Toro* (The Battlements of Toro) we hear the voice of the sentry on the castle walls driving off sleep by the melancholy traditional song:

> *Velador que el castillo velas*
> *Vélale bien y mira por ti,*
> *Que velando en él me perdí.*

> Watchman on the battlements,
> Keep thou strict watch and
> watch for thyself;
> for watching here I met my doom.

Some of Lope's loveliest plays such as *Peribañez*, *Fuenteovejuna* and *San Isidro Labrador* are entirely founded on folk-songs, and the fragments of songs and ballads which abound in his plays are like stray folk melodies used by a great master of musical form, who from them weaves a magic sound-pattern which, in the end, becomes a complete and original work, but through it runs the slender gold thread of those melodies, faint as a ghost of the past, like a sudden glimpse through magic casements.

Lope had the genius to sense the rich dramatic material that could be extracted from the ballads and chronicles of Spain's past history, and through the chronicles the poet reached the ancient Epic, because his dramatic genius led him straightway to the most poetic passages, which were those derived from the old rhapsodic poems. In this way the spirit of the ancient Epic exercised a decisive influence on the nascent theatre of the *siglo de oro*.[2]

The extraordinary life story of Lope de Vega "the Portent of Nature", as Cervantes described him, reminds us of the words used by Havelock Ellis to portray Casanova (who, incidentally was of Spanish origin): "Whatever offences against social codes he may have committed, Casanova can scarcely be said to have sinned against natural laws. He was only abnormal because so natural a person within the gates of civilization is necessarily abnormal and at war with his environment. Far from being the victim of morbidities and perversities Casanova presents to us the natural man *in excelsis*. He was a man for whom the rational world existed and who reacted to all the stimuli it presents to the healthy normal organism. His intelligence was immensely

[1] R. Menéndez Pidal, *The Spaniards in their History*, Introd., p. 62.
[2] W. Starkie, Introd. R. Menéndez Pidal, *op. cit.*, p. 63.

keen and alert, his resourcefulness, his sagacious audacity, his presence of mind, were of the first order. He was equally swift to feel, to conceive and to act."[1]

The difference between Lope and Casanova was that whereas Casanova went through life blindly and selfishly gratifying his instincts without a thought for the morrow and muttering always to himself the defiant challenge of Tirso de Molina's Don Juan Tenorio, *tan largo me lo fiais*, Lope, even in later life, was a Don Juan burdened with a conscience, and after treading the primrose path of dalliance he was beset by remorse and his conscience left him no peace. He would then flog himself till the whitewashed walls of his cell were stained with blood, and he would devote himself to the care of the lepers and the poor in an attempt to mortify his sinful flesh.

Even as a child he was a disconcerting wonder—dictating verses before he could write, learning Latin when he was five. A few years later, we hear of his prowess as dancer, as fencer, as incorrigible truant from school and as juvenile dramatist. At twenty-three his amours were the scandal of Madrid and led to his exile, but insolent as Casanova he retaliated by eloping with Isabel de Urbina, the daughter of a King-at-Arms. The police were unable to catch him, he married the girl by proxy and set sail on the *San Juan* in the Invincible Armada—the famous expedition of the "Sad intelligencing Tyrant", when as Milton said, "the very maw of Hell was ransacked, and made to give up her concealed destruction, ere she could vent it in that terrible and damned blast." And Lope during the lulls in the battle and during the ensuing disaster found time to write the greater part of *La Hermosura de Angélica*, an epic of eleven thousand lines. Later, after his stay in the pleasure-seeking court of Valencia and a period of service in the household of the fifth Duke of Alba, he won fame as a dramatist and became the rage in Madrid. People rushed to see his plays and he wielded the powers of a dictator over the Spanish theatre. In spite of writing incessantly for the stage, he found time to become entangled in a series of scandalous amours in which he rivalled the exploits of Casanova. One after another, his fair victims are conjured up for us in innumerable sonnets, eclogues, elegies, and in the plays that poured incessantly from his pen: Antonia Trillo de Armenta, Micaela de Luján—the Camila Lucinda of his sonnets and mother of his brilliant children Lope Felix del Carpio y Luján and Marcela, who inherited some of her father's genius.[2] Even his second marriage to Juan de Guardo (for Isabel de Urbina had died in 1595) did not make him mend his ways, for the stage had him in its grip and he was unable to break with his past, even though he had moments of sincere repentance. His devotional mood deepened when sorrows came upon him. The death of his beloved son Carlos Felix was followed soon afterwards by the death of his wife. It was then that he wrote the "Four Soliloquies", which with his *Rimas sacras* are among the most moving of all his poems. The full title of the soliloquies is as follows: *Cuatro Soliloquios de Lope de Vega Carpio: Llanto y lágrimas que hizo arrodillado delante de un crucifijo pidiendo a Dios perdón de sus pecados, después de haber recibido el hábito de la Tercera Orden de penitencia del Seráfico Francisco* (Four Soliloquies of Lope de Vega Carpio: Lamentations and tears he shed when kneeling before a crucifix beseeching God to pardon his sins, after having received the habit of the Third Order of the Seraphic Francis). It was then, in a moment of mystical yearning and sincere contrition for his frequent lapses, that he resolved to take holy orders. This, as Fitzmaurice Kelly says, was his irreparable mistake. No man was less fitted to be minister of religion, and in spite of his moments of mysticism and remorse when he felt inspired to write in the vein of the Soliloquies he did not show any sign of a religious vocation. On the contrary, we discover in the long correspondence which he carried on over many years with his patron, the Duke of Sessa that he had acted continually as *alcahuete* or servile pander, forever at his master's beck and call, ready to write the latter's love letters and act as go-between in his discreditable amours. Few more fascinating revelations have been written of the psychology of one of the world's famous writers than the four volumes of correspondence which has been published, with copious commentary, by the late President of the Spanish Academy of History, Dr. Agustin de Amezúa. It is a monument of patient scholarship which is indispensable for those who wish to penetrate into the complex personality of Spain's greatest dramatist. These letters reveal from time to time his agonies of remorse at the shameful part he was playing, and he protests again and again at being made

[1] Havelock Ellis, *Selected Essays*, London, 1936, pp. 60-61.
[2] She entered the religious Order of the Discalced Trinitarians, and under the name Sor Marcela de San Felix, wrote some of the most beautiful mystical verses in Spanish poetry. She lived until 1688.

the intermediary of the Duke's vulgar love affairs. He tells his master also of the terrible quandary in which he was placed every week when he had to face his confessors, who threatened to withhold absolution if he did not renounce his vile services as purveyor of the Duke's lustful pleasures. Then in his fifty-fifth year he himself, who had become a priest in 1614, fell madly in love with the beautiful Marta de Nevares Santoyo, who, as Marcia Leonardo, inspired some of his loveliest poems. Lope de Vega, owing to his success as dramatist and poet and his unexampled popularity among the masses of the people, made a number of bitter enemies, especially Góngora, the leader of the opposition poetical school, who missed no chance of attacking him. By taking holy orders and becoming a Familiar of the Inquisition, Lope had placed himself at the mercy of his enemies who did not spare him. Cervantes in the prologue to the Second Part of *Don Quixote* alludes to him indirectly as a Familiar of the Inquisition, notorious for his "virtuous occupation".

At first, Lope snapped his fingers at his accusers for he was at the height of his fame. Not only were his plays acted on every stage in Spain, but the people who filled the theatres listened spell-bound and followed him through the streets as though he possessed the powers of a wizard, while women leaned out of windows and blessed him as he passed. As a result of his fame his plays filled the theatres in Italy no less than in Spain, and it was said that Italian impresarios had only to print the name of Lope de Vega on the advertisement posters in the streets for the theatres to be packed. His name in Spain and Italy became the synonym for matchless excellence.

Lope's contemporaries were never weary of celebrating his incredible industry, invention and his "Ocean of Plays". It is today impossible to know how many plays Lope de Vega actually wrote, for only a comparatively small number of those that were acted has survived. He was supposed to have written two hundred and twenty plays up to 1603, and by 1609 the total rose to four hundred and eighty-three; in 1618, it reached eight hundred, in 1628, one thousand and seventy and in 1632, fifteen hundred.

After his death his friend and disciple Pérez de Montalbán in a posthumous panegyric asserted that Lope wrote eighteen hundred plays and more than four hundred *autos*, bringing his total output to 2,200. This would mean that Lope never wrote less than twenty-four plays a year, that he usually wrote fifty, that the yearly average rose to sixty as he grew older, and that in the last three years of his life he wrote over a hundred—say, two plays a week. Most of Lope de Vega's plays, however, have perished, and those that are extant today reach the number of four hundred and thirty-one plays and fifty *autos*.

VELASQUEZ, CHRONICLER OF PHILIP IV

No Spanish King is more familiar to us than Philip IV whom his subjects with flattering unction called *Don Felipe el Grande sobre todos los Reyes máximo monarca.*

Through the peerless art of Velasquez we know how he looked at every stage of his life. We see him as a flaxen-haired youth of sixteen with light blue eyes, long face, prominent jaw, and a puzzled, irresolute expression full of melancholy. A little later he becomes more assertive, and the budding moustachios and the pouches beneath the eyes tell tales of dissolute living and late carousals. Ten years later there is more kingly majesty, but the face is listless, and there is weariness in the eyes. One hand rests limply on his sword hilt, the other hangs irresolute by his side. The next portrait shows him on horseback, and we think of Titian's painting of his ancestor Charles V riding at dawn on the day of Mühlberg. The fiery steed snorting defiance only serves to stress by contrast the listlessness of the King holding irresolutely the baton of command in his right hand. In another portrait Velasquez paints the King out hunting with his dog and his gun, and here there is more kingly dignity, more *bonhomie*, but the gloomy profligate face is full of *ennui*, feebleness and failure. When we gaze into those melancholy eyes we do not need to read the tragic tale of official corruption, obscurantism, bigotry, huge taxation, inept finance, sloth, superstition and ignorance.

Those portraits in the Prado tell us more and far more dramatically about the Spanish royal court, and we have only to look at two portraits of Velasquez of the Conde-duque of Olivares to understand the relations

The Fountain of the Tritons in the gardens of the royal palace of Aranjuez: a landscape by Velasquez. From the Prado Museum, Madrid. This was the characteristic setting of many of the seventeenth-century comedies by Calderón and Moreto.

between the favourite and his royal master. The first shows the Conde-duque in 1624, the early days of his power. A square-headed, imperious figure, resplendent in velvet and massive gold chain, he positively gloats with pride and arrogance as he stands before us, and the huge gold key which he prominently displays on his doublet is the most significant symbol of his omnipotence in the palace. Lust for power lies in those deep-set scheming eyes and in the sensual mouth. Ten years later in 1634 the massive figure of Olivares on a prancing horse is the personification of "hybris" and in glaring contrast to the portrait of the listless King on his charger. A later picture of 1638 shows us the *Privado* after fourteen years of personal power. The lined face with pouches under the eyes and deepening furrows, the haunted expression of those eyes reveal the tragedy of "hybris" avenged: overthrown after having driven his country into the ruinous Thirty Years' War and provoked the revolts of Catalonia and of Portugal, which latter recovered its independence. Velasquez, however, gives a certain grandeur and nobility to Olivares for whom he felt sincere gratitude. When he had come to Madrid to study the paintings in the Escorial it had been the Count-Duke who had called him to the palace to paint the King. [1]

As we gaze at these historical paintings by Velasquez we begin to understand the deeper implications of the revolution which he caused in painting.

For the Spaniard the supreme values of life are moral and depend upon personality. Art must concern itself with realities and not with dreams. Life may be, as Calderón held, a dream; but in the Spanish view of the world, when the dream is over, then the individual is still left with his personal responsibility and his yearning for salvation. In this lies one of the profoundest intuitions of the Baroque, but which Spain alone felt with sufficient intensity to raise it to the plane of art. [2]

If Velasquez makes the life of the Court live for us with its underlying note of tragic nemesis, the satirists such as Quevedo and Vélez de Guevara give us the bitter comments that were made throughout the country against its follies and abuses. Quevedo, whose savage indignation rivals that of Jonathan Swift, shows us a King sunk in apathetic despondency, a dictatorial favourite bankrupting the country through his extravagance, and a decadent society in which Faith has decayed and monstrous superstitions have taken its place. Guevara in *El Diablo Cojuelo* makes his devil take us for a ramble on the roofs of the houses in Madrid and give us a remorseless picture of conditions inside each house. Quevedo, like the Prophet Jeremiah, is full of pessimism, for Spaniards no longer wear iron armour unless it is to deck the statues on their tomb, and they dress in effeminate luxury, "repenting that they had been begotten men".

PHILIP IV AND ISABEL, PATRONS OF THE THEATRE

In spite of his extravagance, his extortions and his war-mongering the dictatorship of the Count-Duke of Olivares marked a very important era in the development of music and the drama. Hitherto the drama had been a popular spectacle patronized by the masses in the two *Corrales*, and the attitude of the Church had been hostile, with the result that between 1598 and 1615 a series of laws had been passed reforming the theatre. Philip IV, however, on his accession, at once showed himself a generous patron, for the theatre was his ruling passion. He not only encouraged dramatists but he is said to have actually written plays. Even in 1614, when he was only nine years of age, he appeared as Cupid in a children's play performed for the Court.

According to the chronicler Cabrera, the movement of the car in which Cupid came upon the stage made him ill, and he vomited twice, though no other mishap befell him and it was said that he played his part exceedingly well. [3]

[1] For the personality and career of the Count-Duke of Olivares see the celebrated biography of Dr. Gregorio Marañón: *El Conde-Duque de Olivares (La Pasión de Mandar)*, Madrid, 1936. See also J. Deleite y Piñuelo, *El Declinar de la Monarquía Española*, Madrid, 1947.
[2] E. Lafuente Ferrari, *Velasquez*, London, 1943.
[3] L. Cabrera, de Cordoba, *Relaciones de las Cosas sucedidas en la Corte de España desde el Ano 1599 hasta 1614*, ed. Pascuala Gyangos, Madrid, 1857, p. 547.

Portrait of Queen Isabel of Bourbon, wife Philip IV, on horseback, by Velasquez. At the Prado Museum, Madrid. The Spanish people had a faith amounting to superstition in their Queens who were blessed with the name Isabel. After Isabel the Catholic, Isabel de Valois, the wife of Philip II was the most beloved of Spanish Queens, and Isabel the wife of Philip IV was the deep affection of the Madrid people. She showed determination too, when the moment came to overthrow the Count, Duke of Olivares.

The Count-Duke of Olivares, knowing how eager the King and Queen were to possess a Court theatre, resolved in 1631 to build a new royal residence on a large tract of land adjoining the royal monastery and convent of San Jerónimo. This fantastic palace of pleasure, called the *Buen Retiro* was utterly to eclipse the groves, gardens and ancient palaces of the Pardo and Casa de Campo which had been the recreation of Philip II and Philip III.[1] The palace was surrounded by large gardens, woods and artificial lakes and contained a magnificent theatre. A portion of the site had originally been devoted to a henhouse where the Countess of Olivares kept her choicest flocks of poultry, and the term *gallinero* was often applied either to the theatre or the palace, even in the days of Madame d'Aulnoy's visit.

[1] Mesoneros Romanos, *El Antiguo Madrid*, Madrid, 1881, vol. II, pp. 163 ff. See also M. A. S. Hume, *The Court of Philip IV*, London, 1907, p. 238.

131

Olivares in 1631, before the great palace was completed, organized a monster dramatic entertainment on Saint John's night in the gardens of the Duke of Maqueda and those of his neighbour Luis Méndez de Carrión. Lope de Vega wrote his play *La Noche de San Juan* in three days for the event, and Quevedo and Antonio de Mendoza wrote their play *Quien más miente medra más* jointly in a single day. Both plays were produced by the company of the *autor* or actor-manager Vallejo under the superintendence of the Count-Duke.

🎵 THE ORIGIN OF THE ZARZUELA

The Count-Duke acted as master of ceremonies and Chief Artificer of the royal revels for twenty years, and this was a period of exceptional brilliance in the history of the Spanish theatre, not only because of the great dramatists Lope de Vega, Tirso de Molina and Calderón, but also because of the innovations introduced by Cesare Fontana and Cosimo Lotti, the Italian architects and their disciples, who perfected the stage machinery and scenery in the plays.

Among the performances given to the royal family in the palace should be mentioned Lope de Vega's pastoral eclogue, *La Selva sin Amor*, which was sung before His Majesty some time prior to November 1629.

Ticknor states that this was the first attempt to present dramatic performances with music, and it is significant that the introduction of music went hand in hand with elaborate innovations in Baroque decoration. Already the stage decorators like Cosimo Lotti were beginning to collaborate with the dramatists and musicians in the creation of operas.

In those years, *El Mayor encanto amor* or *Circe*, which was the invention of Cosimo Lotti, was represented at the request of the Countess of Olivares on the great pond of the Retiro on the Night of Saint John, 1634, and and in the following year Calderón's *Los Tres Mayores Prodigios* were given in the open air on separate stages, next to one another (like the French *mansions*), each act by a different company of players. According to the *Anales de Madrid* of Antonio Léon Pineto, under the year 1640, these plays of Calderón were produced upon a floating theatre which the wasteful extravagance of Olivares had erected on the artificial lake in the garden of the Buen Retiro. In the concluding verses of the play Calderón says that "the water was very happy on this gracious night".

Ticknor, however, says that a storm of wind scattered the vessels, the royal party, and the supper that was also among the floating arrangements of the occasion, prepared by Cosmo Lotti, the Florentine architect.

Music in the theatre was still in the seventeenth century the Cinderella of the arts, and in the first attempt at Spanish opera we know of, namely Lope de Vega's *La Selva sin Amor*, the name of the composer of the music is unknown.[1] Probably the music came from Italy and Lope adapted his words to it. In many of the comedias of Lope we find attractive *tonadillas* to which he set the words, and the music was by his friend the distinguished lute-player, Juan Blas de Castro, who had been a member of the Chapel Royal since 1605.

Lope de Vega's next collaborator was the celebrated lutenist Juan Palomero, who had entered the service of the Duke of Alba in 1594, when Lope himself was secretary to the Duke at Alba de Tormes.

In *El Peregrino en su Patria* Lope de Vega, after a learned discussion on music as it was considered by Aristotle and Plutarch, goes on to mention some of the greatest lutenists and singers of his time. Palomero, he says, "on his five strings made all the celestial voices sing". In Lope de Vega plays music serves to create the atmosphere of the comedia. He used music as a descriptive element in the form of a *copla* sung by shepherds or villagers, or of a ballad which was sung by the *dueña* or the maid-servant to soothe her mistress, the princess: or else we find a play on the festivities of Saint John's Night beginning with a noisy rustic chorus of peasants. Lope de Vega, too, was very fond of using the dramatic possibilities of the serenade which the hero sings under the window of his beloved, and he was alive to the humorous possibilities of the satirical street-song with its grotesque effects à la Beckmesser. And again we find him frequently combining singing, instrumental music

[1] J. Subirá, *Historia de la Música teatral en España*, Madrid, 1945, p. 65.

and dancing, as in the sparkling comedia *El Maestro de Danzar*, which might also be included with *La Selva sin Amor* as among the first embryos of Spanish operas.

Nearly twenty years elapsed after *La Selva sin Amor* before Calderón, who had become, since the death of Lope de Vega, the arbiter of the Spanish stage, made an attempt to adapt music to drama. [1]

The occasion was the second marriage of Philip IV to his young niece Marie-Anne of Austria, in 1648. The authorities lifted the ban on theatrical performances which had been in force since the death in 1644 of Philip's first wife, Isabel de Bourbon.

Calderón, who did not possess the spontaneous imagination and gift for improvization of Lope, was in a quandary, for at the moment he had no new plots in mind which would satisfy his insatiable master Philip IV, who was forever clamouring for novelties. The latter had seen all the plays written in the past forty years and was in consequence blasé in his tastes.

At last Calderón resolved to add music to *El Jardín de Falerina* (The Garden of Falerina), a play in two acts. Originally it had been in three *Jornadas*, but one act had to be cut, on account of the amount of time given to singing and dancing. In the second scene a *gallarda* was danced and the actors sang a ballad for which Calderón wrote the words. In the second act a women's choir sang and the hero or *galán* sang with another choir, then Falerina sang with a chorus of nymphs and the performance ended with a grand ensemble of voices and instruments. According to Pedrell and Mitjana, the composer of the music was José Peyró, about whom nothing is known save that he wrote *villancicos* for the Cathedral of Segorbe.

At the end of the same year at the Palace a comedia with music was performed entitled *The New Olympus*, written by Cabriel Bocangel, the librarian of the Infante Cardinal Don Fernando and son of an Italian doctor who had settled in Madrid. It was sung by the professional musicians of the Chapel Royal.

In 1657 Philip had a son by his second marriage; in honour of the event Calderón wrote *El Laurel de Apolo*, in two acts, which he called a *Zarzuela*. [2] *Zarzuela* was the name of a pleasure palace and grounds near the Pardo which belonged to the Infante Don Fernando. When he went off to serve in Flanders, the King added to the small palace, and as there was not much space there for big festivals it became the custom to hold short 'musical comedies' there to which they gave the name *Fiestas de la Zarzuela*, for the palace was called *La Zarzuela* (from *Zarza*, briar bush).

The King would always spend some days of winter residence in his palace of *La Zarzuela* and there *El Laurel de Apolo* was to have been played for him in the month of December 1657, but as he had returned to Madrid before that date the opening performance was transferred to the big theatre of the *Buen Retiro*. In a *loa* or prefatory dramatic sketch Calderón craved pardon of their Majesties for producing so slight a "musical comedy" in such a spacious auditorium. The *loa* was mostly sung: in the second scene of the *Zarzuela* there were two choruses, one of youths, the other of maidens who sang separately at first and then all together, and between the choruses one of the shepherdesses sang solo.

In the fifth scene Cupid and Apollo, whose parts were represented by women, sang and they were followed by a chorus of nymphs, solos by Apollo and a scene between a shepherd and a chorus, which was in the *Jácara* style.

The *Jácara* was a roistering ballad in rogues' dialect, about two hundred verses in length, which was sung by one actor or actress or by several, not only upon the stage, but, to add zest to the show, from different parts of the theatre, for, as Pellicer says, the public was crazy about them *(era perdido por ellas)*. [3] Requests for *Jácaras* in the public theatres generally came from the *mosqueteros* or groundlings in the *patio* or pit, and in case the audience did not demand them, a player used sometimes to be stationed in the *patio*, who called for a *Jácara*. [4] The *Jácara*, in spite of its slightness (it took ten to fifteen minutes), was full of mirth and exuberant spirits.

Like the *loas* and *entremeses* they were a speciality of the celebrated writer of one-act plays, Quiñones de Benavente, who included six of them in his volume of short pieces. [5] They are important in the history of Spanish

---

[1] J. Subirá, op. cit., p. 66.
[2] E. Cotarelo y Mori, *op. cit.*, pp. 16-17.
[3] Ticknor, *op. cit.*, vol. II, p. 533.
[4] Q. de Benavente, *Entremeses*, ed. C. Rosell, vol. I, p. 162.
[5] H. A. Rennert, *op. cit.*, pp. 292-293.

music and the theatre because they are the ancestors of the *tonadilla*, which we shall consider in the eighteenth century.

The second act of *El Laurel de Apolo* is full of music and dancing, and it is interesting to note that one of the shepherdesses sings a *seguidilla*, the characteristic folk-song and dance with a stanza of four or seven verses, which shows how nationally Spanish the *Zarzuela* was becoming, even at this early stage.

Cotarelo, however, warns us that the second act of that *Zarzuela*, as we know it today, was rewritten by Calderón some years later.[1]

In the same year, 1657, Calderón produced a one-act musical play, *El Golfo de las Sirenas* (The Gulf of the Sirens), which he calls an *égloga piscataria*, but it was really a *Zarzuela*.[2] Then in 1659, to celebrate the peace with France and the marriage of Louis XIV to María Teresa, the daughter of Philip IV, Calderón wrote the libretto of an opera in one act entitled *La Púrpura de la Rosa*, which he said would be all music. This opera, which was sung all through, was performed for the first time in the Coliseum of the *Buen Retiro*. So completely had Calderón forgotten Lope de Vega's production of *La Selva sin Amor* in 1629, that he believed *La Púrpura de la Rosa* to be the first operatic work, and in the *loa* he claims to be the pioneer of this musical style.

The Spaniards liked plenty of action in their plays and at first they had been bored by the chanted recitatives. In *La Púrpura de la Rosa*, however, we know from the libretto that the character in the opera sang in recitative style, and there were pieces for vocal duets, quartets and chorus. There was also an orchestra, and in the war-like scenes the trumpets and drums sounded. There were also dances and special scenic devices which enabled ghosts to appear and trapdoors for them to disappear and wires enabling them to fly. The musical score no longer exists, but Subirá believes it was composed by Juan Hidalgo.

On December 5, 1660, another opera was produced in the Coliseum of the *Buen Retiro* with the libretto by Calderón, entitled *Celos aun del Aire Matan* and described as a "great festival of song" *(fiesta grande cantada)*. It was in three acts and was produced after many rehearsals which were held in a house at the corner of the calles de Leon and Huertas hired for the purpose by the Marquis of Liche.[3] With one exception all the male parts were given to women. There was also a female choir of ten and a male choir of six. José Subirá was fortunate enough to discover in the library of the late Duke of Alba the vocal score and figured bass from the first act, and he has given the following transcription of the final chorus:

Subirá in summing up the information concerning Spanish opera and the *Zarzuela* in the seventeenth century points out that the latter like the former was an art-form that developed first in aristocratic surroundings before

[1] E. Cotarelo y Mori, *op. cit.*, p. 18.
[2] J. Subirá in *Historia de la Música teatral en España* notes that this *Zarzuela* was anterior to *El Laurel de Apolo* which was produced in the same year.
[3] J. Subira, *op. cit.*, pp. 68-69.

descending to the public theatre; there was, however, a fundamental difference between both *genres*. Whereas opera sprang from Renaissance Italy in response to aesthetic ideals which had been subtly elaborated, the *Zarzuela* arose at the outset in a haphazard way as makeshift and did not respond to any preconceived plan.

This period in Spanish music is represented in our recording by two *Villancicos* by Juan Cererols (1618-1676) *Son tus bellos ojos soles* * sung by the Antics Escolans of Montserrat, and *Vuela Paloma divina* **, sung by Lolita Torrentó and Asunción Serra (sopranos) with harpsichord accompaniment by Esther Nadal de Janés. It has been adapted by Rafael Ferrer.

Juan Cererols was born at Martorell in Catalonia in 1618 and died at Montserrat in 1676. He was one of the musical celebrities of Montserrat, where he spent most of his life. He was organist, violinist and composer and so famed among his contemporaries that he was always known as "the composer". Dom David Pujol in his work *Mestres de l'Escolania de Montserrat (1500-1800)* devotes three volumes to Cererols.

The *Villancico Son tus bellos ojos solos* is both sophisticated and religious at the same time. It is characteristic of Spanish vocal music in the seventeenth century, and with its complexity it is a contrast to the simpler and more unaffected music of Guerrero and Morata.

Son tus bellos ojos soles que con rayos nos defienden María, y así lo entienden tus esclavos españoles. Son tus bellos ojos soles.

Thy beauteous eyes are suns, which by their rays protect us, Mary, and this is the belief of thy Spanish slaves. Thy beauteous eyes are suns.

The second *Villancico, Vuela Paloma divina* belongs to the intermediary period of Spanish music when Calderón was the monarch of Spanish drama, and poets as well as composers experimented with the operatic and lyrico-dramatic styles.

ஐ CALDERÓN AND HIS AUTOS SACRAMENTALES

Now that we have considered Calderón's important contribution to the creation of the essentially Spanish musical dramatic form the *Zarzuela*, we must turn to another form of Spanish drama in which he was unrivalled, namely the *Auto sacramental*.

After the death of Lope de Vega in 1635 Calderón became immediately the dictator of the theatre, and from that day until his death he reigned supreme. According to professor Valbuena Prat, one of the staunchest admirers of Calderón's dramas, he is the great master of the Baroque era in the theatre. If Fray Luis de León was the poet of the later sixteenth century, and Cervantes of the period between the two centuries, Calderón was the most significant poet of the seventeenth century. Embodying as he did the dramatic ideals of Lope and the decorative elements of Góngoras' poetry and the theological casuistry of the century he is both universal and of his own epoch. But there are two periods in Calderón's works which have to be distinguished; the first in which he follows the trend of Lope's drama, contenting himself with modifying somewhat the technical ideas and style of his predecessor; the second in which he is master of his own muse and strikes out in a new direction. [1] The great Lopesque period of Calderón's work was in his youthful years from 1630 to 1640.

His period of individual creation was in his mature and older years after 1640. Only after that year do we discern the essential Calderón who, like an anchorite, renounced the rebellious ideas of his youth and with self-denial purified his style of all that he considered dross and excessive. This is the Calderón who renounced the world, became a priest and watched from his cell the melancholy decline of the Spanish monarchy and the glorious golden age. In his first period Calderón condenses the plays of Lope, simplifies their language and restricts the number of characters whereas Lope expanded the action of his plays and multiplied the number of characters. In the second and mature period Calderón still simplifies his plots, but he introduces decorative

---

* First Record, *Ancient Music*, side II, No. 3.
** First Record, *Ancient Music*, side II, No. 4.
[1] S. de Robles, *El Teatro Español, Historia y Antología*, vol. III, Madrid, 1943, Introd., pp. 22-23.

Baroque details which are selected with loving care for they create his symbolism. Thus, as Sainz de Robles says, Calderón was in literature what Gracián was in philosophy and Wagner in music. In Lope de Vega's theatre the essence of the drama lies in the conflict as theme: in Calderón's mature epoch the essence of the drama lies in the conflict which takes place in the mind.

Where Calderón modified the theories of Lope de Vega at the outset was in the *Autos sacramentales*, the short religious plays which were performed at the instance of the municipalities of the various cities at the festival of Corpus Christi. In the age of Lope de Vega and in the following one of Calderón they were at the height of their popularity and had become part of the religious ceremonies of the sacramental feast, not only in Madrid, but throughout Spain, for the theatres were closed while they were represented. From the earliest times they were accompanied by music and dancing, and since Lope's time by a *loa* and an *entremés* as well. The *autos* were acted upon movable cars *(carros)*, which passed through the city to various stations where the representations were to take place, and the festival was called *La Fiesta de los Carros* (The Feast of the Cars.) In front of the cars walked strange symbolic figures; a kind of serpent crushed underfoot by "the Woman of Babylon", Giants, a Moor and a colossal negro.

A great deal of money was spent in the preparations for the four customary *Autos* performed in Madrid and Seville, and the splendour of the decorations and costumes made great appeal to the masses.

A stage was built at the various points along the streets where the *Auto* was to be represented, and around the stage the cars were grouped; the stage properties were made of pasteboard, and in accordance with the directions of the poet-dramatists. The costumes worn by the players were of rich materials and sometimes it was stipulated by the city authorities that they were to be of brocade and velvet, damask and satin trimmed with passementerie.

The most celebrated passage describing a company representing an *Auto* comes from the second part of *Don Quixote* where the *Auto* was entitled *Las Cortes de la Muerte*:

"Don Quixote was about to reply to Sancho Panza, but he was prevented by a cart which passed along the road laden with the strangest figures that could be imagined. He who drove the mules and acted as carter was a hideous demon: the cart was open to the sky without wicker tilt or awning. The first figure that presented itself to Don Quixote's eyes was that of Death itself with a human face: next to him was an angel with large painted wings. At one side was an emperor with a crown, to all appearance of gold, upon his head. At the feet of Death was the god called Cupid, without his bandage on his eyes but with his bow, quiver and arrows. There was also a knight armed cap-a-pie, except that he wore no morion or helmet but only a hat adorned with plumes of varied colours. With these there were others of different faces and costumes. At this unexpected encounter Don Quixote became somewhat disturbed, and Sancho was struck with terror. But on second thoughts Don Quixote rejoiced, for he believed that some new perilous adventure was at hand: so, under this impression, and with the firm intention of facing any danger, he halted in front of the cart and cried out in a loud, threatening voice: 'Carter, coachman or devil, be quick to tell me who you are carrying in your coach, which resembles rather the boat of Charon than an ordinary cart.'

"To which the Devil, stopping the cart, answered courteously: 'Señor, we are players of Angulo El Malo's company: we have been acting the play of the 'Parliament of Death' this morning in a village behind yonder hill, seeing that this is the octave of Corpus Christi; and we have to act it this evening in that village which you can see from here; and because it is so near at hand, and to save ourselves the trouble of undressing and dressing again, we go in the costumes in which we play. That lad there goes as Death, the other as an angel: that woman, who is the manager's wife, is the Queen; another one is a soldier: that one is the Emperor, and I am the Devil, and I'm taking one of the leading parts. If there's aught else you wish to know about us, ask me, and I'll know how to answer to the point, for since I'm the Devil, I'm up to everything.'

"While they were talking, chance willed it that one of the company, clad in motley, with a great number of bells and bearing on the end of a stick three ox-bladders fully blown, came up to them."[1]

Angulo el Malo was a well-known *autor* or manager of a theatrical company in the days of Cervantes, and according to Rennert this particular *Auto* was probably one begun by Miguel de Carvajal, finished by Luis

---

[1] Cervantes, *Don Quixote*, part II, ch. XI.

Hurtado de Toledo, published in 1557, and represented in Seville about 1570 and again in 1571.[1] And we should note that even on such a solemn occasion as the representation of *Autos sacramentales* at Corpus Christi there was as much noise and irreverence among the noisy crowds that thronged the streets as in the public performances in the theatre, and many attempts were made by the Corregidor or the mayor of the town to apportion the seats on the *tablado* or platform by seniority.

In the seventeenth century protests were made by the clergy at the introduction of worldly and irreverent *entremeses* and *bailes* into such representations, for the *entremeses* treated of robberies and adulteries, and the *bailes* consisted of profane dances. *Autos* were also performed in bullrings, and they were played in the palace before the King.

The *Autos* had by 1765 lost their appeal, for they were no longer given in the open air before the King and Court and the devout multitude, but were played indoors before an indifferent audience and to ribald remarks.[2]

Clavijo, the writer, who in his articles in *El Pensador Matritense* advocated the suppression of the *Autos*, tells us that on one occasion after the actor who played the part of Satan had declaimed a passage effectively, an admirer in the pit raised a cheer for the Devil: *Viva el demonio!* The Voltairean eighteenth century was completely deaf to the liturgical, religious, poetic and even dramatic implications of Calderón's drama.

We must remember that great as the popularity of the drama was in Spain, and rapid as had been its rise, its decline and fall were almost equally rapid, and by 1650 the Spanish theatre was clearly on the wane. The death of the founder of the national theatre, Lope de Vega, in 1635 was such a serious loss that in a few years the magnificent structure began to totter. It is strange to find that by the middle of the century all the greatest dramatists, with the single exception of Calderón, were dead. Guillén de Castro died in 1631; Alarcón's death occurred in 1637, followed by that of Mira de Amésecua in 1644. Tirso de Molina died in 1648, but he had ceased to write for the stage even before Lope's death. Of the lesser lights of the drama, Montalbán died in 1638, and Luis Vélez de Guevara in 1644. Calderón alone was still writing comedias after the middle of the century, for even his followers Rojas and Moreto had written their last plays by that time. As Rennert points out, here, once more, at the close as at the beginning, the Spanish national drama exhibits a striking parallel to the English, that had also produced all that was best in it before the closing of the theatres in 1642 by Cromwell at the beginning of the Civil War.[3]

Before saying farewell to the seventeenth-century theatre in Madrid let us quote the following spirited description of a visit to the theatre from *El día de Fiesta* by Zabaleta written in the year 1666.[4]

"You must dine hurriedly at noon, and not linger at table if you are going in the afternoon to the theatre and wish to find a seat. The first thing you do when you arrive at the door of the playhouse is to try and get in without paying. The actors work much and as few pay as possible. That is the actors' first misfortune. It would not do so much harm for twenty people to get in for a few farthings but for the fact that many more try to imitate them. As it is, if one person gets in without payment, the others expect to do the same. Everybody wishes to enjoy the privilege of free admission in order that other people may see that they are worthy of it. This they desire with such intense eagerness that they will fight to obtain it, and by fighting they usually achieve their object. Indeed rarely does a man who has managed to enter without paying ever pay on any subsequent occasion. A fine way to reward those who deserve some return for all their sweat and toil in trying to entertain them! And do you think that he who does not pay will be easier to please? On the contrary, if the actor is not properly dressed, those who have not paid insult and hiss him most.

"At last one idler gets into the theatre and asks the person who assigns the seats and benches for a place. He is told that there are none, but that a certain seat that has been engaged has not yet been occupied, and that he had better wait until the guitar-players appear, and if it be still vacant, he may occupy it. Our man argues, but to amuse himself in the meanwhile, he goes into the dressing-room. There he finds women taking off their street clothes and putting on their theatrical costumes. Some are so far undressed that they look as if

[1] H. A. Rennert, *op. cit.*, p. 313.
[2] J. Fitzmaurice Kelly, *op. cit.*, p. 207.
[3] S. de Robles, *op. cit.*, vol. III, Introd., pp. 25-26. H. A. Rennert, *op. cit.*, p. 341.
[4] J. Zabaleta, *Obras*, Madrid, 1692, *El Día de Fiesta por la Tarde*, pp. 296 ff.

they were going to bed.   He stops in front of a woman who, having come to the theatre on foot, is having her shoes and stockings put on by her maid.   This cannot be done without some sacrifice of modesty, and the poor actress must put up with this, and does not dare to protest, because, as her main object is to gain applause, she is afraid of offending anyone.   A hiss, no matter how unjustified, discredits an actress, because people in general believe that the judgment of those who find fault is superior to their own.   In the meantime the actress continues to dress while the idiot goes on staring at her.   Next he approaches the hangings of the stage to see whether the doubtful seat is occupied, and finds it vacant.   As it appears that the owner will not come he takes it, but scarcely has he sat down than the owner arrives and defends his claim.   The other does the same, and they come to blows.   The last comer, as he came to the theatre to amuse himself, finds no fun in shouting and fighting, so he gives in and finds another seat which has been offered him by the peace-makers.

"When all the commotion has subsided our intruder settles down quietly and now turns his eyes to the gallery occupied by women, the *cazuela*, (or saucepan as it was called) staring at their faces one by one until he sees one whom he particularly fancies and cautiously makes signs to her.   'My dear sir, the cazuela is not what you came to see, but the comedia.'   He looks round in every direction, when he feels someone pull his cloak from behind.   He turns and sees a fruitseller, who leans forward between two men and whispers to him that the woman who is tapping her knee with her fan says that she has much admired the spirit which he has shown in the quarrel, and asks him to pay for a dozen oranges for her.   The fellow looks again at the 'saucepan', sees that the woman is the one that caught his fancy before, pays the money for the fruit, and sends word that she may have anything that she pleases.   As the fruitseller leaves, the fellow immediately plans that he will wait for the woman at the entrance to the theatre, and he begins to think that there is an interminable delay in beginning the play.   In a loud and peevish tone he signifies his disapproval, exciting the *mosqueteros*, or groundlings, who are standing below, to break out into insulting shouts in order to hasten the players...

"Women also go to see the comedia.   On feast days men go to the play after luncheon, but women go before.   The woman who goes to the comedia on a holiday generally makes it an affair of a whole day.   She meets one of her friends, and they take a bite of breakfast, postponing the midday meal to the evening.   Then they go to Mass, and from the church straight to the 'saucepan' to get a good seat.   They avoid the front seats, for these are for the women who come to see and be seen; so they take a modest seat in the middle.   Now the fun begins.   The money-takers enter.   One of our friends draws a handkerchief from beneath the folds of her petticoat, and with her teeth loosens a knot tied in the corner of it, and takes out a *real (34 maravedís)*.   While she is doing this the other takes from her bosom a paper containing *10 quartos (40 maravedís)*, and hands her money to the doorkeeper, who passes on.   The one with the *10 maravedís* in her hand now buys a packet of filberts for two *quartos* and, like a child, does not know what to do with the remaining *octavo (2 maravedís)* which she has received in change; finally she drops it in her bosom, with the remark that it is for the poor.   Now the two friends begin to break the filberts, and you can hear them munching them.

"Now more women are crowding in.   One of those who are in front makes signs to two others who are standing behind our two friends, and without asking by your leave she strives to pass between the two, stepping on their skirts and disarranging their cloaks, which annoys them and they exclaim: 'Did you ever see such rudeness!'

"The 'saucepan' being now full, the apretador or doorkeeper enters, and his job is to make the women sit closer so that they may make more room.   He is accompanied by four women, well dressed and thickly veiled, whom he wants to accomodate for they have given him eight quartos.   He approaches the two friends and tells them to sit closer; they protest, he insists, and they reply that the women should have come earlier, when they would have found seats.   Finally the newcomers let themselves fall upon those already seated, who to get away from under them, unconsciously make room.   There is grumbling on all sides, but at last quiet is restored...

"It is now half-past two o'clock, and the friends, who had not dined, begin to get hungry.   At length, one of the women who had been accommodated by the *apretador*, gives to our friends each a handful of prawns and some candied yolks of eggs, saying: 'Come, let us be friends and eat these sweets which some boob gave me.' They begin to eat and want to strike up a conversation, but they say nothing, as they cannot stop eating.   Presently there is a quarrel at the door of the *cazuela* between the doorkeeper and a number of youths who want some women to enter free, and they burst into the 'saucepan', shouting.   A great commotion and uproar ensues.   The women rise excitedly, and in their anxiety to avoid those who are quarrelling they fall over one another.   ... Those who rush up from the patio to help to restore order barge into the surging mass and knock over the women.   All now take refuge in the corners as the best place in the *cazuela*, some on all-fours, others running to seek a place of safety.   Finally the police expel the men, and every woman takes a seat where she happens to be, none occupying the one she first had.   One of the two friends is now on the last bench, while the other is near the door.   The former has lost her gloves and finds that her gown is torn; her friend is bleeding at the nose as the result of the scuffle, and having lost her handkerchief makes use of her petticoat. All is lamentation, when the guitar-players enter, and quiet is once more restored."

NAPLES UNDER SPANISH DOMINATION IN THE SEVENTEENTH CENTURY

Whereas right at the beginning of the century it had been the Italian composers, singers and players who had invaded Spain, later owing to the fame of Lope de Vega, Tirso de Molina, Calderón and their disciples it was the Spanish companies of actors who began to visit Italy in their numbers, so that our seventeenth-century musical journey must finish in Naples, where even today we may relive day by day the annals of the Spanish Viceroys who architecturally and musically transformed Naples into a Spanish city.   It is important, we repeat, to realise that the whole spirit of Southern Baroque music was predominantly Spanish, but since Spain did not happen to produce any great musicians of her own after the death of Victoria, it was only natural that the region which gave the most complete and perfect expression to the Baroque ideals in music should have been the Kingdom of Naples, then a mere province of Spain, ruled from Madrid by a Viceroy, and wholly dominated by Spanish culture and artistic influences.[1]   One of the unforgettable experiences of my life was an evening I spent in the spring of 1919 in Naples, under the guidance of the great philosopher and historian Benedetto Croce.   The Master led me on a historical journey through the Spanish quarter of Naples which began in the days of Alfonso the Magnanimous in the fifteenth and ended in the heyday of the eighteenth century.

During the seventeenth century, Spain with its pompous grandeur, its soul-searching mystics, and its romances of chivalry loomed on the bright horizon of sunny Italy like a dark cloud.   It was Naples that experienced the full intellectual onslaught of its conquerors.   The Spanish Viceroys used to surround themselves with a host of men of letters from their country, and academies were set up for verse and the improvization of plays.[2]

About 1647 the first companies of Spanish actors appeared at Naples, and won great fame, especially among the large Spanish colony that was established there, and among the upper classes.   The plays they represented there were for the most part heroic dramas or plays of the cloak and sword variety. Andrea Perrucci in his book says that the Italians resented the frequent changes of scene, but he also makes the interesting remark that they were praised for having banished masks.[3]   We may take this as evidence showing the gradual decline of the *commedia dell'Arte* in public favour.   Perrucci notes that the Spanish dramas terminated with dances, and were a contrast to the Italian, which ended with blows.[4]

The great success achieved by Spanish drama in Italy was thus one of the main causes of the decline of the improvized, masked play.   It was useless for Captain Matamoros or Pulcinella to ridicule the Spanish swashbuckler: their glorious Harlequinade days among the nobility and gentry were over.   In order to draw the

[1] C. Gray, *op. cit.*, p. 143.
[2] B. Croce, *Teatri de Napoli*, Bari, 1916, pp. 56-57.
[3] W. Starkie, *Carlo Goldoni and the Commedia dell'Arte*, April, 1927.
[4] A. Perrucci, *Arte representiva*, Napoli, 1699, pp. 26-27; 372-373.

public to see a play at that time, the Italian impresario used to print the name of Lope de Vega on the hand-bills. The *commedia dell'Arte* still drew crowds of admirers from the lower classes, the roguish, sunshine-loving populace of Naples, which refused to silence its merry laughter at the blasts of even the most severe agelast from Castile. Thus we find in the seventeenth century that some of the most characteristic and popular *scenari* for improvization are taken from the Spanish.

Tirso de Molina's immortal play, *El Burlador de Sevilla o el Convidado de Piedra*, was translated and represented at Naples in 1652 and immediately became one of the most popular plots for the *commedia dell'Arte*. It is not Don Juan, proud, swaggering hero of Spain that we meet in these *scenari*, nor a forerunner of Molière's atheistical hero, but a prancing clown whose antics and *lazzi* excite roars of laughter.[1] Don Giovanni has very little of the jaunty insolence of the Spanish original: his *zibaldone* is full of the most artificial flourishes and *chiusette* of the Marinistic style. His flourishes are a marked contrast to the stupid antics of his follower *Arlecchino*, who shivers apprehensively. No scene could better show the burlesque nature of the play than the final scene of the banquet to which Don Giovanni has invited the statue of the Commander whom he has killed. The scene is a solemn one in the original—the scene of final punishment, and yet in the *scenario* it starts with Arlecchino's attempt to eat maccaroni. His comic attempts remind us of Charlie Chaplin's adventures with the same food. The laughter in the seventeenth century, we may be sure, was just as hilarious as that of modern audiences. Suddenly there is a knock at the door; Arlecchino goes with lighted candle in his hand to open it, but at the sight of the stranger he falls down. However, by one of the acrobat tricks that the masked actors were fond of playing, perhaps owing to their association with mountebanks and tumblers, he jumps up without putting out the candle. Then, ghostly and terrible, dressed in a white sheet, the phantom of the Commander walks up towards Don Giovanni, and accuses him of the wrongs he has done. The tragic muse does not hold the stage for long, for, suddenly remembering that no scene must lack its *lazzi*, he commands Arlecchino to sing. The singing of the trembling Arlecchino must have produced comic effect, especially as he entreats his master to send the phantom away. In the next striking scene the tables are turned: it is Don Giovanni who is the guest of the Commander, and this time the action takes place in the sepulchre and serpents are served up on a dish for the dinner. The play ends with the descent of Don Giovanni to the lower regions by means of a trap-door, and morality is satisfied by the final words of warning given by him—as he sinks into the flames—to men of his like on earth that they should repent in time. Arlecchino follows him shouting: "For pity's sake, what about my salary? Must I follow you to Hell to get paid?"

This play is typical of the *commedia dell'Arte* owing to the frequent *lazzi*, but it reflects certain features of Spanish drama. Spanish plays frequently ended with a moral axiom or lesson generally put in the form of a trite saying, suitable for the members of the audience to carry home with them. In this *scenario* the author wanted to reproduce the Spanish atmosphere and also to avoid the vigilance of the Inquisitors.

The *commedia dell'Arte* did not confine its attention only to parodies of foreign dramas; it also joined forces with the spirit of music and produced *Opera Buffa*, the Neapolitan counterpart of the *tonadilla Madrileña*. Scherillo, the authority on the *Opera Buffa*, states that the first experiments in it were made when the masked comedy was at its zenith and when companies of actors wandered through Italy improvizing in every city and village before audiences that knew not what to make of plays imitated from Latin.[2] In the last years of the sixteenth century *Opera Buffa* sprang to life, when Orazio Vecchi produced at Venice in 1597 a play in verse accompanied by music, called *Amfiparnaso*. This *commedia harmonica*, as it was called, introduced masks from the *commedia dell'Arte*, but the music was limited to five musicians, for performance in a room, not a theatre. This musical comedy had no success at the time and *Opera Buffa* for many years was neglected, though serious Opera which had started so dramatically with Monteverdi's *Orfeo* continued its triumphant progress. More than a century elapsed before *Opera Buffa* rose to favour again, and then it is not at Venice, but at Naples that we meet it.

The same causes that worked against the *Commedia dell'Arte* worked against the *Opera Buffa* during the artificial seventeenth century. Just as the upper classes sought eagerly the representation of heroic tragedies

[1] W. Starkie, *op. cit.*, pp. 56-57.
[2] M. Scherillo, *Opera Buffa Napoletana*, Roma, 1916, ch. I.

in the Spanish, so even in their lighter moods they delighted in melodrama [1] with demure shepherdesses and pastoral lovers, who piped their languid music. Scherillo defines the style of this melodrama thus: "Melodrama", he says, "sprang to life amidst the bleatings of the lambs of the pastoral fables at the end of the sixteenth century, and it has all the faults of its origin. It is not serious as a tragedy, nor is it comic or satiric: it is soft and effeminate. It resembles a pretty, dapper youth of the aristocracy, an only son, brought up on sweets and confectionery, languid and drooping, one who says that he is dying of love because he has read about the heart pangs of the heroes of the romances." What a contrast this fantastic rural world of melodrama is to the gross, indecent *commedia dell'Arte* with laughter holding both its sides! In the melodrama as in the poems of Marini, Love held complete sway—not the pure love of the troubadours, but rather a romantic, platonic love. Gravina says that this platonic love, which was but a cloak to wantonness, had excluded all variety from the theatre, and it had come to pass that on the stage there appeared bands of noble knights who did naught but breathe sighs and fill the theatre with their tears. [2] It is characteristic of the times that Andrea Perrucci, whose work on the *commedia dell'Arte* is the most authoritative contemporary one we possess, should also have been famed as a writer of melodrama.

[1] By melodrama we naturally mean the ancient plays with music. In modern days in England the word melodrama is used in the restricted sense of a macabre blood-and-thunder play.
[2] G. V. Gravina, *Della Tragedia*, Bk. I, ch. 20, in *Opera Italiana*, Napoli, 1757.

Chapter XIII

THE EIGHTEENTH CENTURY

The War of Spanish Succession brought with it an invasion of foreigners, owing to the fact that the armies of France, England and Austria fought on Spanish soil during the first fourteen years of the eighteenth century, followed by the arrival of hosts of Italian or French courtiers, ministers, technicians who under the new dynasty of the Bourbons took part in the government and the life of Spain. The forces of innovation if they did not level the traditional walls of Spanish isolationism, yet breached them in many places and allowed influences to percolate from abroad. Spain, as Menéndez Pidal says, found that the great events of history had definitely decided against her, for a new concept of public life had grown up in the two countries that had been the bitterest enemies, namely England and Holland, and had spread throughout Europe. The religious question which had caused such bloodshed in the two preceding centuries, could not be solved on this field of battle or by state compulsion, and so had to be left to the individual conscience. Spain, owing to its isolated life, was enormously backward in comparison with other countries, and this was noticed by large sections of the people, who in former days had been muzzled and unable to express their views. From now on we shall notice two antagonistic ideologies in operation in Spain and the struggle would in the end always turn on religious motives. In the days of the Catholic Monarchs the mediaeval toleration was restricted in the interests of national unity that the Spaniards might launch out into great enterprises. Now in the eighteenth century when national unification was no longer possible under militant Catholicism, we find intolerance among the partisans of the two antagonistic factions: the *nacionistas* or "antinationals", as they are called, who were so exaggerated in their admiration for foreign nations and foreign fashions that everything in their own country seemed to them uncouth and barbarous; and on the opposite side the chauvinists who believed that their land contained all the treasures and virtues that were to be found in the world, and looked down with scorn upon the other nations, making fun of their advances in art and science, for they believed that foreign books brought nothing but futile frivolities.

When Philip V had come to Spain as King in 1701 he knew hardly a word of Spanish and he only stayed in Madrid about seven months before setting out for Barcelona to receive his bride María Luisa of Savoy. As she knew no more Spanish than her husband the prospect ahead for Spanish literature was not promising as far as royal patronage was concerned. At court nothing was spoken but French, and the King, owing to his love for his Italian wife, preferred Italian actors and singers to any other, and gave special privileges to an Italian theatrical company which was called *Los Truffaldines* after the celebrated masked personage of the *Commedia dell'Arte*, Truffaldin, whom we met in the last century.   The works performed by this company were all in Italian and were melodramas in three acts consisting of opera and ballet.   In addition to playing in the royal Coliseum of *El Buen Retiro*, they hired a *corral* in the Calle de Alcalá at which they performed daily except on the days they played at the *Retiro*.

🐌 PHILIP V AND ELIZABETH FARNESE

Twelve years after Philip's accession to the throne, in 1713, the treaties of Utrecht were signed, which were to set their mark upon the map of Europe for a century and to solve most of the questions which had made Europe a vast camp for the greater part of two hundred years. [1]

Philip V was now for the first time really King of Spain and as his patriotism and energy in the war had made him popular among his subjects there was every hope that Spain would advance by degrees to happiness and prosperity.   Unfortunately, at this moment his beloved wife, who had played so devoted a part in the grim years of struggle, collapsed as the result of her unceasing labours and anxieties and died at the beginning of 1714. The King, who had been completely under her domination, gave way to grief and retired to the palace at Medinaceli, where he would see no one but the *camarera mayor* of the late Queen, the Princesse des Ursins.   The Princess, who was in daily communication with the King, soon realized that he must marry at once or he would lapse into morbid melancholia and lose his reason.   She had been in communication with an ambitious Italian abbé called Alberoni, who had come to Philip's court as an envoy of the Duke of Parma.   Alberoni suggested to the Princesse des Ursins the name of the Duke of Parma's niece and step-daughter, Elizabeth Farnese, as the future Queen of Spain, and the proposal appealed to the scheming Princess as Elizabeth was the daughter of Dorothea, sister of the Queen Dowager of Spain, the widow of Charles II.   One of the main advantages in the proposal was, too, that there was no male heir to the throne of Parma and the Princesse des Ursins saw the possibility of strengthening Spanish power in Italy again and at the same time securing a wife for Philip, who would act under her influence.   Philip, who was sunk in deepest melancholy, accepted Elizabeth Farnese as his wife and on September 16, 1714, he was married to her by proxy in Parma.

To explain the deep depression of Philip which settled upon him like a leaden pall after the death of his first wife, we must consider his early life in Versailles under *Le Roi Soleil* and contrast it with the life he had to endure in Spain at the outset of his reign.   When he arrived in Madrid to take up his crown he was shocked by the incredible backwardness of a country that for wellnigh forty years under Charles II had remained static and changeless.   Even the periwig, which the French had introduced all over Europe, never reached Madrid, and Charles like Philip IV, his father, wore the long natural hair and the stiff starched collar which had been laid aside two generations before.   Spain seemed to the Frenchman the most barbarous country in the world and its food a further proof of the "sauvages" in whose company he was doomed to spend the rest of his life. [2] Philip's tendency to melancholia, which was congenital, developed more acutely when he became older and at times reached a crisis, and there were long periods during which he became insane.   One of his obsessions was his terror of being poisoned, another was the conviction that he was dead.   He would lie in bed for months on end, without speaking to anyone, without eating, gazing fixedly at the ceiling with mouth agape. The only occasions when he would rouse himself from his lethargy was when someone brought news from France, for then his eternal hopes would revive of one day returning to Versailles to occupy the throne of his grandfather, Louis XIV.   The other way to rouse him was through music, for when he heard soft melodious singing, he would straightway awake to normal life and recover his good sense.   Elizabeth Farnese, who was a termagant, at first devoted herself so wholeheartedly to her personal ambitions that she had little time left for Philip. In any case, possessing, as she did, the character of a virago, she despised the weak nature of her husband.

[1] M. A. S. Hume, *op. cit.*, pp. 344-345 ff.
[2] S. Sitwell, *Southern Baroque Art*, London, 1924.

144

With the help of the Machiavellian Alberoni, however, she determined to dominate her husband completely, so that she might be able to carry out her designs for her family. In order to gain ascendancy over Philip she sacrificed her life of ease and devoted herself to his passion for hunting, and knowing how uxorious he was by nature, she made herself necessary to his hourly existence. She was absolutely successful in this, but some of the credit must go to Alberoni who spurred on her ambition and checked her extravagance. Philip, in the end, had no will of his own and let the country be ruled as an Italian state and to serve Italian ends, for Elizabeth's plan envisaged a future when her sons should rule over the States of Parma and Tuscany under Spanish influence.

THE STORY OF THE KING, THE MINSTREL AND THE POET

Elizabeth Farnese kept watch over her husband as he lay sunk in lethargy, slovenly, dirty in habits, unshaven, vacant in mind, save occasionally when he raved of the French crown and of his enemies who wished to poison him. She knew that there was only one cure that had always proved infallible, and that was music. If only she could discover some superhuman minstrel possessed of such a magic *duende* that he could charm the distracted King out of the dismal depths of his madness. It was then that reports came to the court of an extraordinary Italian singer, Carlos Broschi, who sang under the name Farinelli.

He was the elder son of a Neapolitan music-master and composer, who became a *governatore reale* or treasurer of Monatea and Cisternino, and was born at Andria in Apulia in 1705.[1] In the older biographies on the famous singer it was stated that when a child he fell from a horse and had to undergo an operation which turned him into a *castrato*, but according to Fétis most of the celebrated *castrati* in the eighteenth century used to tell similar stories to excuse the cruelty of their families in maiming them in this way for the benefit of their voices. There is no doubt that eunuchs were in vogue in the seventeenth and eighteenth centuries and always remained an almost exclusively Italian product, for they were often employed in the church choirs of Rome and elsewhere in Italy, but became the fashion on the stage, and exercised their greatest influence in Italian opera in the eighteenth century. Probably boys were chosen for the beauty of their voices, and were then prepared for the calling of adult choristers. Incidentally, the training of professional *castrati* could begin at an early age and proceed uninterruptedly, and although their voices had a high pitch, the quality was of a characteristic type and their lung capacity and force of expiration were equal to, if not greater than that of a mature man.

This was the cause of their extraordinary popularity, and with Italian opera their fame spread all over Europe. Even in countries like France and England they were accepted as an artistic necessity as long as composers of opera, including Händel, wrote for them.

Farinelli, after studying with his father, became a pupil of Porpora who was master of the Neapolitan conservatorio di Sant' Onofrio. As a singing teacher Porpora was unrivalled and counted among his pupils at this period some of the most famous *castrati* such as Antonio Uberti, known as *Il Porporino* and Caffarelli.

Even at the age of seventeen Farinelli was famous in Southern Italy under the name of *Il Ragazzo* (the boy), and on August 28, the seventeen-year-old youth took the part of Medoro in *L'Angelica* by Pietro Metastasio to which his teacher Porpora set the music.[2]

Thus in Naples that night were united for the first time the three great pioneers of poetry, music and singing of the eighteenth century. The friendship between Farinelli and Metastasio was to last for over fifty years, and the latter used to call the former *caro gemello* (dear twin) or "adorable twin" and to recall the old days in Naples where he used to write to him in Neapolitan dialect. Porpora, his teacher, he would meet again in London in 1734.

After leaving his master's guidance in 1724, he proceeded to take Vienna by storm and from there he went to Venice where he sang for the first time in Albinoni's *Didone albandonata* before returning to Naples. We

[1] R. P. Giovenale Sacchi, *Vita del Cavaliere Carlo Broschi*, Venezia, 1784. The most complete biography of the singer. See also E. Cotarelo y Mori, *Orígenes de la Opera en España hasta 1800*, Madrid, 1917, pp. 101-110.
[2] B. Croce, *Teatri di Napoli*, p. 150.

next hear of him in 1727 at Bologna, where he sang in a vocal duo with the celebrated Bernacchi, known as "the King of Singers", but was defeated. Nevertheless he was wise enough to beg his rival to give him lessons, and enriched by the latter's experience he visited Vienna again when he had the privilege of receiving advice and guidance from the Emperor Charles VI.

Vienna in those days attracted crowds of artists from foreign countries, for it was then at it greatest period of building. Only a short time before, the Turks had been driven back from its walls in their great invasion of Eastern Europe, and the sense of security was the reason for the building of great palaces in the city by the rich Austrian nobles.

The Emperor Charles had then in his service the architect Bernard Fischer Von Erlach, a student of Bernini, who, as Sacheverell Sitwell says, did his best to foster Caesarean approbation by building Vienna into the semblance of an improved Rome, and as Italy at that time was too poor to retain the services of her best artists they were forced to emigrate. Among the families of vagabond Italian artists living in Vienna were the Bibbienas from Bologna, who carried the scheme of Von Erlach still further in imagination, and, as Sitwell says, "it is as though the Italians having matured their plans so far in earlier times, now that their imagination was unfettered and had the skill to play how it liked, found themselves without the money to realize their schemes, and so were forced to take opportunities abroad and produce in plaster and canvas that which they had planned in brick and marble".

Farinelli learnt from the Emperor and Von Erlach one lesson from which he would derive great profit in the future, namely that opera required a stage setting which would reflect the emotions of the play and the vocalization of the singers, and soon he began to travel about with hosts of Italian scenic decorators, who in a moment could create fantastic palaces of plaster and cardboard out of which he would sing to his audience in the theatre.

It was in 1731, as a result of meeting Metastasio in Vienna, that Farinelli changed his style from one of mere brilliance and bravura, which he had hitherto practised as a faithful pupil of Porpora, to one of pathos and simplicity. Some say that the change was due to the wise counsels of the Emperor who advised him to cast away all fireworks and technical tricks and hide his technique under a style of absolute simplicity; but we believe that the change was suggested by the example of his most intimate friend his *gemello adorabile*, Metastasio, who as he composed verses sang them, accompanying himself on the clavicembalo. Metastasio had more influence over musicians in the eighteenth century than any poet and as Marmontel said, *tous les musiciens se sont donnés à lui.*

After a further Italian tour Farinelli made his first journey to London in 1734 at the very moment when the Prince of Wales and his friends had deliberately sponsored a new opera company as a counterblast to Händel and Heidegger's company at the King's theatre. The new venture was housed in the Lincoln's Inn Fields Theatre and was called the "Opera of the Nobility", and was under the musical direction of Porpora with Senesino, formerly Händel's best *castrato*, as chief singer. The enterprise, however, did not prosper and it was then that Porpora engaged his star pupil to appear in *Artaserse*, the music of which was mostly by the latter's brother Ricardo Broschi, and Hasse.

The singing of Farinelli in that opera, in *Polifemo* and in other operas by Porpora created such enthusiasm among the aristocratic audience in Lincoln's Inn Fields that Hogarth in *The Rake's Progress* immortalized the famous exclamation of a lady in one of the boxes: "One God and one Farinelli!"

It was in London that Farinelli received the royal invitation from the Queen of Spain, and after a triumphal farewell to his London audience he departed laden with gifts in 1737. On the way to Spain he stopped in Paris where he met the veteran actor and author Luigi Riccoboni, who in his *Reflexions* describes the extraordinary sensation the young singer made upon the King and Queen and the court at Versailles. "Not only", said he, "is he far superior to the celebrated Faustino Bordoni, but he has reached the highest grade of artistic perfection. Italy has never produced and, perhaps, will never more produce so perfect a musician." [1]

This criticism by the eclectic Riccoboni is all the more significant as among the countries in Europe France was the one that made the strongest opposition to Italian influence. Nevertheless Italian influence did exercise

---

[1] L. Riccoboni, *Réflexions historiques et critiques sur les Différents Théâtres de l'Europe*, Rome, 1738.

predominance over artists and society generally in Paris.   But we should not forget that Italianism, which was vigorously supported by the Philosophers of *L'Encyclopédie*, such as Diderot, Grimm, and especially Rousseau, led to veritable warfare among the musicians, and ended by winning a partial victory for Italy, for in the second half of the eighteenth century, as Romain Rolland says, French music, like a conquered country, became the prey of three great foreign composers; Piccinni, an Italian; Gluck, an Italianized German, and Grétry an Italianized Belgian. [1]

Farinelli reached the royal palace of La Granja in the mountains of Segovia in August 1737, and on the twenty-fifth of that month King Philip heard him for the first time.   The King had been for some time in one of his periods of hopeless melancholia and neglected the affairs of State, refusing even to preside at the Council. The Queen, now that she had procured, at a fabulous price, the human nightingale, arranged with the courtiers and the doctors a concert in the room adjoining that which the King occupied, and invited Farinelli to sing there a few tender and pathetic airs.

No sooner did the King hear the first notes of the magic voice than he remained spellbound.   As the notes floated into his consciousness he felt soothed and enchanted and life began to awaken in him as if through some miraculous power.   When Elizabeth presented the healer to him, the King in an outburst of heartfelt gratitude begged Farinelli to name any reward in the world he pleased, but the latter, who possessed a noble nature devoid of mercenary greed, answered that for him it was sufficient reward to know that he had relieved His Majesty of his sufferings.   All he would ask would be to see the King shed his sadness and return to his court to direct the affairs of State.   Philip straightway consented and allowed himself to be shaved for the first time for many weeks, and invited Farinelli to a feast in the palace, announcing to all the court that he had been cured by the Prince of Song.

Farinelli had intended returning to London where he had many engagements but the Queen succeeded in persuading him to renounce them, and there and then his fabulous career as a virtuoso ended and he became like a nightingale in a golden cage.   Henceforth he would live in Spain attached to the court at a huge annual salary. And so, five days after the king had heard him sing, he signed a decree nominating Don Carlos Broschi, called Farinelli, to his royal service and to that of the Queen, "on account of his remarkable talent and skill in singing", and granting him 1500 guineas in English money, paid regularly in sums of 135,000 reals alloy, every year, without discount of any kind, the said sums to run from the twenty-fifth day of each month onwards.   Also he was to be supplied with a coach and two mules for his personal service in Madrid, and a train of mules to enable him to accomplish the necessary journeys of the court from place to place; also fitting and adequate living apartments for his person and his family in the royal palaces.

The list of presents lavished on the singer by the royal family in the days after his arrival at La Granja, which is to be found in a manuscript in the National Library in Madrid, includes such gifts as portraits of the King and Queen framed in diamonds, gold boxes studded with diamonds containing gifts of money, diamond rings and chains, and gold watches ornamented with diamonds. [2]

In spite of the high salary and the gifts lavished upon him by his patrons the price that Farinelli had to pay was very high, for he had to sacrifice his career of world fame as virtuoso and agree to be bound by a strict contract to sing for the King and for no one else.   On one occasion Elizabeth Farnese even refused to allow him to sing specially for the Prince of Asturias and his wife, the heirs to the throne.   He became the exclusive property of the King and for ten years soothed Philip's distracted mind with the same few songs.   He told Burney at a later date that until the death of the King he sang the same four songs to him every night without any change.   Two of these were *Pallido il sole* and *Per questo dolce amplesso* by Hasse, and a third, a minuet, on which he improvized variations.   He thus repeated the same songs about three thousand six hundred times.

As Farinelli initiated in music the extraordinary vogue of the virtuoso which culminated in the fantastic personality of the violinist Paganini in the nineteenth century, he marks an important epoch in the history of music and the theatre.   It is, however, hard to imagine how the voice of Farinelli sounded, for already he and his voice and his personality had become idealized and transmuted into a phantom inhabiting a vast Churrigueresque

[1] R. Roland, *Voyage musical au Pays du Passé*, Paris, 1922, pp. 172-173.
[2] F. Barbieri, *Crónica de la Opera*, p. XLIV.

Elysium with airborne palaces, colonnaded avenues and terraces overlooking glassy pools and leafy gardens peopled by countless sylphs. As Sacheverell Sitwell says, "the exaggerated femininity, with its redoubled skill, of a *castrato*'s singing was something that transcendentalized the voice as we recognize and hear it now. It was not like human singing at all, but like some strange and foreign variety of insect keeping up an incessant praise of its easy life under the help of the summer sun. And his technical resources must have been no less miraculous, for Barbieri copies out two cadences, in one of which we find a hundred and fifty notes sung to one syllable of the song. This gives us some ideas of the extraordinary rapidity of his vocalization and his breath control. The other qualities of his voice have been well analyzed by the contemporary musical historian Arteaga, who exalts the teaching methods of Farinelli's professor, Porpora. It was Porpora who developed the extraordinary faculties of the boy, and in addition to educating his natural voice, taught him to explore countless forms of singing that were unknown to the artists of the day. According to Arteaga, Farinelli, in addition to his perfect intonation and his incredible technical agility, possessed a classical sense of balance and an aristocratic elegance musically, which he displayed in the light style as well as in the serious and pathetic. He also possessed the gift of being able with infinitely subtle gradations to increase or diminish his tone when he sang his arias.[1]

During the reign of Philip V Farinelli did not intervene personally to any large extent in the musical performances in the Royal Coliseum of the *Buen Retiro*, for the Director was a fellow Italian, the Marquis Annibale Scotti, who for many years had wielded the powers of a dictator, but the King and Queen did consult their court virtuoso, who advised them what singers should be brought from Italy, and how the operas should be staged. Nevertheless, it was chiefly owing to his methods of directing and staging the operas that Farinelli became afterwards significant in the history of the eighteenth-century Spanish theatre.

The theatre where Farinelli had sung in Vienna formed part of the buildings of the Royal Palace in such a way that the palace gardens lay directly at the back of the stage, and it was possible on occasions of great splendour to take out the back of the stage and prolong the scene indefinitely into the garden behind, so that the avenue could be reinforced with a row of painted trees, and plaster fountains could play among those of marble. When we examine one by one the wonderful collection of stage designs which constitute the unique treasure of the Vienna Opera House, we can visualize the settings Farinelli created for his incomparable voice, with their interminable colonnaded avenues down which the actors and singers arrived, and in which the perspective was so skilfully exaggerated that, as Sitwell says, the journey down them seemed of such length as to require a railway train to negotiate them. So carefully had Farinelli and his fellow-singers practised the art of entrance on the stage that they came on as though they had just arrived from some other planet, and, dressed in their stylized heroic Roman costumes, they appeared like immortals. According to the portraits of Farinelli painted by Hogarth and Amiconi he was abnormally tall, broad and full-breasted like a prima donna, and must have been a striking figure on the stage. Sacheverell Sitwell evokes the scene that follows:

"Down one of the corridors there came a low whispering note, like the wind beginning in the dead of night. It came a little louder, and now a shadow, closely followed by a huge figure could be seen walking down the portico on to the boards. The voice grew louder and louder until it reached a climax as Farinelli reached the candles and stood there in full view, shaking every ear with his sound. All the glasses of the chandeliers rattled and his voice was taken up and echoed by every bar and piece of metal in the theatre. While the hand-rails were still tingling and the note in the glass lights was dying away like a loud bell, Farinelli diminished the note, drawing it away again through the dying bells. Their life ebbed quickly away, and his note was left, not so much dying itself also, but going away—fading farther and still farther from the colonnades into the landscapes behind. No sooner had its sound completely vanished, even the echo being no longer audible, than Farinelli started again, singing with such speed that the orchestra found it impossible to keep pace with him. Following their guide as best they could the orchestra reached the end of their journey and were landed in safety by the middle of Farinelli's acknowledgment of the applause. But it was a world of skill and not of art, of sexless insect-like accomplishment rather than of natural and true flowing."[2]

[1] Fer. Arteaga, *La Rivoluzione del Teatro musicale Italiano*, Bologna, 1783, vol. I, p. 304.
[2] S. Sitwell, *op. cit.* p. 172-173.

Baroque eighteenth-century stage design drawn by Juvarra, theatre decorator in Vienna, taken from *Denkmäler des Theaters* by Joseph Gregor, formerly director of the theatrical section of the Vienna National Library. The operas produced and interpreted by Farinelli at Madrid had similar designs with the same perspective and depth.

Beside that description, which in style and imagination recaptures the magic of the Baroque period, we might set a parallel passage by Vernon Lee describing the triumph of the Italian burlesque in the eighteenth century, which took place simultaneously in the popular theatre: "Everywhere swarmed new varieties of masks, acrobats, jesters; grotesque, terrible; obscene and ludicrous shapes only half human, suggesting the broken egg-shells, melon rinds and bundles of rags of their native dust-holes and drain-vaults. Spanish Rodomonts—wondrous indeed with slashed jackets and cobwebbed swords, of names without end—swaggered about with bristling whiskers and mangey plumes before the Spanish garrisons, boasting that they were sons of Earthquake and Thunder, Cousins of Death, and bosom friends of Beelzebub; Trivellinos, Fritellinos, Formicas, Coviellos, dancing, fiddling, kicking creatures with long noses and slit mouths, tumbled about singing heathen songs with jargon burdens." [1]

Such was the Italian operatic and theatrical world that invaded Spain in the eighteenth century, making of the country, as Romain Rolland says, an Italian music colony. For the moment Spanish individuality and *casticismo* was overwhelmed and the natural drama lost ground as Spaniards travelled abroad and returned home with complete contempt for everything national. Ignacio Luzán, a pupil of Vico, published his *Poética* in 1737, the year of Farinelli's arrival in Spain, in which he stated his object was "to subject Spanish verse to the rules which obtained among cultured nations" and proceeded to call Lope and Calderón old barbarians "whose day is over and who must make way for children of the light". [2]

Nevertheless a great change occurred in 1746 on the death of Philip V, for the new king Ferdinand VI and still more his wife María Barbara de Braganza, both of whom had been cruelly persecuted by the former's step-mother, Elizabeth Farnese, were determined to pay off old scores. For sixteen years both had been scorned, abused and purposely kept in the background. Now was the moment when they could spread their wings freely after their confinement. The haughty termagant Queen, even at this juncture, believed that as mother of the heir to the throne, the then King of Naples, she could go on living at the Royal Palace, brow-beating and governing as she had done before the death of her husband, but she soon realized her mistake. At first it was politely hinted that it was customary for Queen Dowagers to retire to some religious house where they could mourn their loss, and though she was allowed to reside in Madrid in the palace that formerly belonged to the Duke of Osuna, the place became such a hot-bed of intrigue and gossip that she was plainly notified that her best course was to withdraw to La Granja which she and her late husband had converted into a Spanish Versailles.

Elizabeth Farnese broke out into a fit of furious recrimination, saying that she considered this tantamount to exile, but she had to acquiesce, and murmuring threats she departed to La Granja, where she and her children nursed their spite to keep it warm and waited day by day for the death of the King and Queen whom they considered intruders.

Ferdinand VI was of kindly disposition, well read and a great lover of music. He was fortunate in having efficient ministers, especially the celebrated Marqués de Ensenada, and he was satisfied to leave most decisions to them as he was not interested in public affairs. Like his father he was liable to acute fits of depression, which would eventually end in madness in the last year of his life, but he placed all his reliance upon his wife, who while possessing the courage and tenacity of the widow of Philip V, was more sociable and of a far higher moral nature. Modest and affectionate in manner, she possessed quick intuitions, and plenty of determination, once she had made her mind up. In moments of crisis, calm and level-headed, she always maintained the dignity of the monarchy and was liberal and unprejudiced in her dealings with her subjects. She and her husband during their long years of royal apprenticeship as Prince and Princess of Asturias had not allowed their natures to become embittered at their humiliating treatment by the Queen and by the courtiers, who toadied for royal favour. Doña Barbara's many good qualities made up for her ugly face, pitted with smallpox, her small eyes and her large mouth. She was, however, of elegant figure and had beautiful hands. She was most accomplished in music, for she sang well, and played the clavichord like a professional. One lesson she had learned from her predecessor and that was devotion to her husband's whims, and she made herself into a great huntress and

[1] Vernon Lee, *Studies of Eighteenth Century Italy*, London, 1880.
[2] J. Fitzmaurice Kelly, *A New History of Spanish Literature*, London, 1926, p. 404.

horsewoman simply because Ferdinand VI, like his step-brother Charles III, was an inveterate killer of stags, wild boar, wolves and vixens.

When Elizabeth Farnese retired in high dudgeon from the Royal Palace into private life, she wished to take Farinelli with her, but Queen Barbara refused to allow this and made her husband issue a decree stating that the great singer would continue to enjoy the same emoluments as before, but to those he would add many extra privileges. The principal privilege that the King bestowed upon Farinelli and one which he had been coveting for a long time, was to have the sole management of the Royal Palace entertainments, a post that hitherto had been held by the dictatorial Marquis Annibale Scotti.

Now begins the great and significant period in Farinelli's career. This was the moment for which he had been waiting patiently all through the years during which he had repeated the six songs night after night, thousands of times, to soothe the demented King. He had dreamed of this moment when he had been at the court of Vienna listening to the Caesarean Emperor discuss operatic schemes with the Bibbienas, or when he had argued interminably about the problems of music and drama with his beloved "twin", Pietro Metastasio. For this reason many of Farinelli's biographers, from Dr. Burney onwards mistakenly repeat that by accepting to remain with the King of Spain as his personal singer at a huge salary, he separated himself "from the world of art for ever". On the contrary, it was now in the reign of King Ferdinand VI and Queen Barbara de Braganza that Farinelli entered into the higher reaches of the world of art, for during the next eleven years, until 1758, he would create for his royal master, in the *Buen Retiro*, with the help of his legions of Italian singers, players, designers, and decorators a universe of musical illusion, rivalling the one he had seen in Vienna in the Imperial Palace of Charles VI. And today, in the library of the Royal Palace of Madrid, we may consult the precious manuscript written in his own writing, wherein he describes for the King and Queen his grandiose plans for festivities during those years.

The manuscript is a large volume luxuriously bound in red leather with the royal arms and lettering in gold.

The text of the manuscript is primarily a glorified financial estimate drawn up by Farinelli of the royal entertainments, but here and there, he discusses subjects of interest to all theatre directors and producers, and tells humorous anecdotes in a strange half-Italian, half-Spanish jargon. [1]

Speaking about the companies of opera singers who visited Madrid, Farinelli is most insistent that visiting singers should be treated with urbanity and courtesy and given dinner and supper during the first eight days at the King's expense (other theatres only do so for two days, he adds). This concession should be continued afterwards but the expense should not exceed three doubloons (about seventy pesetas) daily.

During their period of engagement in Madrid the singers live rent free, and Farinelli insists that the furniture in their apartments should be attractive and comfortable *(muy decentes)* but should only be renovated every three years, and if the living quarters assigned to the singers be not to their liking they should be given an equivalent sum of money enabling them to rent them.

Prima donnas were paid a thousands reals for each performance of the opera or serenata, and men were paid four hundred and fifty reals. These payments were in addition to their regular fixed salary. They were also supplied with the costumes they wore in operas or serenatas.

The singers were served on silver table services which varied according to their category as artists. Incidentally, the silver table services were returned to the palace at the end of their engagement. The silver table service of the chief prima donna consisted of twenty-four plates, four cups, six complete sets of knives, forks and spoons, two ladles, two big dishes, two trays, two salt cellars and four candlesticks. The second prima donna received six plates and two candlesticks less than the first lady. The three principal male singers were given the same as the second lady.

---

[1] This manuscript is in the Library of the Royal Palace, Madrid, and its number is 412. The full title is as follows: " *Descripción del Estado actual del Real Teatro del Buen Retiro de las Funciones hechas en él desde el Año 1747, hasta el presente :* de sus individuos sueldos y encargos, segun se expresa en este Primer Libro. En el segundo se manifiestan las diversiones que annualmente tienen los Reyes Nros Sres. en el Sitio de Aranjuez. Dispuesto por Don Carlos Broschi Farinelli. Criado familiar de Ss Mes. Año de 1758. " There is another copy of this important manuscript in the library of the College of San Clemente in Bologna from which Leandro de Moratín published an extract in vol. 2, *Obras Póstumas.*

Whenever there was an operatic performance or rehearsal the *Gefe del Ramillete de la Reyna*, or "Master of the Queen's Bouquet" served the singers with broth and cooling drinks in silver cups. They were also given carriages on Sundays and feast days to take them to Mass.

Farinelli, taking into account the severe nature of the Madrid climate, with its subtle air that will not extinguish a candle, yet will kill a man, and where the women and children cover their mouths with hand-kerchiefs and the men muffle themselves up in their cloaks, arranged closed carriages to take the virtuosi to the theatre and back on the nights they performed, and knowing by experience how liable a prima donna or a primo tenore is to envy and jealousy, he recommends the coachmen and grooms not to make any distinctions between one singer and another.

Even more interesting are the details Farinelli gives of the daily life of the singers under his care, and the method that must be adopted in conducting the rehearsals of operas. Here the author writes as one who has rubbed shoulders with singers all over Europe and enjoys having a joke or two behind the scenes with his fellow artists, and so we find him playfully twitting his chief musical assistant Maestro Niccolò Conforto.

"Maestro Niccolò Conforto", he says, "or whoever it maybe, when he is setting a play to music, or composing a Serenata should follow the good old custom of rehearsing separately the solo voices, so that the virtuosi may be quite sure of their parts. And he should see to it that Signor Porreti turns up at all these rehearsals, for as he with his violoncello and his brilliant technique is a whole orchestra in himself, there is no need of calling the rest of the instrumentalists."

Nevertheless Farinelli adds that when arias had to be rehearsed, two first and two second violins, two viols, two horns, an extra oboe and a double bass should assist at the rehearsal of the voices. After those special rehearsals it was only necessary to call two or three rehearsals with the full orchestra, but three or four days' rest should be given to the virtuosi before the performance. Throughout Farinelli makes many bantering allusions to Maestro Conforto, who evidently must have expressed great irritation at the continual demands made on him by the singers and managers, and he calms him down, saying:

"Ever since 1745 professional musicians behave in a different way than they used in the 1730's. This is due to the enormous increase in the number of theatres that have arisen all over Europe, for it has given them a more exalted notion of their own merits and has changed their way of thinking. All now prate of *Fedeltà* or fidelity of interpretation and all worry the chapel-master to put on this or that piece of music which the prima donna or the virtuoso has sung in the Canary Islands, in Dresden, in Venice, Naples, Bologna, Milan, Florence, Turin, Vienna or Prussia. If Maestro Conforto and others do not patiently and complacently play up to their whims and caprices and let them show off their trills and pet bravura passages they find themselves cold-shouldered and in disgrace. 'And so, my dear Maestro Conforto', says Farinelli. 'You must possess your soul in patience and try to please them. You must, in fact, become blind and deaf and clamp a muzzle on your mouth. Silence is your best policy.' "

After enumerating the professional musicians of the Chapel Royal who take part also in the performances in the palace of Aranjuez, Farinelli details the duties of the members of the orchestra and the days they have to give to performances at Aranjuez. The orchestra, which was conducted by Maestro Conforto, consisted of a leader and three first violins, seven second violins, two violas, four oboes, two horns, two double-basses, two harpsichords and two bassoons.

At the end of Part I of this manuscript there is a charming description of Farinelli surrounded by the singers of the chorus in the stage tailor's workshop, supervising the fitting of the costumes.

At the end with justifiable pride the great singer exclaims: "No theatre in Europe can compare with the Royal Court Theatre of Spain either in wealth, variety of scenery or richness of costumes, yet the cost of upkeep of this theatre is relatively small, for we have not thrown away our stage sets but stored them for future use, and for this reason the three great store-houses in the *Retiro* are not large enough to hold all our stage effects. And the same is true of the theatre at Aranjuez. In pursuit of economy we have reduced the high cost of illuminating the theatres by constructing brass tubes shaped like candles, which enabled even the candle ends to be used.

By this exceptionally interesting manuscript report on the theatres under his direction Farinelli showed himself not only a practical man of the theatre and a consumate director, possessing a knowledge of every detail in stage craft, but also a true father of his company, forever alive to their interests.

152

Nicola Porpora

Pietro Metastasio

Queen Marie Louise of Savoy

King Philip V.

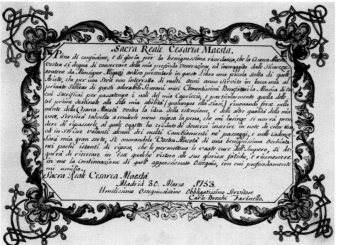

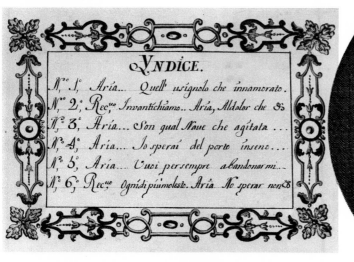

Three pages from the manuscript which Farinelli sent to the Emperor Charles VI of Austria containing some of the songs which he sang every evening for ten years to King Philip V. From the Österr. Nationalbibliothek, Vienna.

Carlo Broschi, called Farinelli, 1705-1782, world-famous singer who came to Spain at the invitation of Elizabeth Farnese to cure the melancholia of her husband King Philip V. The engraving is after the contemporary portrait by Amigoni. It is in the Österr. Nationalbibliothek, Vienna.

154

Farinelli showed his noble moral qualities not only in the theatre within the precincts of the royal palace, but also in Madrid generally. Being devoid of mercenary greed he wished through the royal favour he enjoyed to help the humbler artists, musicians and dramatists who struggled to earn a mere pittance, and his purse was forever ready to assist them. But more remarkable still was his constant attempt to help the Spanish actors of the companies who played in the ancient teatro de la Cruz and teatro del Principe. Those details we learn through a series of letters which Cotarelo y Mori discovered in the National Historical Archives. The letters were written by the Infanta Doña María Antonia, who was twenty years of age, to her mother, Elizabeth Farnese, giving her day by day an account of court gossip, Madrid scandal, plays and concerts. The correspondence covers a period of four months from December 18, 1748, to April 13, 1749. [1]

All through that correspondence there is an undercurrent of bitter hatred, for the infanta María Antonia, like the rest of the family, had been brought up by her mother to hate Barbara de Braganza and Ferdinand VI and she loses no opportunity of backbiting. She always refers to the King as "he" and to her sister-in-law the Queen as "she" in her pitiless diary, and we can imagine the glee with which the revengeful old Dowager received from her daughter the bulletin of the increasing infirmities of Doña Barbara. The correspondence is also interesting as it shows how wise and tolerant was the policy of Farinelli in varying his operatic programmes with the national Comedias by such authors of the golden age as Lope de Vega and Moreto played by the Spanish actors of the two ancient theatres of the capital.

The Infanta Doña María Antonia became in 1750 the centre figure in court celebrations on the occasion of her marriage to the Prince of Piedmont, afterwards King Amadeo III of Savoy, and on that occasion her sister-in-law Queen Barbara, whom she had so bitterly reviled in her letters, heaped coals of fire upon her head, for she and the King behaved towards her with the utmost generosity and arranged the most elaborate festivals of their reign out in the *Retiro* in honour of her marriage.

Those festivals, which were held during the month of April 1750, were all directed by Farinelli with the assistance of the stage designer Yolli and the composers Mele and Corselli.

As a climax to the festival the *Armida Placata* was produced with great splendour in the Coliseum of the *Retiro* with the music by Farinelli's Neapolitan friend Giovanni Bautista Mele and the decorations by Yolli. The last scene represented the Temple of the Sun with its lofty transparent columns of red and white crystal. Apollo's paradise was all suffused in pink, and by innumerable globes of variegated crystal and hundreds of silver stars all revolving in continual movement it produced the impression of celestial spaces traversed by the chariot of the sun which stood in all its resplendent gold and crystal in the centre, drawn by its swift steeds poised on revolving globes of clouds, and driven by Apollo. Throned in the clouds above were the Twelve Signs of the Zodiac and various deities, and behind the chariot of Apollo blazed the face of the Sun, which was of crystal, all in one piece, five feet in diameter, with two rows of spiral crystal rays revolving in opposite directions and blazing so brightly that the eyes of the audience were dazzled by them and by the glow of the lights in the theatre which exceeded eighteen thousand in number. All this immense phantasmagoria rose little by little until it disclosed a crystal gateway with vistas beyond of the Park of the *Retiro* with coloured lights twinkling in the branches of the trees and flashing patterns of fireworks, while Apollo sang his address which brought the festival to a close.

This was the culminating point of Farinelli's career, and His Majesty, desiring to pay tribute to the great artist, conferred upon him there and then the Cross of Calatrava studded with diamonds, and the Queen gave him a gold box containing a ring in which was set a brilliant of great value.

For these years we turn to the vivid correspondence which passed between the two friends. To Metastasio, Farinelli confesses all his troubles with his singers and asks his advice as he would from a kindly tutor. Metastasio writes back, sometimes as a poor relation would to the rich member of the family, praising the latter's generosity and hinting his sore need of money.

Farinelli shows himself all through generous, trusting and naive; Metastasio on the contrary is cynical, witty and full of the worldly wisdom of an Italian abbé of the eighteenth century. Farinelli was too simple and trusting a mortal to be able to cope with such a capricious prima donna as La Mingotti. Being a sly

---

[1] Archivo Historico Nacional, Estado Lo. 2577. Summaries are quoted in Cotarelo y Mori, *op. cit.*, pp. 134-139.

puss she had no compunction in breaking her contract and disappearing from Spain on the eve of the first performance of the Serenata.

When Farinelli wrote bemoaning his sad experience, Metastasio replied in a letter of June 18, 1754: "What else could you expect from our Mingotti? Is it only now that you are beginning to understand the grotesque character of our Tragicomic sirens? I am more amazed at your amazement than I am at her conduct. She has only behaved as she should have done *secundum ordinem* of all singers; and you have fooled yourself into thinking that you could make a reasonable girl out of her. Send her your fatherly blessing and leave her to repent at leisure."

Few musical correspondences are as entertaining as those thirty-eight letters which passed between these two masters of the theatre, each supreme in his own line, and the letters are as significant an indication of the eighteenth century as the celebrated correspondence between Richard Strauss and Hoffmannsthal is of the nineteenth. The charm of these letters springs from the fact that Farinelli's vivid picture of the Spanish court in Madrid, La Granja and Aranjuez is counterbalanced by the picture the poet Metastasio gives of Vienna and its opera and the plays in the royal garden of the palace of Schönbrunn. In many cases the operas and serenades represented in Vienna were afterwards repeated in Madrid by Farinelli, though sometimes with special music written by his friend Maestro Conforto, the conductor of the orchestra.

The audience who attended the theatrical performances in the *Retiro* or in Aranjuez generally consisted of the official world and the nobility, and cards were sent as invitations and metal medals were given as entrance tickets. When it was noticed that there were vacant seats in the theatre, royal servants were sent to the promenade of the Prado to invite passers-by to the opera, and they were given free seats. This custom was adopted because Ferdinand VI always wished to see the theatre full. This was the only possibility the general public had of seeing the opera, for the performances, though given gratis, were only open to those who presented invitations.

As the performances at Aranjuez took place in the spring and summer when the court moved to the palace there, the ingenious Farinelli devised a new form of musical entertainment which would find its setting in nature itself. He ordered the construction of a squadron consisting of a royal barge *(La Real)* sixty feet long and fifteen feet broad, and three frigates *El Respeto*, *San Fernando* and *Santa Bárbara*, each forty feet long. The *Santa Bárbara* was equipped with sixteen miniature cannon, and there were eleven other boats of smaller dimensions, two of them being nine-oared and seven-oared respectively, and two more of grotesque shape, for one represented a peacock and the other a stag.

The boats glided slowly and gracefully down the four miles of river below Aranjuez, where the Tagus coils like a snake through the countryside amidst woods and gardens. Farinelli's river festivals combined the two favourite Bourbon pastimes, hunting and music, for the guests from the deck of the barges marked down wild boar or other game beaten up by the huntsmen in the woods, or else they fished from the side with rod or net and the smaller boats held miniature regattas. During the expeditions after sunset the wooded banks of the river were illuminated, and amid displays of fireworks the miniature cannon would fire salvos.

The Queen, who was dressed like an Amazonian huntress, stood on deck, gun in hand, and with great skill shot the wild boar, stag or fox that was beaten up by the huntsmen and plunged into the river.

The expeditions began generally at six o'clock in the evening and lasted until nine or ten at night when the whole Sotillo or grove, which was the haven of the boats, became like an enchanted forest lit up by forty thousand lanterns artfully placed here and there amongst the trees. On the royal barge, *Le Real*, a lofty cabin had been built in the shape of a small temple with silken hangings, and there the King and Queen and Farinelli sat surrounded by a number of lords and ladies of the palace, listening to the playing of an instrumentalist. It was then that the courtiers in the boats and on the banks had occasion to hear the incomparable voice of Farinelli in arias accompanied by the Queen on the harpsichord.

To hear in the silence of those summer nights that peerless voice floating over the waters as the barges glided by like phantoms was a memory never to be forgotten, and from the second part of Farinelli's manucript to which we have already referred we can recreate in our minds the vision of those "Venetian Nights", which were for the great singer and artist the apotheosis of his whole life. From those stray notes which describe day by day the music festivals on the Tagus we can see how fortunate Farinelli was in his royal patrons. It was, however, the Queen who was the moving spirit and the bountiful Fairy Godmother. She was by nature profoundly musical and she had the good fortune to meet Domenico Scarlatti in Lisbon and became his pupil. After her marriage she took him with her to the Spanish court, where he spent all the rest of his life. As a result of Scarlatti's teaching the Queen became a highly cultivated performer on the harpsichord, and she not only accompanied Farinelli, but sang duets with him at the river festivals.[1]

The last excursion on the river was on July 14, 1758. One month and few days later, on August 28, Doña Bárbara, the Fairy Godmother, whose gracious patronage enabled Farinelli for eleven years to create a fantastic world of Music, Drama and the sister arts, breathed her last and never again was the voice of Farinelli heard within the palace, nor was the royal harpsichord ever again opened to accompany his celestial arias. The King lapsed back into his brooding melancholia and became so violent in his madness that he had to be confined in Villaviciosa de Odón, where on August 10, 1759, he passed away, one year after his wife's death.

Now it was the turn for the exiles of La Granja to sing their paean of triumph, and the vindictive Dowager Elizabeth Farnese began to rule imperiously again in Spain's capital, while her son Charles III made his preparations to leave Naples and take possession of his Spanish Kingdom.

No sooner did he land on Spanish soil, however, than he gave orders that his mother should not in any way intervene in the government of the country.

One of the new King's first acts was to exile Farinelli, but he allowed him to continue receiving all his salary and to keep all his previous emoluments, saying that he was all the more pleased to do this as Farinelli had never abused the favours and the generous treatment which he had received from the preceding monarchs.

And so with heavy heart the celebrated musician left Spain where he had lived uninterruptedly for the previous twenty-two years. He retired to Bologna, which in the eighteenth century was, as Romain Rolland calls it, the headquarters of Italian art, the brain that reasons and directs. In Bologna lived the greatest musical authority in Italy in those days, whose expert knowledge was not only recognized by the Italians but also by the masters in all Europe—such as Gluck, John Christian Bach and Mozart—the venerable Padre Martini. In Bologna, too, was the chief music academy of Italy, the celebrated Philharmonic Society, founded in 1666, wherein Dr. Burney met Leopold Mozart and his little prodigy of a son whom Padre Martini had admitted as a student.

In the outskirts of Bologna Farinelli built a sumptuous palace where he collected together the countless works of art and souvenirs which the Spanish monarchs had bestowed upon him. According to Armona in his *Memorias chronológicas* he kept there open house for all his Spanish friends and acquaintances, who became his guests on their journeys to and from Spain and France to Rome and Naples. He entertained them all in princely fashion and placed his wealth at their disposal. In that calm retreat he lived for another twenty-two years and passed away quietly on July 15, 1782, three months after his beloved Metastasio.

DOMENICO SCARLATTI (1685-1757)

Generous as Queen Bárbara de Braganza was in her patronage of Farinelli, she was still more of a fairy godmother to his fellow Neapolitan Domenico Scarlatti, who was not blessed with this world's goods, and having a family of nine children to feed was always in debt. In addition, he was an inveterate gambler. From Giovenale Sacchi's biography of Farinelli (1784) we learn that Scarlatti was an agreeable man, but so addicted to gaming that he was frequently ruined. He was, however, as frequently relieved by his royal patroness, the Queen of Spain, who was a staunch admirer of his original genius and incomparable talents. He died in very poor circumstances, leaving his wife and two daughters totally unprovided, but the charitable Queen settled a pension upon them.

[1] R. P. Govenale Sacchi, *op. cit.*, vol. II. See also G. Antonio de Armona, *Memorias Cronológicas*. He was corregidor of Madrid for many years in the eighteenth century. His mss. chronics. quoted by Caparella, *op. cit.*

Trend, who calls Domenico Scarlatti one of the greatest composers who ever lived in Spain, considers that in view of the number of years he spent there and the amount of music he wrote, it would be no more unreasonable to describe him as a Spanish composer than it is to describe El Greco as a Spanish painter. "Scarlatti's music glitters like hot Spanish sunshine, illuminating impartially, but not unkindly, tragedy and comedy alike. There can be tragedy leading to despair, as in the incomparable Sonata in B minor; yet even the shadows are hard and clear, not only in outline, and the faintest approach to sentimentality is interrupted by a dry cackle of laughter from across the way." [1]

Domenico Scarlatti becomes for us on our musical journey through the eighteenth century the most significant link with the preceding period, first of all through his father, Alessandro, in whose operatic arias all the Italian schools of the seventeenth century culminate. Domenico, who, according to Cecil Gray, belongs rather to the Rococo than to the Baroque period of the preceding age, transformed the grandiose arias of his father with their luxurious stretches of melody into precise and epigrammatic aphorisms in music, and when we listen to a series of his little sonatas, or *essercizi* as he called them in the aggregate, with the sudden glimpses they give us of gaiety or tragedy, we are reminded of Oscar Wilde's lines:

> But strange that I was not told
> That the brain can hold
> In a tiny ivory cell
> God's heaven and hell.

His genius was recognized at an early age by his father, as is shown by the following passage from a letter written in 1705, introducing the youth to Ferdinand de Medici. "I am sending my son away from Rome, since Rome has no roof to shelter music that lives here in beggary. This son of mine is an eagle whose wings are grown: he ought not to stay idle in the nest, and I ought not to hinder his flight... He sets forth to meet whatever opportunities may present themselves for making himself known—opportunities for which it is useless to wait in Rome nowadays."

After presenting that letter, which is now in the Medici archives in Florence, to the Prince, Domenico continued his journey to Venice where he studied with Gasparini and made the acquaintance of Händel. With Händel he returned to Rome, where Cardinal Ottoboni, the munificent patron of "The Father of the Violin", Arcangelo Corelli, held a competition in which Händel and Scarlatti drew even as regards harpsichord playing, but in the organ Scarlatti himself admitted the marked superiority of the German. They both became fast friends and remained together as long as Händel was in Italy, and they met in later years in London. Both always had the greatest admiration for one another, and in his later life in Spain whenever anyone admired Domenico Scarlatti's playing he would utter the name Händel and cross himself.

It is significant that the vogue of the great harpsichord players arose in the Rococo age. The plastic arts in Italy yielded the palm to music, and after Michelangelo came a whole series of minor painters whose affectations like those of their colleagues in the neighbouring countries are expressed in a term which is significant in key-board music, namely *manieren* in German and its French equivalent *agrément* which conveys a touch of gallantry to style, for Rococo in France is a form of decorative art. The decadence of Caracci, Guido Reni, Domenichino and Caravaggio culminates architecturally in Bernini, whom Louis XIV called to Versailles, and the golden age of Rococo in music in the salons of *Le Roi Soleil* succeeded to the Baroque era of Henry IV, and Louis XIII with its painters, such as Rigaud and Mignard who portray for us a galaxy of gorgeous blue-stockinged ladies with their powdered wigs, their studied smiles, their billowing silks and furbelows. [2]

But that cold and pompous art with its ostentatious elegance quickened into vigorous life in the eighteenth century after the death of Louis XIV, when the Italian players returned to Paris and music triumphed in the Couperin musical dynasty. Such concerted music prepared the way for Watteau (who was a devotee of the

[1] J. B. Trend, *Manuel de Falla and Spanish Music*, New York, 1929.
[2] A. Salazar, *op. cit.*, vol. II, pp. 225-226. See also S. Sitwell, *A Background for D. Scarlatti*, London, 1935.

masques of the commedia dell'Arte), Boucher, Fragonard, and Chardin, whose realism and tender irony is reflected musically in *La Poule* of Rameau and *La Fine Madeleine*, *Le Réveil-Matin*, and *La Divine Babiche* of Couperin. The glory of the eighteenth century was the art of the *clavecin*, as it was called in France, which reached perfection as an instrument for embellishing music by its *agréments* and surpassed the clavichord by its greater sonority.

The suites of François Couperin "le Grand" (1668-1733) mark the summit of fame reached by the French *clavecin* in the eighteenth century and his concertos entitled *Gouts réunis* were unrivalled in the realms of concerted music in Italy or England.

It is noteworthy that the lives of the three great composers, who wrote for the harpsichord, clavecin or clavicembalo in the second half of the seventeenth and first half of the eighteenth century, coincide with each other: Purcell who was born half way through the seventeenth century in 1658 dies at its close in 1695: François Couperin, who belongs to the following generation, died in 1733, and Domenico Scarlatti, who was born three years before François Couperin, outlived him by over twenty years, but his last years, when he was living in poverty in Spain, were unproductive.

Nevertheless Domenico Scarlatti is a far more universal figure than François Couperin, for in a sense he was the founder of modern keyboard technique, and his influence may be traced in Mendelssohn, Liszt, and Verdi *(Falstaff)*. In Spanish music he is still more significant because he arrived in Spain at the moment when what we today call the "Spanish style" in music was being created. Scarlatti was alive to the Spanish national reaction that had arisen in the eighteenth century against the dictatorship of Italian virtuosi and the Italian opera. During his years in Madrid he became familiar with the street songs and the dances that had survived from the days of Lope de Vega, Tirso de Molina and Calderón, when the *Zarabanda* and the *Chacona* had shocked the moralists. In his later years he heard everywhere the *Tonadillas*, which were short musical plays, full of street-cries, folksongs and tavern dances, and which were the musical counterpart of the sparkling one-act *sainetes* of Ramón de la Cruz, which portrayed the Madrid of the *Majos* and *Manolas* whom Goya was to paint.

Domenico Scarlatti is regarded as the founder of Spanish pianoforte style and he made great use of the crossing of the hands and produced new effects by these means. The earliest of the manuscript volumes of the sonatas, which is dated 1747, and is to be found at Saint Mark's, Venice, contains, in addition to the harpsichord sonatas, twelve sonatas for violin with *continuo* for the harpsichord on the lower line. Scarlatti himself only published one book of thirty sonatas entitled *Esercizii per Gravicembalo*, but forty-two *Suites de Pièces pour le Clavecin* were published in London under the supervision of his friend, Roseingrave. Nevertheless the first definite step forward in the Scarlatti cult did not take place until Ricordi published in ten volumes an edition of over five hundred sonatas edited by Alessandro Longo. Today Domenico Scarlatti has been fortunate in his most recent biographer, Ralph Kirkpatrick, who has discovered new material and brought the number of extant sonatas up to 555. By his evocative harpsichord playing he has done much to spread the cult of the eighteenth-century master. [1]

ANTONIO SOLER (1729-1783)

The tradition of Domenico Scarlatti was carried on by a monk of the Order of Saint Jerome, Antonio Soler, who became organist and choir-master at the royal monastery of the Escorial, where he remained until his death. Born in 1729 at Olot in the mountains of the province of Gerona, he studied first of all at Montserrat, where he learnt the organ from a pupil of Juan Cabanillas, the celebrated organist of the seventeenth century and composer of the beautiful *Missa de Angelis*, and while very young became chapel-master of the Cathedral of Lérida. After his appointment at the Escorial in 1752 he devoted himself to music, teaching and composition. Among his pupils were members of the Spanish royal family. According to Santiago Kastner, Padre Soler had been in contact with Domenico Scarlatti during the last five years of the latter's life. Certainly

---

[1] Ralph Kirkpatrick, *Domenico Scarlatti*, Princeton and London, 1953. Ralph Kirkpatrick, *Domenico Scarlatti's harmony (The Score*, Nos. 5 and 6, 1951-1952).

the influence of the Neapolitan master is evident in Soler's compositions, especially the sonatas for harpsichord which show the same cult of Spanish folk rhythms, but there is undeniable originality in the Catalan composer's melodies and rhythms. Some of his sonatas were printed in London by Robert Birchall. [1] Soler also composed church music, and six concertos for two organs have been edited by Santiago Kastner from manuscripts which remain in the Escorial, and published by the Biblioteca Central, Barcelona. In the musical archives, too, of the Escorial is music which Soler wrote for plays and interludes of Calderón and other dramatists of the seventeenth century. He also published a treatise on musical theory entitled *Llave de Modulación y Antigüedades de la Música* (Madrid, 1762). In recent years the sonatas for harpsichord were introduced with great success to the French musical public by the distinguished Catalan pianist and composer Joaquin Nin who published a group of them in his *Classiques du Piano*, volumes I and II.

Of all the music of Padre Soler that has come down to us, the most evocative are the six Quintets for organ and strings which have been edited by Roberto Gerhard and published by the Biblioteca de Cataluña in 1935. They are most effectively written for the various instruments, and make an admirably balanced ensemble. As an example of the melodic charm to be discovered in Soler's music there is the *Allegro Pastorile* * of the third Quintet which is a gem of eighteenth-century chamber music. This latter is included in our recording. It is performed by the Chamber Music of Barcelona with Esther Nadal de Janés at the harpsichord.

There is a further example of eighteenth-century Spanish music which we have included in our recording** : *Villancicos de Navidad* or Christmas carols by Francisco Morera, a celebrated *maestro de capilla* of Valencia Cathedral, who composed masses, psalms, motets and many *villancicos* in four, eight and twelve voices. The exquisite carol which is sung with such freshness and balance by the little singers of the *capilla clásica* is only part of the whole *Villancico*. Like most *villancicos* of Morera's epoch it includes an instrumental introduction, arias and recitatives. Although it is a quasi-sacred work it is full of laughter and gaiety, and we are in the Mozartian world, enlivened by melodies and rhythms from the east coast of Spain.

[1] *XXVII Sonatas para Clave, por el Padre Fray Antonio Soler*, London. Robert Birchall (British Museum, Cambridge, Univ. Lib. Fitz-William Collection).
* First Record, *Ancient Music*, side II, No. 7.
** First Record, *Ancient Music*, side II, No. 6.

Well-known torero of the XVIIIth century. Mentioned for the first time in the history of bull-fighting around the years 1775 to 1790. He is one of the toreros who gave the bull-fight the rules which are still in use.

D. Juan de la Cruz sculp.

Joaquin Costillares. Le Fameux Joaquin Costillares.

Chapter XIV

THE SPANISH REVIVAL
IN DRAMA AND MUSIC

Goya's fine portrait of King Charles III shows a keen, ascetic and vigorous man dressed as a hunter with his gun and his dog, and he soon showed that he was what the eighteenth century called "an enlightened prince." He was a follower of the French Encyclopédistes, entertained liberal views and was resolved to govern his country himself. The government supported the ideas of "Enlightenment and Progress" which were inspired by the French: they encouraged the sciences, arts and industries, with the result that foreign technicians were introduced and young Spaniards were sent abroad to study.

Charles made the "Family Compact" with France in 1761, whereby the Bourbons bound themselves to resist the encroachments of England, who although she was fighting France for domination in North America and India, adopted a hectoring tone to Spain and hampered her trade with her colonies. Charles III soon realized that England was Spain's worst enemy because in extending her dominions in the New World she was obliged politically and economically to try to weaken Spain. Even the wife of Charles, Queen Amalia, who was friendly disposed to England, recognized the English danger. "London", she said, "needs to be given a lesson, otherwise there will be no dealing with her, and she will think herself mistress of the world." As long as the Queen lived she prevented an overt breach with England, but after her death in 1760 Charles, irritated by the English squatters in Spanish fisheries in Newfoundland and Honduras, was delighted to strengthen his family pact by a treaty with France in 1762, and war was declared between Spain and England. In 1763, the following year, peace was made, but the Treaty of Paris did not settle the outstanding problems between the two countries, for there remained a resentment which was bound to lead to further hostilities.

Such was the general state of foreign affairs in the reign of Charles III. Let us now consider the internal situation in Spain. Here Charles III was much more successful. When he arrived in Madrid with his favourite the Marquis of Squillace (Esquilache) and his ministers and friends of the French school they all were greatly shocked at the backward appearance of the city and its inhabitants. Madrid at this time was one of the filthiest capitals in Europe: the people swaggered in the streets armed to the teeth and the Marquis of Esquilache said that the men in their broad-brimmed hats and long cloaks all looked like conspirators. The King at once set his ministers to work to clear up the city and turn the inhabitants as far as possible into Frenchmen. The streets were paved and swept, pipes and gutters were made to carry off the drains. In religious matters, however, the King remained conservative and his first act after taking the oath to the united Cortes was to proclaim the Virgin of the Immaculate Conception the official patroness of Spain, but his Neapolitan followers made no

163

attempt to conceal their contempt for the priests and monks that thronged the capital and made large claims upon the royal prerogative.[1]

The Madrileños resented the reforms introduced by Esquilache, such as the laws compelling them to wear cocked hats, bagwigs and coats instead of *chambergos* (wide-brimmed hats), *guedejas* (sidelocks) and long cloaks. In 1766 those sumptuary laws were strictly enforced on pain of imprisonment, and police were posted in the streets with shears to clip the cloaks to the regulation length. At last on Palm Sunday 1766 a popular revolt broke out in the Plaza Antón Martín. When those who paraded in the offending cloaks and *chambergos* were challenged they resisted and a crowd gathered from all sides to assist them. "*Viva España* and death to Esquilache!" was the cry of the mob as they sacked the hated minister's house. When the Walloon guards of the King fired on the crowd, bands of insurgents attacked the them, murdered every one they could find, and the heads of the Walloons were carried through the streets on poles. After two days of street slaughter the King was forced to bow to the popular will. Esquilache was sent away disguised to Naples, foreign ministers were dropped and the Spaniards were allowed to wear the hats and cloaks they wished.

The King, though he gave way on externals, was grimly determined to have his own way in the government of the country. Knowing that the clergy were at the back of the resistance by the people against his decrees he appointed as President of the Council, Count Aranda, who was a zealous reformer and anticlerical. As a result, in 1767 the Jesuits were suddenly expelled from Spain, and six thousand unfortunate fathers were driven from their monasteries to various ports and shipped to foreign countries. Simultaneously orders were given to the Spanish colonies to drive out their Jesuits likewise. The Society founded by Saint Ignatius Loyola at Rome in 1540 had spread Christianity and Civilization all over the globe, but in the eighteenth century many enemies had risen against it. The Universities were jealous of the well-run Jesuit Colleges, the liberals and Voltaireans looked upon them as champions of Obscurantism, France and Portugal had already expelled them. The news of the Spanish expulsion, which Charles III explained as an "indispensable economical measure" fell like a thunderbolt upon Spain and the Papacy. The Holy Father Clement XIII preferred to abandon the Jesuits to their fate, though he had just defended their cause in a papal bull. His successor, Clement XIV, judging discretion the best policy, suppressed by decree the Society of Jesus throughout Christendom.

THE MADRID OF RAMON DE LA CRUZ

The reign of Charles III has always been considered the lull before the storm in the last years of the century, but it was by no means a period of tranquillity, for Spain was at war with England most of the time and in Madrid the riots against the hated foreigner Esquilache showed that the temper of the people was not to be trifled with, even in matters of dress. The riots, however, taught the King a lesson and he ceased to interfere with the traditional customs of the Madrileños, who, owing to increased prosperity under an able government, became welded into a compact society. Fortunately we are able to recapture the vigour, the charm and the animation of that society through the *sainetes* and *zarzuelas* of Ramón de la Cruz, who was acknowledged by all critics to be not only the greatest master of the one-act play, but also the greatest historian of Spanish social life and culture as it existed in the second half of the eighteenth century, and the immortal companion of the painter Goya.

Ramón de la Cruz y Cano was an aristocrat with democratic leanings and he began his career conscientiously endeavouring to write tragedies according to the French formula in vogue, but he soon became wearied of the *afrancesados*, who held their *cénacle* in the *Fonda de San Sebastián*, where they carried on the gallicizing traditions of the *Academia de Buen Gusto* founded by Luzán. Rámon de la Cruz soon recognized his own limitations and he realized that he would only succeed as a dramatist by shunning the literary dogmas of the day, by returning to Spanish traditions and writing with realism and humour as Spain's greatest writers had done. He chose as his form the *sainete*, which was one of the most ancient types of play in the Spanish theatre, for it went back

[1] M. A. S. Hume, *op. cit.*, p. 394.

through the *entremeses* of Quiñones de Benavente and Cervantes, to the primitive *pasos* of Lope de Rueda, when Spanish drama was in its swaddling clothes.

The origin of the word *sainete* is instructive and explains the significance of this theatrical genre. *Saín*, from which *sainete* is divided, was the piece of marrow which the hunter reserved for his falcon when it had brought down its prey, and from this it was applied to any dainty tit-bit agreeable to the palate, or to the sauce that seasons food. Finally, the word was used as a kind of dramatic tit-bit at the end of a full-length play. Ramón Pérez de Ayala, the celebrated modern novelist, in one of his witty essays compares the classical theatrical performances of the Spanish Golden Age to a copious and Lucullian banquet. First, he says, came the *loa* or apéritif; then the comedia with its three big *jornadas* or acts which corresponded to the joints. Between *jornada* and *jornada* there were the *entremeses* or *entremets* (the same word incidentally is used in Spanish restaurants today), and the *sainete* came at the end as *postre* or, as we would say, dessert. Ayala adds that the Spanish are a sober people and believe in abstinence, but when they do sit down to dine they do not stop eating until repletion (*no se detiene hasta el hartazgo*).[1] The *pasos* of Lope de Rueda, whom Jacinto Benavente calls "the Father of Spanish Drama", were simple "incidents", mostly of a humorous nature, and they were developed by Cervantes into such miniature masterpieces of universal appeal as the "Judge in Divorces" and the "Mayors of Daganzo". After him came Quiñones de Benavente (1589?-1651) who was called the Lope de Vega of the *entremés*, for he gave it its definitive form. He was a kindly man "who never spoke ill of a poet". All dramatists sang his praises, and they were right to do so, for a Benavente farce between the acts of a mediocre play used to be called the crutches which propped up its tottering carcase and saved it from disaster. Quiñones de Benavente, according to Cotarelo y Mori, wrote about nine hundred of these tiny farces and he was equally effective in supplying the verse of *bailes* or dramatized dances that were introduced in the seventeenth century at the end of the *jornadas* of a comedia.[2]

Ramón de la Cruz, in opposition to Moratín and the *afrancesados*, who wished to relegate Lope de Vega and Calderón to the background, strove to revive the ancient Spanish tradition by rejuvenating and amplifying these small-scale one-act plays, which do not last for more than twenty or twenty-five minutes. As Fitzmaurice Kelly says, Ramón de la Cruz's collection of these plays is a huge whispering gallery where we hear all the political and social gossip of the day; all the middle and lower classes of Madrid flit past us in a vivid and picturesque panorama, light-hearted, full of impertinent grace and wit.[3] But it is more than that, for Ramón de la Cruz gives us all the elusive poetry of Madrid life at a moment when the Madrid populace, under the wise and patriarchal government of Charles III, began to revive like plants in the spring after the long winter and find self-expression in their picturesque local festivals of song and dancing. Ramón de la Cruz laid the scene of most of his *sainetes* in the Plaza de Lavapiés, Plaza de Cebada, Calle de Toledo and the other streets that branch off the majestic Plaza Mayor, the scene of Spain's pageantry in the Golden Age.

After his first work for the stage, which was a *zarzuela* entitled *Quien complace a la Deidad*, Ramón de la Cruz wrote his first *sainete La Fingida Arcadia*, which, in spite of its technical flaws and crudities, is a characteristic little sketch of Madrid life describing the streets on a day of fiesta, the pilgrims on their way to the shrine of San Isidro, the labourer Saint of Madrid. The play contrasts the false artificial life of the aristocratic Arcadia of the eighteenth century, where we see shepherdesses à la Watteau, pirouetting ceremoniously and flicking their fans as they listen with bored expressions to the dull pastoral poems of their shepherd swains.

Nevertheless, these *madamas* and *petimetres*, as they were called in the fashionable Gallicisms of the day, became wearied of those tedious *tertulias* and they would prick up their ears when they heard in the distance the thrumming of the guitars in the street. The ladies would then shed furtively their party frocks, put on the short skirt and mantilla of the *manola* or *maja* and the men their ceremonious dresscoats, their waistcoats, wrap themselves up in the cloak and swagger-hat of the *manolo* or *majo*—and off they would hasten in search of the guitars. Even today we may follow those *majos* and *majas* through the Madrid of Ramón de la Cruz and Goya, for certain streets and squares are still haunted by the ghosts of the playwright, the painter and their heroines.

---

[1] R. Pérez de Ayala, *Máscaras*, Madrid, 1919, vol. II, pp. 131-132.
[2] E. Cotarelo y Mori, *Migajas de Ingenio ; Colección rarísima de Entremeses, Bailes y Loas*, Madrid, 1908.
[3] J. Fitzmaurice Kelly, *op. cit.*, p. 418.

The *majo*, let us not forget, was the street gallant of the eighteenth century and dressed himself in a costume reminding us of that of a bullfighter today but less gorgeous, more workaday. The *maja* was the incarnation of Goya's ideal of feminine beauty. In character she resembled the sparkling Colombina of Goldoni's Venetian plays—a playful, mischievous chatterbox, who flirted her way through life. Goya immortalized her in his two pictures the "*Maja* clothed" and the "*Maja* naked," which hang in the Prado, but the type appears again and again through his pictures of Madrid life. It was popularly believed that the beautiful Duchess of Alba, Madrid's heroine of the later eighteenth century, was the painter's mistress and malicious tongues gossiped indiscreetly. Although Aureliano Beruete the authority on Goya, refuted the idle tittle-tattle, it will not die, for what beautiful woman in history has not inspired *chroniques scandaleuses* about her private life? Probably if the ghost of the fair Duchess descended on earth from the Elysian Fields she would turn on the learned Beruete and rebuke him sharply for trying to deprive her of her supremacy as Madrid's ideal heroine.

When we consider the *maja* as the heroine of Spain, it is unfair to give all the credit to Goya, for Ramón de la Cruz in his one-act plays described her on the stage as brilliantly as the painter did on canvas. Ramón de la Cruz fought the battle for Spanish nationality no less than Goya did. He lived in the eighteenth century when Spain alternatively bowed the knee to France and Italy. He lived through the era of Farinelli and Voltaire, when Spanish serious drama was a weak imitation of foreign models, producing hundreds and hundreds of those little plays which are a treasure-house of wit and fancy. The life of the poor but picturesque people who lived in the neighbourhood of Plaza de Lavapiés and the descending street called the *Ribera de Curtidores* (the Bank of the Tanners) and today the Rastro, is the theme of these playlets. On moonlit nights those streets are still haunted by *majas* and *majos*: we still hear the sound of guitar and *bandurrias*, and in the distance we see the girls in their skirts and mantillas, flicking fans as they pass. By their sides swagger youths in white frilly shirt, tight fitting trousers and red sash. The air resounds with little folk songs called *seguidillas* and everyone dances. There is gaiety and joy in Lavapiés square, in spite of continual bickering. If a grumbler puts his nose out of a café and tells them all to stop laughing and shouting, he is hounded away like the *Refunfuñador* (the Growler) who has given his name to one of the amusing *sainetes* of the master. In each of these little plays we enter the lives of the humble inhabitants of these squares and streets, who spend nearly all their lives in the open. In one called the *Fandango de Candil* we watch them dancing under the moon; in *Las Gitanillas*, we take part in a gypsy revel which shows us how the Romanichals were transformed into "New Castilians" by Charles III's law. Instead of being excluded as pariahs and wild beasts they had come into the cities and were capitalizing their talents for singing, dancing and humorous guying and mimicry.

Other *sainetes* describe the great battles that sometimes took place between the *majas* of Lavapiés and the neighbouring streets and those from other quarters of the city.

One brilliant *sainete* of this type called *Los Panderos* (the Tambourines) is full of charm and humour. The battle begins when the girls from Barquillo invade Lavapiés singing and dancing to their tambourines. This annoys the leading *maja* of Lavapiés who calls herself Pantaleona. The *majas* from the two factions then challenge one another in verse, and there is a noisy tussle between the rival Amazons. The excitement spreads to both sexes and some *petimetras* or society ladies who are indulging in local colour become frightened and faint. But a round of night watchmen approaches and the fight stops. There is a procession, peace is made between the two warring bands and the *majas* dance with the *petimetras* who have recovered from their fainting fit.

Madrid has never lost its ancient tradition of the local festivals, which are called *verbenas*. The word *verbena* is a proof of antiquity, for the word originated with the fragrant plant. In the time of the ancient Romans the priests used to carry a branch of verbena as a symbol of their faith. They used to gather it on the second night of the summer solstice the twenty-third of June. Later on, the Christians converted the fiesta into a *romería* or religious festival, and a *romería*, we must remind the reader, was not all prayers and psalms as is proved by the old proverb, *Romería de cerca mucho vino y poca cera* (where there's a *romería*: plenty of wine but scarce a candle). There are *verbenas* in Madrid for all the sunny months of the year, in order to give the good-humoured populace of Madrid the excuse of going to the bullfight in the afternoon, the taverns in the evening and dancing in the plaza all the night until dawn.

166

Ramón de la Cruz did not limit himself to the *majos* and *majas* of the Lavapiés or Maravillas quarter: all social classes and all walks of life are depicted in his one-act plays. From the crowded streets we often find ourselves transported into the dressing-room of a lady of fashion, a *petimetra*.

But Ramón de la Cruz, like Goya, was the first to see that the real strength of Spain lay in the primitive and spontaneous qualities of the lower classes, and he was most attracted to his *majos* and *majas* of the people. Nevertheless, he was not a revolutionary and did not flatter the mob. On the day of the popular rising against the hated reformer Esquilache, Don Ramón had occasion to witness mob passion, and by irony of fate, he was forced to flee for refuge to the *Fonda de Sebastián*, where the cénacle of his inveterate enemies the neoclassic writers held their meetings.

The society described in the *sainetes* can be illustrated by earlier pictures of Goya which show us the *Pradera de San Isidro*, the *Romería* of San Antonio de la Florida, the flower-sellers, the popular picnicking on the banks of the Manzanares, the blindman's buff and the popular scenes he painted in 1780 for the royal tapestries. In the prosperous years of 1783 to 1792, Goya and Ramón de la Cruz were both patronized by the two queens of Madrid society, the beautiful young Duchess of Alba, Doña Maria del Pilar Cayetana de Silva y Alvarez de Toledo and the Duchess of Benavente and Duchess of Osuna, Doña María Josefa Pimental, "the most distinguished lady of Madrid", according to Lady Holland, and who had as much right to be considered a queen of Madrid Society in her time as Doña Cayetana. Indeed, the Countess of Yebes in her charming biography, which appeared in 1955, shows that the spirit of eighteenth-century Madrid was incarnated in those two ladies equal in rank though so unlike in temperament. [1] No two members of society excited greater interest or were the cause of so much gossip in aristocratic circles and among the people as these two friends and protectresses of Goya during his happiest and most triumphal period. The Duchess of Benavente was not beautiful but she possessed supreme elegance, and her wit and charm made her the arbiter of courtly life in the capital. Her greatest pleasure lay in striving to be like Madame de Rambouillet, a *Bas bleu*, presiding over literary academies and *tertulias*. Indeed, the *tertulia* as a literary gathering came into special predominance in her days, and inspired her protégé, Ramón de la Cruz, to make it the subject of a play. In the halls of Maria Josefa's palace in Madrid, or on the lawns of the Alameda de Osuna, on the outskirts of the city, which was called "the Caprice" (a name imitated from *les folies* of French aristocratic ladies) lovers of the artificial pastoral paradise of Rousseau and Bernardin de Saint Pierre used to gather, and Goya the primitive Aragonese was welcomed and encouraged to spread the wings of his genius.

We must now observe the great contrast between Goya's temperament and that of Ramón de la Cruz. The latter, too, possessed the faculty of "seeing at every pore" and when he was at a loss for the plot of a *sainete* for the theatre or for the private theatricals of the Duchess of Benavente in her palace in calle de Alcalá, all he had to do was to stroll out in the fashionable promenade of the Prado beneath the trees. In his pocket he had his notebook, in which he would jot down with a pencil the incidents that struck his fancy and later, at home, he would work up his play. Early next morning, the theatre copyists collected the manuscript. He drew his plays directly from life surrounding him, and in the introduction to the ten-volume edition of his works, he writes proudly the words: *Yo escribo y la verdad me dicta* (I write and truth dictates to me). What Ramón de la Cruz saw was the external truth, the outer mask of humanity, but not the deep underlying causes of events to come. He described the bright scenes of festive Madrid at a moment when there was a certain "insouciance" in the people, but he only rarely noted beneath the surface the signs of the coming storm.

Goya the Aragonese was of sterner mettle and was conscious of the tragic sense of life in the Spaniard. He was in many respects an unfathomable man and all the elegance of the Alba and Benavente palaces with their gay, frivolous society did not dispel his gloomy foreboding. He was fascinated by tales of spooks and witches and was spurred on to paint a series of macabre pictures by *La Dunciade, ou La Guerre des Sots* of Charles Palissot de Montenoy and the novel of Gaston d'Abad entitled *L'Antimystère, ou Les Sorcières de l'Espagne*. Goya, however, was no recluse: he used to spend long periods as guest in the Alameda and in one of his letters to Zapater, he boasts of his prowess as a sportsman with the gun.

[1] Condesa de Yebes, *La Condesa-Duquesa de Benavente, Una Vida en Unas Cartas*, Madrid, 1955, pp. 92-93.

The Duchess of Benavente, like the Duchess of Alba, was a great supporter of the theatre and music. While Doña Cayetana favoured Maria Rosario Fernández, known as La Tirana, who excelled in classical tragedy, Doña María Josefa inclined to the genuinely popular *sainete*. She erected a little theatre in her palace for which Tomás Iriarte wrote *zarzuelas* or musical plays. But her most assiduous callers were the two dramatists Leandro de Moratín and Ramón de la Cruz, who consulted her when they were writing their plays. To Ramón de la Cruz, her palace must have seemed a paradise, for his days were spent in drudgery in the State Accountant's office, and he and his family lived in a state of penury. It is remarkable how intimate were the relations between actors and actresses who lived the lives of vagabonds *sur la branche* and the great ladies of Spanish society. Some of the most interesting letters published by Countess Yebes are those that passed between Doña María Josefa and these wandering artists.

Ramón de la Cruz rendered another great service to the national theatre in the eighteenth century by his popularization of the *zarzuela*, the form which evolved out of the *entremés cantado* or miniature comic opera of Quiñones de Benavente in the previous century.

Rodriguez de Hita, who was, as the Spaniards say, a *madrileño legítimo*, and grew up in the atmosphere of the *majos* and *majas*, became a close collaborator of Ramón de la Cruz. The two produced a *zarzuela heroica* entitled *La Briseida* on July 11th, 1768, in the Teatro del Principe which marked an epoch. It was an attempt to write an opera with Spanish words and Spanish music, but with reminiscences of Italian operatic style. It was one of the first public performances in Spain which were given at night. In 1896 when the centenary of the death of Ramón de la Cruz was celebrated at the Ateneo, Madrid, Pedrell conducted the overture and some numbers of *La Briseida* which contain charming music.

In 1768 Ramón de la Cruz and Rodriguez de Hita achieved still greater success with *Las Segadoras de Vallecas*, a comic opera or *zarzuela burlesca* full of folksongs and with rustic characters from the villages near Madrid. In the following year 1769 the composer produced his masterpiece *Las Labradoras de Murcia* which deserves to be heard today, for no work evokes the popular atmosphere of Spain in the eighteenth century so effectively. It was revived by Pedrell in 1896. The plot is woven round the silkworm industry in Murcia, one of the provinces in Spain that has preserved unspoilt its folk traditions. In the *zarzuela* the *huertanos* or husbandmen play their native instruments and sing their folksongs in chorus in order to prevent the silkworms from hearing the thunder, which according to the old belief, damages them.

In the second half of the eighteenth century a new musico-dramatic genre became very popular in Madrid called the *Tonadilla escénica*. It was a kind of miniature comic opera and only lasted at most twenty minutes. Like the *sainete* or the seventeenth-century *baile* it served as an interlude between the acts of a full-length play. Ramón de la Cruz wrote the libretto for many of them, as for instance the *tonadilla* with music by Blas Laserna, which was sung and spoken by the Duchess of Alba herself, and accompanied by violins, oboes and horns. The little monologue describes her meeting with a handsome muleteer on her journey from Andalusia through La Mancha, who sang love songs accompanying himself on the guitar, and when she went to bed in the inn she stayed awake listening to him singing *seguidillas* below her window. According to José Subirá, whose volumes on the *tonadilla* are a treasure-house of eighteenth-century music, this art-form went through five stages of evolution: it appeared first of all in the year 1751 and, it is said that it was invented by the composer, conductor and woodwind-player Luis Misón (Missón). His first *tonadilla* was a simple musical dialogue between the landlady of an inn and a bohemian, but it became so successful that the composer was encouraged to write many more, always taking as his subject a simple scene of popular life in Madrid, and inspiring himself in the folk *seguidillas*. As J. B. Trend says, Missón's little works are genre pictures, the musical counterpart of the paintings and tapestries of Goya. After the second period of development in the years 1757-1770, we came to the apogee of the *tonadillas* in the years 1771-1790 when they were played to the music of Pablo Esteve, Blas Laserna, Pablo del Moral and lastly Manuel García, who is our link with Spanish music in the nineteenth century. After 1790 the *tonadilla* became more elaborate and infected with Italian virtuosity, and so lost its national popular characteristics that by 1810 it was in full decadence, though it did reappear from time to to time obscurely until 1850. [1]

[1] J. Subirá, *op. cit.*, p. 148.

As the *tonadillas* were an essential element in the creation of "Spanish style in music" which was largely a creation of the eighteenth century, it is important to note that they arose as a national reaction against the dictatorship of Italian singers and the Italian opera, for they could only be performed by singers born and bred in Spain and more particularly in Andalusia, such as *La Tirana*, the singer immortalized by Goya, *La Caramba* and Manuel Garcìa.   The *tonadilla* gave a glorious sense of freedom to the composer, for in it he could indulge in every variety of song or dance, and the stranger the name he could invent for his dance rhythms, the more applause he would win from the high-spirited tavern audiences of the *baile de candil*.   The Gypsies, who were famed throughout Andalusia for their skill in dancing, and had been for centuries engaged by the city council of Granada for the traditional dances in the Corpus Christi processions, exaggerated the wild, picaresque note of these dances, and even gave Gypsy names to some of them; as for instance to the lascivious *manguindoy* or begging-dance.   Henry Swinburne, an eighteenth-century traveller, says that it, as well as the *fandango*, had been imported from Havana, being both of negro breed.   Luis Missón in his *tonadilla*, *Lo que pasa en la calle de la comadre* (1760), includes the following characteristic *fandango*, which is sung off stage:

And in another *tonadilla* entitled *Los Ciegos* (1758), we have the following *jota* written for oboes, violins, voice and bass:

The *Tonadilla* was an elastic form and possessed immense variety: sometimes it consisted only of one character, as in the case of that sung and spoken by Doña Cayetana, the Duchess of Alba: but there were others for two, four and more characters, even up to twelve, and occasionally choruses were introduced.   At first many of them were markedly satiric and they depicted the folklore of diverse regions of the country, but in later days their defect was too much moralizing and preaching.   In the golden age of the *tonadilla*, composers like Esteve and Blas Laserna, following the procedure adopted by Ramón de la Cruz in writing his little plays, went out into the promenade of the Prado at sunset or in the crowded quarters of Lavapíes or Embajadores, when the streets rang with the street cries of pedlars, the songs of blind men at corners and the *boleros* and *seguidillas* of *Manolos* and *Manolas*. Take the following *Tirana del Zarandillo* from the *Tonadilla, Los Novios y la Maja* by Pablo Esteve y Grimau (1779) in which the *Maja* dances and sings as she hawks her baskets of oranges. She proudly claims that she is friendly to every man in the world, for she wheedles the old fogeys, makes fun of the youngsters and dazzles them all by her roguish pranks:

In our recording of the music of the eigthteenth century we have included a song from a *tonadilla* by Pablo Esteve (1730-1792). The song, *Alma sintamos**, is sung by Lolita Torrentó, soprano, with orchestral accompaniment under the direction of Raphael Ferrer.

Pablo Esteve in his early days scorned the *tonadilla* and consigned its authors and composers to perdition, but through the influence of Ramón de la Cruz and others he was tempted to try his hand at writing music for them, with the result that he and Blas Laserna (1751-1816) wrote over four hundred of them. Those two composers raised the *tonadilla* to its highest pitch of development and so successful were they that over a century later those works inspired the great composer Enrique Granados to create his *Goyescas*, which evoke the haunting beauty of eighteenth-century Madrid in the epoch of Ramón de la Cruz and Goya.

No song is better calculated to show the wide range of the *tonadilla* than the lovely song *Alma sintamos*, which might serve for the tragic aria in a grand opera by Gluck. And it is in this sense that the melody has been treated by the composer Joaquín Nin, who has heightened the tragedy of the song by the resources of modern orchestration.

There is an interesting story referring to the aria *Alma sintamos* explaining its tragic melody. One of the most celebrated singers of *tonadillas* was Maria Antonia Fernández (1751-1787) known as *La Caramba* because of the big bright-coloured bow she wore in her hair on the stage. She was unrivalled in wild Andalusian, Gypsy *polos* and *siguiriyas*, and especially for her magical way of intoning the long *Ay, Ay...* with which those songs always begin. In 1781 she married a Frenchman, but her volatile Gypsy temperament soon made life impossible for both, so she left him and returned to the Madrid theatre under the direction of Pablo Esteve. Her return to the stage was made the subject of a *tonadilla* which bore the title—*El Luto de Garrido por la Muerte de la Caramba* (The Mourning of Garrido for the Death of La Caramba) with music by Esteve. In the *tonadilla* the tenor (whose name, incidentally, was Garrido) laments over his poor Caramba who has just died, when she suddenly

* First Record, *Ancient Music*, side II, No. 8.

appears before him wrapped in a mantilla and her bright red bow, warbling in her inimitable way the *melismas* of an Andalusian Gypsy song.[1]

Occasionally, however, her gagging in her *tonadillas* landed her into trouble, as on one occasion when she hinted that the two rival queens of Madrid society, the Duchess of Alba and the Duchess of Benavente, were having love affairs with the two rival bullfighters Costillares and Pedro Romero. The two duchesses then appeared together before the Corregidor, demanding exemplary punishment for the actress, but she deftly shifted the responsibility on to the shoulders of her Maestro, Pablo Esteve, who was left to cool his heels in gaol, vowing he would never write another *tonadilla*.

It was characteristic of eighteenth-century irony to discover a genuinely tragic aria portraying a mock-tragic situation. The words are as follows:

> *Alma, sintamos! Ojos llorar!*
> *a mi Caramba que murió ya.*
> *Ay pobrecita! toda bondad,*
> *que no tenía pecado venial.*
>
> *Alma, sintamos! Ojos llorar!*
> *a mi Caramba que murió ya,*
> *a mi Caramba que murió ya,*
> *que murió ya, que murió ya.*

> Heart of mine suffer, eyes of mine shed your tears!
> for my Caramba has just passed away.
> Alas, poor thing, she was Goodness unalloyed,
> not even a venial sin her soul defiled.
>
> Heart of mine suffer, eyes of mine shed your tears!
> for my Caramba has just passed away,
> for my Caramba has just passed away,
> just died, just died.

 GOYA

In 1789, the year of the French Revolution, Goya not only became the Court Painter but the supreme arbiter of art in Spain and he was fêted everywhere by the aristocracy. The portraits he painted in those years show a dispassionate interpretation of Spanish history: we see the ministers of the Crown who strove to steer the ship of state: Aranda, the impulsive reformer, enemy of the Jesuits, and who had frequented Madame du Deffand's salon in Paris and had known Voltaire: Floridablanca, bright-eyed, intelligent, but with his beliefs still rooted in the old regime and unable to steer the ship in a storm: Manuel Godoy, the Queen's lover, to whom she entrusted all the affairs of state. Goya in that portrait painted in 1800, before the hurricane broke, shows Godoy as Lady Holland described him in her journal (1803): "Godoy", she says, "is a large, coarse, ruddy-complexioned man with a heavy, sleepy, voluptuous eye." The painter, however, was fairer to him than Richard Ford, who in later days compares him to "a foul beast of prey, always craving and swallowing". Probably the fairest judgment was given by Lord Holland, who after the Prince of Peace's fall wrote: "His manner, though somewhat indolent, or as the French term it, nonchalant, was graceful and engaging. In spite of his

---

[1] Joaquín Nin, *Quatorze Airs anciens d'Auteurs espagnols*, for music and words of the song. See also Grove's Dictionary, article on *La Caramba* by J. B. Trend.

education, which I presume was provincial and not of the best, his language appeared to me elegant, and equally exempt from vulgarity and affectation. Indeed his whole demeanour announced, more than that of any untravelled Spaniard I ever met with, a mixture of dignity and politeness, of propriety and ease... He seemed born for a high station—without effort he would have passed in any mixed society for the first man in it."

Goya in those years divided his time between his duties as Court Painter and being lionized by the aristocratic hostesses, all of whom were eager to be painted by him. Those years belong to what Beruete calls the master's grey period—the period when he was obsessed by the beauty of the Duchess of Alba. According to the biographers, he fell seriously ill in 1792 and was unable to paint until April 1794. This was his most serious illness since 1777 when his deafness came upon him. In a celebrated letter written in January 1794 to Bernardo Iriarte he describes how his infirmity, by keeping him apart from human society, actually drove him, as he said, to occupy his imagination, which was so mortified by the contemplation of his own infirmities *(para ocupar la imaginación, mortificada en la consideración de mis males)*. The works to which he here refers are those which today are exhibited in the Academia de San Fernando in Madrid, and Goya in the same letter describes them as works of a new kind in which the artist allowed caprice and invention to widen his vision. The words *imagination, caprice, invention* and *widening vision* are significant, for they show that Goya's infirmity had all of a sudden brought him face to face with a visionary personality within himself, whose existence he had not previously suspected.[1]

Such was the origin of the "Caprices" in which Goya expressed in satirical form the strange visions of his mind. The "Caprices" first revealed the coming Romantic movement, but they maintained the macabre mood of Goya's witch pictures. It is strange that these "Caprices" which we find today so difficult to interpret, did not cause greater sensation at the end of the eighteenth century, but this was probably because German writers like Bürger and such English writers as Mathew Gregory Lewis and Mrs. Radcliffe had already created a European vogue for tales of mystery and horror. One of the characteristic etchings of the "Caprices" shows the Duchess of Alba dressed as a *maja* with butterfly wings sprouting from her head, and with arms extended holding a cloak: she seems to be flying through the air upheld by a group of three bullfighters. The "caprice" is entitled *Volaverunt* and the painter must have meant by it to reproach the duchess for her giddy and variable temperament, for in the comment he says: "There are some heads so full of inflammable gas that they fly without any need of balloons or witches." This "caprice" is a reminder of the interest the duchess took in bullfighting, but according to her biographer Ezquerra del Bayo, although she enjoyed the colour and drama of the *corrida*, she was revolted by the slaughter of the animals. She showed preference for the theatre and during those years she became the pupil of the most famous tragic actress of the age, María del Rosario Fernández, *La Tirana*. *La Tirana*, we should add, received her nickname from her husband, the actor Francisco Castellanos, who specialized in playing tyrant parts. The duchess also was very fond of music and attended the Italian opera performances in the theatre of *los Caños del Peral*. Her husband, the Duke, was an accomplished clavecinist and lover of Haydn's music and had been a pupil of Padre Soler. In one of Goya's portraits we see him leaning against a clavecin holding an opened music score in his hands. In 1796, the Duke fell ill and he and the duchess left Madrid for their palace of *Las Dueñas* in Seville and there he died a few months later.

We next hear of the duchess at her palace at Sanlucar de Barrameda, where she spent a long period of convalescence after a serious illness. Although she was in mourning, her arrival at Sanlucar attracted many visitors, for as the traveller Fleuriot de Langle, who had visited Spain in 1784, says in his *voyage: Remplie de grâces et complètement belle, la duchesse est un prodige. Au Prado, au Retiro, à l'église, dans quelque lieu qu'elle soit, on court auprès d'elle, on ne voit qu'elle. Quand elle passe, tout le monde se met aux fenêtres: et les enfants mêmes quittent leurs jeux pour la regarder.*[2] It was in Sanlucar that Goya painted the famous picture of the Duchess in mourning, which

---

[1] E. Lafuente Ferrari, *Breve Historia de la Pintura Española*, Madrid, 1946, pp. 291-292.
[2] F. de Langle, *Voyage en Espagne*, 1784.

SEGUIDILLAS BOLERAS. Eighteenth-century dance print, from a series containing the main figures of the Seguidillas Boleras. This one shows the *Pase*.

UN PASAR DE LAS SEGUIDILLAS BOLERAS

hangs in the Museum of the Hispanic Society of America. Doña Cayetana is dressed as a *maja* in a black costume with a yellow jacket, a scarlet and gold sash about her tiny waist, and a black mantilla draped over her black curls. Her graceful aristocratic figure stands against a background of delicate blue sky and trees painted in tones of pale grey. On her right hand, she wears two rings: on one the name Alba is inscribed and on the other Goya. The painting was probably painted on the banks of the river Guadalquivir, near the woods of the Coto Doñana which in the sixteenth century had belonged to Doña Ana de Silva y Mendoza, the daughter of the Prince and Princess of Eboli.

The sudden death of the Duchess of Alba in 1802 came as a great shock, and the populace of Madrid, who were aware of the hostility that existed between her and María Luisa, believed that she had been poisoned by the Queen or by the latter's lover, *El Choricero*, as Godoy was nicknamed. So insistently did the public rumour grow that the King had to order an investigation, as is proved by the letter written by him to Godoy, which was discovered by the Marquis of Lema in the archives of the Royal Palace. The letter states that disloyal servants of the duchess had, after her death, rifled the safe containing her private papers. According to Ezquerra the motive of the royal letter to the Prince of Peace was to enable the Queen and Godoy to seize any compromising document that had been in the possession of the duchess, and to frighten her heirs into selling or presenting to the Crown the most famous pictures in the late duchess's gallery. Furthermore, María Luisa, who possessed the instincts of a vulture, sent a message before the funeral to the judge of wills saying that their Majesties wished to examine the pearls and diamonds left by the duchess. And so the Queen had the satisfaction of wearing publicly the jewels that had belonged to her hated rival. As for the pictures such as those of the *Majas*, they found their way to the gallery of the Prince of Peace.

In recent years the distinguished physician, Dr. Blanco Soler, who was the doctor of the late Duke and Duchess of Alba, has destroyed the legend of the Duchess of Alba which had been created by French romantic writers of the nineteenth century, who followed the biographies of Zapater and Goya's son.

What was not legendary, however, was the craving Goya felt for Doña Cayetana's divine beauty. She became for him the ideal symbol of womanhood. Her spirit tranquillized him when he was haunted by spooks and vampires from the tomb. He adored her with all the obstinacy of the true Aragonese *baturro*, for Aragonese he was by birth, though spiritually he was a Madrileño, as is shown by his ferociously satiric picture of the family of Charles IV, which makes all of them knavish in their malevolence. The fact that Goya was a mere painter and Doña Cayetana was Duchess of Alba is no proof that a love affair could not have taken place between them, and there is no doubt that the people in Madrid believed that Goya was a caprice of the duchess and allowed the painter to paint her in the nude, as a gesture of condescension of a great lady to a plebeian painter, but not because she was in love with him. It was an immodest *coup de tête* to dazzle the infatuated man, for she was tempted to test coldly to what limits the painter would go, who even when he painted her clothed seemed to undress her with his devilish paint brushes.[1]

In the end, we must agree with the Colombian writer, Eduardo Caballero Calderón that problems of historical interpretation are not transcendental, and an anecdote when it reveals a psychological reality is much more valuable. Historical data catalogued in a library are tombstones covering a corpse, whereas legend is like a ghost, all the world talks about it though nobody has seen it; it floats in the air and may reappear suddenly any dark night.[2] The legend of Doña Cayetana stamped her forever in the memory of the Madrid people and today, on Sundays, when the Prado gallery is visited by rich and poor, the greatest crowd always gathers round the Goyas, and as we walk through the streets of Madrid near the rebuilt Palacio Liria everyone thinks of Goya's Duchess; her legend spread from the *Maja desnuda*, although, according to a categorical statement in the official catalogue of the Prado, there is no doubt that the Duchess was not the model of either the naked or the clothed *maja*, and it adds that in the catalogue of Godoy's pictures, the two *majas* are called *gitanas*. Surely the divinely beautiful Cayetana—enthroned in Elysium among the other goddesses—must smile sweetly at the thought that here on earth her hated rival transformed her into a gitana. Legend or no legend the *maja* and the Duchess meet in Goya, for Cayetana could mix with the *chulos* and the *golfos*, as the street arabs are called

[1] Dr. C. Blanco Soler, *Esbozo psicológico, Enfermedades y Muerte de la Duquesa María del Pilar Teresa Cayetana de Alba*, Madrid, 1946.
[2] F. Caballero Calderón, *Ancha es Castilla*, Madrid, 1954, 3ª edición, p. 167.

175

in Madrid, without ever ceasing to be a duchess. The *gracia* or charm of the *maja* was genuinely Spanish and signified qualities of soul as well as body, and in the language of the Flamenco *aficionado* "the clothed Maja" has *angel* "the naked Maja" has *salero*, and both these qualities combine to create the mysterious power which García Lorca defined as *duende*—the melancholy little demon not bigger than the size of an unripe almond that made Descartes, when bored with lines and circles, go roaming along the banks of the river to hear the drunken sailors sing. Doña Cayetana, too, possessed that power which no philosopher can explain, and it is because Madrileños ever since have recognized the playful little demon in Goya's picture of the naked *maja* that Doña Cayetana, Duchess of Alba, remains eternally Madrid's ideal heroine. And when we listen to the *Goyescas* of Granados which the great composer recreated from the little folk *Tonadillas* of eighteenth-century Madrid the gran' Duchess presides amidst the *Majas*.

Goya's painting changed after the death of the Duchess, for when the break-up came and Spain was precipitated into war by the French invasion he used, as Beruete has pointed out, a gloomy, intense tonality in his military portraits which was in complete contrast to his "grey period". In the painting done in this period of the organist Pedro Mocarte, who posed dressed as a bullfighter in reddish-brown cloak, grey jacket embroidered in blue, black and silver, we note the atmosphere of gloom which envelops the scene.

After the battle of Trafalgar and the complete destruction of the Spanish fleet, Godoy's enemies turned to the Infante Fernando, and the people of Madrid rallied round him, with the result that the "Prince of Peace" was arrested and Charles IV abdicated in favour of his son Fernando on March 19, 1808. Napoleon, who had sent Marshal Murat with French troops to Madrid gave him orders to sow dissension between Charles IV and his son Fernando by hinting that the Emperor of the French would favour the old King's return to his throne. When Don Fernando first, and later Charles IV, María Luisa and Godoy had been enticed to Bayonne, Napoleon obliged Don Fernando to abdicate in favour of his father. But the father, through the infamous Godoy, had already signed a treaty with the Emperor whereby he renounced the throne and disinherited his sons and their descendants. At Madrid matters had gone from bad to worse, for Murat's haughtiness and high-handed methods had aroused public indignation. The explosion came when, in accordance with the Emperor's wish, Murat despatched Charles IV's grandson Don Francisco to France.

On May 2, when the carriage was ready to take the boy away, the populace of Madrid cut the traces, and the French troops fired on the mob. The fighting at first took place in the Puerta del Sol, but later shifted to the artillery park where two patriot leaders, Captain Luis Daoiz and Captain Pedro Velarde were killed. The heroism of these, the first two victims of the War of Independence, is perpetuated by a great statue in the Plaza de la Lealtad. Conde de Toreno, who was an eye-witness of events in Madrid that day, and tried desperately to secure the release of friends who had been arbitrarily arrested in the streets by Murat's soldiers, describes the grim silence of that night of May 2, when all that could be heard were the cries of the hapless victims, the rattle of the guns of the firing squads and the occasional distant booming of cannon.

But more vivid than any written description is the memorable picture which Goya painted of the execution next morning which he had witnessed. It is just before dawn but the sky is still blue black, and the yellow light of a lantern placed upon the ground illuminates the scene of horror as the troops of Murat mow down a small group of Spaniards, clustered upon the hill. The celebrated Catalan philosopher and art-critic Eugenio d'Ors has described the significance of the picture as follows: "In the centre of the group, the simple rustic stands erect with outstretched arms and the light from the lantern shines full on his chest, through the open shirt. He is hairy, almost black, grotesque, yet sublime; bumpkin, yet archangel, unknown, yet immortal: this rebellious Madrileño is for us the Revolution. I do not mean simply the political Revolution. He is this, but he is the other also—the revolution in culture, in art, the revolution that the Past tries to shoot and cannot. What do we see in this picture, looked at as a story? An execution. What do we see ideologically? The contrary, an apotheosis: a triumphal shout of liberty."

According to Eugenio d'Ors, Goya brings us to the extreme limit of romanticism. Painting ceases to exist: it is hardly even drawing. Here again, as in the painting of El Greco, the contemporary of Victoria, Music, the ruler of the subconscious reappears. Behind, immediately behind Goya is literature, and history, psychology, ethnology, folklore, satire, morals, humour... Nobody, as Eugenio d'Ors says, has been more instinctively a painter than Goya the psychologist, and nobody biographically so immoral as this moralist.

Even if Goya had not become the living symbol of Spanish painting, he would always be that of kaleidoscopic Spain. For this reason, Goya signifies Spanish painting for the great Spanish public, and they have come for almost a century to see the portraits of the Bourbons, and to see how the Spaniards attack the Bourbons, and to see how the Spaniards attack the French in Madrid on May 2 and how the French shoot the Spaniards on May 3.[1]

Old Spain perished in the cataclysm of the Napoleonic invasion and the War of Independence, and for Goya, who was sixty years of age in 1808, there followed many years of chaos and misfortune, in contrast to his former life of prosperity and adulation. What had happened to his other protectress, the witty Duchess of Benavente, for whose sunny artificial paradise, the *Alameda de Osuna* he had painted may graceful frescoes, and many macabre pictures, too, of warlocks and of witches' sabbaths? She and her husband had lived in Paris during the years of tension, when Napoleon on his return from his campaign in Egypt had been shouted down in the Council of the Five Hundred and only saved by the calm judiciousness of his brother Lucien. María Josefa and the Duke had been unpopular with Queen María Luisa, owing to their hostility to the favourite Godoy. But now after the rising of the Spanish people against the French invaders, the Duchess of Benavente became again the leading spirit among the ladies of the Spanish capital, and we can follow the vicissitudes of popular opinion through the comments of her servants and retainers which María Josefa details with gusto in her letters. She herself organized hospitals for the troops and first-aid shelters for the civil population of Madrid to whom she devoted herself indefatigably. She was a convinced partisan of England, and she said: "We good Spaniards must pray God to complete the ruin of Bonaparte, and let those with evil minds think what they please." Goya, whose whole life was darkened by the War of Independence, and who was old and deaf, retired to his country house *La Quinta del Sordo*, on the outskirts of Madrid, the walls of which he decorated with fantastic mural paintings.

Many subsequent writers have called in question Goya's patriotism in these war years, accusing him of accepting appointment as one of the court painters of King Joseph Bonaparte, of painting the portraits of French generals, and of painting the effigy of the French usurper which is still preserved in the Madrid City Hall. To all these accusations which are mean and irrelevant, Goya could reply that at such a time, when forces beyond human control were in the ascendant, all that was possible for him to do was merely to live, and live without indignity. We might, moreover, defend the patriotism of Goya, too, by recalling that between the first and second siege of Saragossa he was invited there by Palafox to paint the heroic exploits of his fellow countrymen, but, as Enrique Lafuente rightly says, such retrospective reputation-clearing is an insult to the memory of the great master.

The truth is that Goya's reaction to the bloody spectacle of total warfare was nobler and more honourable than any resolution taken by a party man. The works in which he shows his vision of the cataclysm are not a national chronicle of a war of liberation, but a terrifying document revealing man's bestiality and his capacity for evil. The heroism of Goya consisted in not lying and in condemning the cruelty and crime lust of mankind, without letting himself become intoxicated by rhetoric.[2]

With the exception of a small number of portraits, most of the artistic activity of the master between 1808 and 1814 was devoted to drawing and engraving *Los Desastres de la Guerra*. These sombre etchings of battle scenes, savage attacks, maimed and mutilated victims reflect the hopeless and endless misery of war. In one of them, selected at random, we see mutilated soldiers being carried away by their comrades on stretchers, and underneath the painter has written sardonically: *Aún podrán servir* (They still may serve). Ramón Gómez de la Serna, one of the recent biographers, who has penetrated most deeply into Goya's mind, has stressed the underlying humour in the work of Goya. He was a humourist, but one like Jonathan Swift, for it was savage indignation that inspired him to depict those terrible scenes. Like Swift, he was tortured by the daily vision of *la bête humaine*, and in his pictures he did not see with the limpid eyes of Velasquez. Goya like Swift believed that

[1] E. d'Ors, *Tres Horas en el Museo del Prado*, Madrid, 1940, pp. 81-82.
[2] E. Lafuente Ferrari, *op. cit.*, pp. 295-296.

there is no animal uglier than man: Swift calls him in *Gulliver's Travels*, Yahoo, and he prefers the wise horses —the Hounyhms. Because all flowers are beautiful, an artist thinks that all women should be beautiful, but in the human species flowers are rare, and for one lovely Duchess Cayetana we meet a swarm of hideous monsters whom Goya reproduces in his "Caprices". The hideousness of old age, sickness, decay and the eerie visions of ghosts, witches, vampires and devils tormented the mind of the Spanish painter night and day as they did the half-insane Irish writer and clergyman Swift, when he was writing his "Journal to Stella". The tendency towards the macabre goes far back in Spanish literature, even to the Middle Ages, but it became an obsession when the paintings of Brueghel and especially Jeronymus Bosch (one of the favourite painters of Philip II) were the fashion in Spain. Quevedo in his *Sueños* is the great forerunner to Goya in the cult of the macabre, but we even find traces in Velasquez, whose luminous conception of life did not banish the many grotesque dwarfs who throng his gallery. In fact their quaint deformities served to set off the tender beauty of the Infanta Margarita in *Las Meniñas*. Cervantes, too, did not neglect the macabre, for into his colloquy of the "Dogs", he introduces the grisly description of the witches Camacha and Cañizares. After Goya, the tradition continued in painting up to our days, in Zuloaga's Segovian dwarfs and Picasso's fantasies whose literary counterparts are the grotesque *esperpentos* of the Celtic poet Ramón del Valle Inclán. Goya had created the symbol of all that cult of the macabre in the "caprice" *El Sueño de la Mentira y de la Inconsciencia*, wherein we see grotesque witch-monsters, with bat's wings flying round the nymph Cayetana.

The sublime bumpkin of Goya's picture *The Shootings of May 3* is Emperor of the seething, haunting mob of ragamuffins, *majas*, dandies, beggars, bandits, bullfighters, soldiers, friars, nuns, harlots, witches, hobgoblins, donkeys and the rest of the grotesque phantasmagoria which, as Goya himself tells us in the caption of one of his etchings, surge up in the mind when reason dreams.[1]

[1] E. d'Ors, *op. cit.*, 1940.

Goya (born at Fuendetodos, Aragón, 1746, and died at Bordeaux, 1828).
Self-portrait, Frontispiece of the Caprices.
Scene of shooting from "The Disasters of the War", Etching by Goya, 1810.

179

Parochial festival at Valencia 1862.   An engraving by A. Rouargue of a theatrical performance in a courtyard.
It recalls the *corrales* or vineyard of the ancient Spanish comedia.

Chapter XV

THE SPANISH MUSICAL
DEMON SPREADS ITS WINGS

We have reached now the end of our journey through the eighteenth century, and with Goya as guide we are launched into the nineteenth century which was an age of chaos, disintegration and civil conflict for Spain.

The personality of Goya radiated influences all over the Spanish world in art, music and literature, but these influences did not produce their full effect in the nineteenth century with its increasing faction-fights within Spain, and we note them in more marked fashion in foreign countries like France, England, Germany and Russia that were quicker to seize the implications of the Goya revolution.

It was not until our century that we find in Ortega y Gasset's *Meditaciones del Quijote* (1914) a clear distinction between the two great currents of European thought, the Germanic and the Latin.[1] The term Latin culture, he says, has given rise to a fundamental error.   The Latin races of today, the French, the Italians and the Spanish, have the weakness of considering themselves the heirs to the Greek spirit, and up to recent times Greece and Rome were always called the two classical peoples.   Nowadays, since philology has advanced in knowledge, it is recognized that Greece stands outside as the directing force of European culture, whilst Rome, in spite of its imitative qualities, was never able to collaborate with the Greek spirit.   "The Romans are a Mediterranean people, and theirs is not a Latin but a Mediterranean culture."

"For twenty centuries", Ortega continues, "the people of the Mediterranean have enrolled their artists beneath the banner of impressionist art.   For the Greek the object seen is governed and corrected by the thought, and it only becomes of value when it ascends to be a symbol of the ideal.   For the Mediterranean peoples this ascension becomes a descent: the Mediterranean is a perpetual justification of sensuousness, of appearance, of surface, of the fugitive impressions which react on our nerves when moved.   Mediterraneans do not think clearly, they see clearly.   For the Mediterranean the most important is not the essence of a thing but its presence, its actuality.   To things he prefers the lively sensation of things.   The result of this impressionist culture in Spain, at any rate, has been to impede progressive culture.   For each impressionist starts, as it were, from scratch, and has to create his own world, unlike the man who can seize the torch from his predecessors and continue from that point the race.   Such has been the history of Spanish culture."

[1] J. Ortega y Gasset, *Meditaciones del Quijote*, Madrid, 1914.

In speaking of Goya, Ortega writes: "Our great men are characterized by Adam the first man; a man without age or history. Goya represents—like Spain, perhaps—a paradoxical form of culture; the primitive culture that knew no yesterday, without any progression or security for the future; a culture perpetually struggling with what is elemental, and fighting daily for possession of the ground on which it stands. In a word, frontier culture."

And the great significance of Goya the Adam was not fully understood until today, and he must be considered the great link between the age of Farinelli and Ramón de la Cruz, the era of virtuosi and the nationalistic *tonadilla* and the revival in the later nineteenth century with Pedrell, Albéniz and Granados leading to Manuel de Falla. Goya exercised as deep an influence over music and the theatre in the nineteenth and the twentieth centuries as he did in painting, for even before he passed away in 1828 in Bordeaux the inhabitants of the Spain he had painted had begun to cross the frontier to other lands. In 1820, when Fernando VII felt quite sure that he had crushed all opposition and could reign henceforth as absolute monarch, he received the news of the revolt of Riego at Cabezas de San Juan and two months later the liberal movement had extended to the whole country. This was the first blow against the political system imposed by the Holy Alliance after the final rout of Napoleon and it was celebrated by Shelley in his Ode to Liberty:

> A glorious people vibrated again
> The lightning of the nations: Liberty
> From heart to heart, from town to town, o'er Spain,
> Scattering contagious fire into the sky,
> gleamed...

The Liberal revolt, which was based on the Constitution of Cadiz in 1810-1812 (when the word "liberal" was used for the first time and spread from there to France and England) produced its first counter-movement of reaction in Austria under Metternich and then in 1823 in France, when the "Sons of Saint Louis" invaded Spain on a "crusade", as it was called by the author of *Les Martyrs du Christianisme*, and reimposed the reactionary old order. "To be a liberal in Spain", said Larra later, "is to be a potential émigré, and a number of those who had to flee into exile in 1823 were doing so for the second time in ten years."[1] The "émigrés" in those years found Gibraltar a convenient stepping-place to their home in exile, England, and through the Rock they maintained their contacts with the Liberals in Andalusia and the east of Spain. The expatriation of the Liberals lasted about ten years and, during the first six years, London was their main political centre, but in consequence of the July Revolution of 1830 most of the exiles went to live in France. The "émigrés" were of all classes and conditions of men.

While in Spain Fernando VII imposed his absolutism by all the means granted to him by bayonets, censorship and the Inquisition, the intellectuals, who acquiesced in the tyranny, hid their lack of talent under the cloak of another absolutism, namely, the tyrannical pseudo-classical rules of the French, and openly expressed their abomination of the ancient Spanish literature. They ruled in Spain, but the distinguished patriots who were driven abroad by persecution verified the truth of Victor Hugo's dictum that Romanticism is liberalism in art. Of no country is that saying truer than of Spain, says Menéndez Pidal in his passionate review of this period of his country's fortunes. "In the Peninsula", he adds, "the great romantics were also the great liberals, who suffered persecution under Fernando VII, in contradistinction to France where it so happened that the romantics were absolutists and the classicists were rebels."[2]

The expatriated writers found to their surprise in London an important movement in progress in favour of the ancient Spanish literature which was so despised within Spain's frontiers, and by a curious coincidence the movement started at the same time from England and Germany. In England from the very first year of the nineteenth century the poet Robert Southey had made Spanish legends and epics the source of his poems, and he had also translated the *Poem* and *The Chronicle of the Cid*, the *Amadis* and the *Palmerin* and rebuked the

---

[1] V. Llorens Castillo, *Liberales y Románticos: Una Emigración Española en Inglaterra*, Mexico, 1954, pp. 15, 31, 58.
[2] R. Menéndez Pidal, *La Epopeya Castellana*, pp. 215-216.

Spaniards for not revering the first monument of their literature. Then came Walter Scott with his poem, *The Vision of Don Roderick* (1811). Simultaneously in Germany, Herder, who was enchanted by what he called "the voice of peoples", produced an adaptation of the Cid ballads (1802) which became a classic. And at the same time the brothers Schlegel delivered public lectures on the ancient theatre of Spain, and one of the two, Frederick, produced at Weimar a tragedy based on the old ballad of Count Alarros, which, he claimed would lead to the creation of a true German national drama.

As a result of this pioneer movement in Germany and England, the French, too, began, though later, to consider the Spanish epic themes as an essential part of their romantic movement and it is interesting to note that the invocation of the *almogávares* to their sword: *Hierro despiértate* (Iron awake!) is the motto of one of Victor Hugo's *Orientales*, and the Spanish word *hierro* was the war cry adopted by five hundred writers of La Jeune France, when dressed in Spanish cloaks they paraded for battle on the first night of *Hernani*.

It was England, however, that became the favourite refuge of the Spanish "émigrés" and, as Menéndez Pidal says, the initiator of Spanish Romanticism. He explains, however, that Romanticism in Spain was more in the nature of a restoration than a revolution, for its fundamental idea was the rehabilitation of literature and national traditions.

For this reason the "émigrés" in London devoted themselves enthusiastically to the arts, especially to music. In instrumental music the most Spanish of all instruments, the guitar, was already so popular in England that the great virtuoso Fernando Sor (1778-1839) was invited to play at one of the Philharmonic Society's Concerts, and became a fashionable teacher in London. He like Padre Soler was a pupil of the *Escolanía* at Montserrat and produced with great success his opera *Telémaco* at Barcelona in 1795. From Madrid, where he composed quartets and songs with guitar, he set out for France and enlisted in Paris as a volunteer in the army of Napoleon, reaching the grade of captain. At the end of the war he settled in Paris, where he became celebrated as a guitarist and enjoyed the protection of Cherubini and Méhul. During the Napoleonic invasion of Spain in 1809 he fled to London.[1] His studies for the guitar have received world-wide recognition through being included in the programmes of the great guitarist Andrés Segovia.

THE MUSICAL DYNASTY OF THE GARCIA FAMILY FROM 1775 TO 1946

Among the "émigrés" in London in the early nineteenth century nobody enjoyed greater prestige than the celebrated Sevillian singer and composer Manuel García, who arrived there to sing in opera accompanied by his son Manuel and his two daughters, María Felicia (afterwards Madame Malibran) and Paulina (afterwards Madame Viardot).

Manuel García was an extraordinary personality, and as he created a most important musical dynasty which lasted until our own days it is necessary to describe his origins. Like so many other great Spanish musicians whom we have met on our musical journey through Spanish history he grew up in the shadow of the First Master, Saint Isidore, for he was a chorister in Seville Cathedral and was educated in the *Escolanía* by Juan Almarca and Antonio Ripa. He showed such extraordinary talent in singing that at seventeen he was given a contract to sing in the theatre at Cadiz and took part in a *tonadilla* which he himself had written for the occasion. A few months later he went to Malaga where he produced with great success his first opera *El Preso*. In Madrid in 1779 he made his debut as tenor and won instant popularity owing to his magnificent voice and his Andalusian charm in singing *tonadillas*. It is important to stress the success García won by his *tonadillas*, for these short musico-dramatic compositions were destined to be the link between the ancient Spanish music and the modern, and created what we know today as "Spanish Style".

From Madrid he went to Paris where he won his great triumph with his opera *El Poeta Calculista*. It contains the celebrated song of the smuggler entitled *Yo que soy contrabandista*, which became immediately

[1] A. Miro-Bachs, *Cien Musicos célebres Españoles*, Barcelona, 1942, p. 87.

popular all over France and Spain and was published in the wellknown collection of Spanish songs by Ocón. From Paris García passed to Italy where he won fame in Naples, Turin and Rome as singer and orchestral conductor. It was in Rome that he made friends with Rossini who wrote specially for him the opera *Elizabetta*, and entrusted him with the part of Count Almaviva in the first performance of the *Barbiere di Siviglia* in 1816. There is a tradition in Italy that the serenade sung by the tenor in the first act was by García, who sang it to his own guitar accompaniment. Such success did Manuel García win in Italy that the King of Naples, Murat, nominated him first tenor and Maestro of his Chapel Royal, and owing to this honour his opera *The Caliph of Bagdad* was produced in the Teatro San Carlo in Naples. We next find him in Paris where he sang with great success in *Il Matrimonio segreto* of Cimarosa in *Le Théâtre italien*, and from there he went to London.

Many amusing stories are told by contemporaries of García's methods as teacher of singing and director of opera. Like Leopold Mozart he took infinite pains with his children's musical education and trained them himself from the tenderest age, but his singing-lessons were generally accompanied by a tempest of pinches and slaps which he bestowed indiscriminately upon his son and the two young prima donnas María Felicia and Paulina. The two girls were not only exceptionally talented in music, but also in dancing and painting, and were able to play a sonata of Bach with the same ease as they sang an aria of Rossini. As for folk-songs, their repertoire varied from Scottish to Neapolitan and songs from their land of origin, Andalusia. In addition, they spoke the chief European languages fluently and were bright and witty in conversation.

According to the English actress Fanny Kemble, the "début" of María Felicia on June 7, 1825, was "the absolute conquest of a nation", and many of the "émigrés", even those who could ill afford it, turned up in the theatre because the ex-bullfighter Muselina sold to them at a low price the tickets that had been given to him by Manuel García.[1] As a result of her triumph María Felicia was engaged for the remainder of the season (about six weeks) at £500. Manuel García then founded a company to perform operas in New York, and set out in 1825 with his wife, his son and two daughters and a number of Italian singers. The début of the company at the Park Theatre, New York, was such a triumph that in the course of the season the company performed nine new operas, and in 1827 went to Mexico where after two years of uninterrupted success they prepared to return to Europe with their earnings. Alas, on the way to Vera Cruz to embark for Europe, they were waylaid by bandits and robbed of all their possessions, including £6,000 in gold. Manuel García, however, possessed the personality of a conquistador, and was undaunted by adversity. We next find him in Paris striving to compete with the most famous tenors of the day. Feeling, however, after a time that his voice was failing, he devoted himself to teaching, and published a *Complete Treatise on the Art of Singing*, which was regarded universally as a masterpiece. He died in Paris on June 2, 1832. Manuel García, in addition to his great powers as singer and actor, possessed original talents as composer and librettist, and wrote both music and words with equal facility. His prolific genius was characteristically Spanish, and according to the catalogue published by Fétis he composed forty-four operas.

[1] Llorens Castillo, *op. cit.*, p. 58.

From an unpublished picture of La Malibran. A painting of the English school belonging to Mr. Edward Whettnall, great-grandson of the celebrated singer, who has kindly authorized its reproduction. It was Alfred de Musset who sang the praises of the great prima donna in a poem published in the *Revue des Deux Mondes* (Oct. 15, 1836). He mourns her early death due to her sacrifice of her life to her art:

Oui, oui, tu le savais, qu'au sortir du théâtre,
Un soir dans ton linceul il faudrait te coucher.
Lorsqu'on te rapportait plus froide que l'albâtre,
Lorsque le médecin, de ta veine bleuâtre
Regardait goutte à goutte un sang noir s'épancher,
Tu savais quelle main venait de te chercher.

The extraordinary success of his eldest daughter Felicia enhanced the fame of Manuel García's family in Europe and America. In New York she appeared in Mozart's *Don Giovanni*, Rossini's *Otello*, *Tancredi* and *Cenerentola*. The last named work, which was written for a mezzo-contralto, is an opera that requires exceptional qualities in technique and range of voice, but Felicia took the public by storm, and, in addition, her father wrote two operas for her entitled *L'Amante astuto* and *La Figlia dell'Aria* which increased her popularity with American audiences. Manuel García, however, was a despotic father, and in the midst of all his daughter's success he married her off to Malibran, an elderly French banker who masqueraded as a man of great wealth. The marriage was an unhappy one and only lasted a year, for Malibran went bankrupt and Felicia, as soon as she could obtain a separation, left the old curmudgeon and returned to Paris, where she triumphed in Rossini's *Semiramide*. In London when she appeared in 1829 she shared the honours with Henrietta Sontag, the great Austrian singer who had taken part in the first performance of the *Ninth Symphony* in the presence of Beethoven. When Sontag married and retired from the stage María Malibran had no rival and sang each season in Paris and London with unfailing success, and on many occasions such was the enthusiasm of the audience at the performances that her horses used to be taken from her carriage, which was drawn to the hotel by the enthusiastic crowd. At Venice her arrival at the theatre was announced by a fanfare of trumpets. In Paris she fell in love with the celebrated violinist Charles de Bériot, and when her marriage to Malibran was annulled she married him and they built a villa near Brussels to which they used to retire between her tours. She was also attached to Alfred de Musset, who wrote one of his most lyrical poems to her beauty and artistry.

She belonged to the generation of Bellini and in her singing personified the divine Italian melody of that genius who was 'fair as the corn, sweet as an angel, young as the dawn', as his black-eyed mistress Giudetta Turina said of him, and whose restless, consumptive genius wore itself out before its time. Death, which his friend Heine called his *jettatore*, withered both with fatal glance, for only a year after María Felicia had stood weeping at Bellini's graveside in Paris with Cherubini, Chopin and Rossini she herself ended her brilliant life in September 1836 during the Manchester festival.

Her voice was exceptional owing to its musical range from soprano to contralto, which enabled her to sing with ease such operas as *La Cenerentola*, but her contemporaries continually refer to the moving timbre of her voice and to her extraordinary talent for improvization. It is interesting to add that in our days *La Cenerentola* was revived in London by another famous Spanish prima-donna, Conchita Supervía, whose brilliant virtuoso qualities as a soprano-contralto were enhanced by the peculiar Spanish pathos of her voice which endeared her to her audiences.

María Felicia's younger sister Paulina (1821-1910) was no less precocious as a child and played her father's accompaniments at his singing lessons, but did not appear in public as a singer until 1837, after her father and sister were dead. Nevertheless she became at once a celebrity in Europe, owing to her amazing vocal technique which enabled her to sing even such bravura songs as the *Cadence du Diable*, which was based upon Tartini's *Trillo del Diavolo* violin Sonata. In Paris when she was engaged by Louis Viardot, the writer and critic of the *Revue independante* and Director of the *Théâtre italien*, she shared the triumphs of such singers as Lablache Tamburini and Grisi. After her marriage to Viardot she appeared regularly every year in Paris and London, especially in the chief role in *Le Prophète* by Meyerbeer, which according to Moscheles, owed half its success to her singing and acting. After retiring from the stage, Madame Viardot-García became celebrated as a teacher and transmitted the methods she had learned from her father to a number of singers, such as Marianne Brandt and Antoinette Sterling who achieved world fame. It is interesting to note that Schumann dedicated to her his song Cycle op. 24., and she was the first to take part in Brahms's *Rhapsodie*, op. 53. Even at the end of her life Madame Paulina Viardot-García was the chief member of a literary and artistic coterie and many writers from all over Europe have described their visits to her salon in Paris.

Manuel Patricio García (1805-1906), the brother of Felicia and Paulina, made his début in New York in 1825 in the *Barbiere di Siviglia*, playing Figaro to his father's Almaviva, his mother's Berta and his sister María Felicia's Rosina. Four years later, however, in Paris he gave up the stage and devoted himself to the scientific problems of vocal production. As a result of his researches he invented the laryngoscope, the value of which has been universally recognized by physicians and artists. In 1842 he was appointed professor of singing at the Paris Conservatoire where he trained some world-famous prima-donnas, including Jenny Lind, Mathilde Marchesi and Catherine Hayes.

Summing up his own father's teaching methods he published two books which attained world celebrity and were translated into Italian, German and English: *Mémoires sur la Voix humaine* (1840) and *Traité complet de l'Art du Chant* (1842). In 1848 he was appointed professor at the Royal Academy of Music in London and held the post until 1895. In 1905 his hundredth birthday was celebrated by a banquet, and his portrait painted by J. S. Sargent was presented to him.

Thus Manuel García père, originally a singer, was first to spread "the Spanish Style" to Europe and the American continent through his own works and through his family, who constituted a dynasty of song lasting over a hundred and seventy-one years until the death in 1946 of Albert García, grandson of Manuel II, baritone and professor of singing at the Royal College of Music in London. The García dynasty began in the days of Goya and Ramón de la Cruz, in the heyday of the *tonadilla*, when the English traveller William Beckford visited Madrid in 1787 and described in his diaries the contrast between the Spanish and Italian music of the day.

The passage in the diaries of the celebrated author of *Vathek* is worth quoting, for it explains the distaste felt by the classical musicians for the exotic rhythms and chromaticism of Spanish folk music.

The party which Beckford attended was given in the palace of a wealthy Portuguese gentleman in Madrid, Pacheco by name, and the Duchess of Osuna, our familiar friend María Josefa, had lent the conductor of her private orchestra, Maestro Boccherini, the famed composer, for the event.

From the outset the eccentric Englishman scandalized the aristocratic gathering assembled in stiff gala costume by appearing in what he called his "dancing dress", which was that of a *majo*, "with ties and tags and trimmings and buttons, redecilla and all".

After listening to some doleful oriental music which had been arranged for the Turkish minister, Beckford insisted on dancing a *bolero* and the Spanish musicians came down from their formal orchestra, only too happy to escape from its trammels. As for the foreign regular musicians they went away, taking vehement pinches of snuff, with the most unequivocal expressions of anger and indignation.

Beckford describes the scene as follows: "A circle was soon formed, a host of guitars put in immediate requisition and never did I hear such wild, extravagant, passionate modulations.

"Boccherini, who led and presided over the Duchess of Osuna's concerts, and who had been lent to Pacheco as a special favour, witnessed these most original deviations from all established musical rule with the utmost contempt and dismay. He said to me in a loud whisper: 'If you dance and they play in this ridiculous manner I shall never be able to introduce a decent style into our musical world here, which I flattered myself I was on the very point of doing. What possesses you? Is it the devil? Who could suppose that a reasonable being, an Englishman of all others, would have encouraged these inveterate barbarians in such absurdities? There's a chromatic scream! There's a passage! We have heard of robbing time; this is murdering it. What! again! Why, this is worse than a convulsive hiccup, or the last rattle in the throat of a dying malefactor. Give me the Turkish howlings in preference; they are not so obstructive and impudent.'

"So saying he moved off with a semi-serious stride and we danced on with redoubled delight and joy. The quicker we moved, the more intrepidly we stamped with our feet, the more sonorously we snapped our fingers the better reconciled the Sublime Effendi appeared to be with me. He forgot my critiques upon his vocal performers; he rose up from his snug cushion and nodded his turbaned head, and expressed his delight not only by word and gesture, but in a most comfortable orientalist sort of chuckling. As to the rest of the company, the Spanish part, at least, they were so much animated, that not less than twenty voices accompanied the *bolero* with its appropriate words in full chorus and with a glow of enthusiasm that inspired my lovely partners and myself with such energy that we outdid all our former outdancings.

"'Is it possible', exclaimed an old fandango-fancier of great notoriety, 'is it possible, that a son of the cold North can have learnt all our rapturous flings and stampings?'—'The French never could or rather never would', observed a Monsieur Gaudin, one of the Duke de la V.'s secretaries, who was standing by perfectly astounded."

The above passage from Beckford is an excellent illustration of the century-old contest in Spain between the classical music introduced from Italy into the aristocratic salon and royal theatre and the traditional music which continued its impetuous course among the people of Spain through the dancing of the *majos* and *majas* in the *sainetes* of Ramon de la Cruz and the *tonadillas* of Blas Laserna and Pablo Esteve. Already Doña Cayetana Duchess of Alba, under the influence of Goya, had been converted to the *boleros* and *seguidillas*, and now we find as early as 1787 an eccentric Englishman shedding his national phlegm and falling victim to the devilish rhythm like one of the Bacchants haunted by the god Dionysus. Even he was surprised at his own temerity, for he adds: "Who are so virulent against their former sect as fresh converts to another? This was partly my case; though my dancing and musical education had been strictly orthodox, according to the precepts of Mozart and Sacchini, of Vestris and Gardel, I declared loudly there was no music but Spanish, no dancing but Spanish, no salvation in either art out of the Spanish pale, and that, compared with such rapturous melodies, such inspired moments, the rest of Europe afforded only examples of dullness and insipidity: the British and American ministers, who were standing by the whole time, enjoyed this amusing proof of Spanish fanaticism in its profane mood. Pisani, the Venetian ambassador, inclined decidedly to the Southern side of the question. He was bound, heart and soul, by a variety of silken ties to the Spanish interest, and had almost forgotten the fascinations of Venice in those of Andalusia. Consequently I had his vote in my favour. Not so that of the Duchess of Osuna, Boccherini's patroness. She said to me in the plainest language: 'You are making the greatest fool of yourself I ever beheld; and as to those riotous self-taught hoydens, your partners, I tell you what, they are scarcely worthy to figure in the third rank at a second-rate theatre.'" [1]

William Beckford was the first enthusiastic convert to the Spanish rhythms, and soon the Spanish war of Independence, the revolution of Goya and the vagabond dynasty of Manuel García and the Spanish "émigrés" would carry the Andalusian *duende* or demon all over Europe and the Americas. During the course of the nineteenth century we find certain *castizo* Spanish authors devoting themselves to the close study of the traditional dances of the various regions of the Peninsula. Among them none more suggestive than Estébanez Calderón *(El Solitario)*. As Salillas says, he was one of the Spaniards who by his temperament and literary style seemed to be a survivor from the past ages when Spain was triumphant. Estébanez Calderón, in a very significant essay entitled *Baile al Uso y Danza antigua*, states that in Spain, which was the crucible in which so many races and peoples were fused together, it is possible to find relics of the ancient methods which men have used to express their passions and affections, whether fierce and bloodthirsty or else soft and voluptuous. In the *jota* of Aragon and in other dances of Catalonia and the Pyrenees, he says, we still discover traces of the Greek dances of antiquity. In the Basque provinces he agrees with the patriarchal folklorist Itzueta (in the latter's *Guipuzcoaca Dantza*) that the *Zortzicos* and other martial dances show reminiscences of the Iberian and Celtic dances. As for the *crótalo* or castanets, they recall the festivals which the people of Latium held in lonely wooded glens and valleys, in honour of the god of gardens. In Andalusia, on the other hand, we meet oriental influences and discover relics of ancient *Zambras* mingled with dances which have come from the remote districts of the Eastern and Western Indies. Even before *El Solitario*, the English traveller Swinburne, who like Beckford was a pioneer of the "Spanish style", has stated in his *Travels in Spain in 1775 and 1776* that the Gypsy dance he saw in Cadiz called the *Manguindoy* and which he calls "a lascivious and indecent *fandango* prohibited under severe penalties, was imported from Havannah, being both of them of negro breed." "Whatever may have been the birthplace of the *fandango*", continues Swinburne, "it is now so thoroughly naturalized in Spain, that every Spaniard may be said to be born with it in his head and heels: I have seen a child of three years of age dance it to the mother's singing, with steps and turns scarce to be credited in an infant of that age. Towards the close of the great balls given heretofore in the theatre, when all the company appeared drooping with fatigue and over-powered with sleep it was a constant trick of the fiddlers to strike up the *fandango*. In an instant, as if roused from the slumbers of enchantment by the magic touch of a fairy's wand, everybody started up and the whole house resounded with the uproar of clapping of hands, footing, jumping, and snapping of fingers."

El Solitario in his brilliant book *Escenas Andaluzas* divides the Spanish dances into three classes. First of all there are the dances of Spanish origin. They may be recognized by the quick rhythm of $2/4$ which accompanies coplas consisting of four or five octosyllabic lines. They resemble the *jota* of Aragon and Navarre. Secondly there are those of Moorish origin, which can be recognized by their melancholy music and by alternate slow

[1] W. Beckford, *Italy; with Sketches of Spain and Portugal*, London, 1834, vol. II, pp. 332-336.

188

Leloir, del.   Imp. Lemercier, Paris.   Bocquin lith.

Marchand d'eau.   Gens de Valence.   Gitanos   Homme de Burgos

DANCE SCENE IN THE STREETS. French colour print which shows the picturesque side of Spanish life, as imagined in the nineteenth century.

and lively dance movements. Thirdly there are those of American origin, which had migrated from Spain to America centuries ago and then returned to Spain transformed.[1] The special undulation which we see in the genuine *Baile Flamenco* is not sensual: the dance is too classical in its movements for that. But the national tendencies of the dance have been changed in America and exaggerated to the point of sensuality by what *El Solitario* calls *una ondulación de retorno*.

America has had a two-fold influence on the Andalusian dances: it has exaggerated the passiveness of the individual dances in exciting surroundings and it has exaggerated what was originally a slight tendency to eroticism. But those influences of America were introduced in the later eighteenth or the first half of the nineteenth century, for the dances of the Gypsies at Granada and Guadix are traditional and are regularly performed at the feasts of the *Calés*—Baptism, Marriage and Wake.

El Solitario contradicts the opinion of Pellicer who held that many of the ancient dances such as the Spanish *Zarabanda* and the *Chacona* had disappeared, and he maintains that those dances survived but with other names, or else entered into the steps and variations of other dances. This he proves by his analysis of the eighteenth century *bolero*, which, he says, does not go back further than the middle of the eighteenth century and is a variant of the *seguidillas*. Some said it was invented by a Manchegan nobleman called Don Sebastian Cerezo; others held that it was invented by a Sevillian coachman, Antón Boliche by name. It was, however, according to *El Solitario*, a *baile de escuela y cuenta* which Philip IV's dancing master Juan de Esquivel considered "a dance fit for gentlemen", not one *de botarga y cascabel*, which was danced by the populace in the streets. Whoever invented it did no more than adapt to the *bolero* the most attractive features of the ancient *Fandangos*, *Polos*, *Tiranas* and other dances.

In Cadiz, however, the traditional home of dancing, a dancer called Lucero Chinchilla introduced into the *bolero* variations called *glisos* which became a dazzling display of footwork. Then a medical assistant in Burgos added a further variant known as the *mata-la-araña*, and a dancer from Chiclana called "Juanillo the innkeeper" invented another offshoot called *El Laberinto* or *La Macarena*, which was still more acrobatic and complicated. *El Solitario* finds in the *bolero* steps derived from the ancient *chacona* and the traditional *bureo*, and he insists that the *Jacarandina* and even the *Zarabanda* (a genuine Moorish dance in his opinion) became later the *Olé* and the *Tirana*, but the *Zarabanda* could still in his days be heard sung and played on the guitar in all its primitive purity in certain places of Andalusia. The *bolero*, however was "all leaps and jumps" and so acrobatic that most of the dancers who specialized in it ended their days with broken legs, with the result that the Murcian dancer Requejo preferred that the dance should be purged of its "pernicious and unhealthy" elements *(todo lo pernicioso y antisalubre)*.

This suggestion caused an uproar among the *bolero* experts and they retaliated by inventing as a protest wilder dances such as the *Zorongo*, the *Fandanguillo* of Cadiz, the *Charandá*, the *Cachirulo* and other exotic dances which we ourselves have seen danced by Gypsies thirty years ago in grimy taverns in Andalusia.

What is important to note in all this evolution through the nineteenth century of the ancient popular dances is that in spite of the tendency of the dances to sink in the social level to the *Hampa* or gathering-place of the picaroons, Gypsies and the rabble, which Salillas calls *hampa delincuente*, where the moral distinction between gentleman and picaroon disappears, there is always a basic stratum of nobility and historic tradition in the dances which is characteristic of Spain.[2] It is this basis of nobility and tradition that gives the peculiar power to such manifestations of Spanish *casticismo* all over the Hispanic world. In a former book *Spanish Raggle-Taggle* (1934) we have analysed this hard ascetic element of *nobleza*, not only in the patriarchal Castilian of the Meseta like the Cid Campeador, the Conquistador or the spiritual knight, but also in the degenerate type of Don Juan Tenorio, the gallant flushed with pride and in the hungry ragged rascal Lazarillo, who with bright eyes and jaunty manner has that remnant of dignity and *nobleza* which he inherited from the race.[3]

It is that basic quality which gave such significance and impulse to the Goya revolution. How powerful that basic *nobleza* has been in the Spanish race may be gauged by the fact that Spain at the intersecting point

[1] S. Estébanez Calderón, *Escenas Andaluzas*, Madrid, 1883. See also H. Swinburne, *Travels in Spain in 1775-1776*, Dublin, pp. 243-244.
[2] R. Salinas, *Hampa*, Madrid, 1898, vol. I, p. 101.
[3] See also W. Starkie, *Don Gypsy*, p. 369.

between Europe, Africa, Asia and the Americas has acted in the world as a gigantic shock-absorber of Eastern and Western forces.   She is the only country that has been able to act as a sounding-board for oriental races, who usually give their richest sounds in it, for as Salvador de Madariaga has said significantly, Spain brought to a high degree of excellence no less than three oriental races—the Arab, the Jew and Gypsy.   It was in Spain that Arab civilization rose to its highest brilliancy; the Spanish Jews were the greatest luminaries of Hebrew civilization since Biblical times; and as for the Gypsy, the superiority of the Spanish type over any other is not to be proved by books, but by the observation of the living specimen which may be found in Andalusia.[1] But Spain is no less important today as a sounding-board for the countries in the Western Hemisphere with their Indian and coloured populations, which during the centuries of colonization have fused together and created Hispanic nations.   At the beginning of the nineteenth century, when the dramatic change occurred which transformed the destiny of the whole Hispanic world, Spain was caught as in a vice by a gigantic cultural, tactical and economic crisis—the rivalry between England and France, and that crisis descended upon her while she was in full process of evolution.   Spain alone could not fight against the two foremost powers in Europe as she had done in the sixteenth century.   Napoleon, according to the historians, lost his crown in the Spanish War of Independence, but the Peninsula was sacked and the nation was ruined.   And for many years Spain and America were without responsible government and without point of contact.   Nevertheless, in spite of the unstable political situation which lasted all through the nineteenth century up to our period, and the difficulties arising out of the lack of adequate communications, the Hispanic world forms one body socially, intellectually and even up to a certain point economically, and in our days the situation has begun to change radically owing to the new methods of transport, electricity and the wide extension of industry, which have brought about a gigantic transformation.

For this reason as we emerge from our time journey through Spanish history into the contemporary world and fly in our plane from Hispano-America across the Atlantic Ocean and descend upon the Pentagonal Island covered with its tawny bull's hide, as Strabo said two thousand years ago, we must remember that the Peninsula is the bridgehead of a great association of peoples who today influence one another mutually in a modern life of human progress.

[1] S. de Madariaga, *Spain*, London, 1946.

Throughout our musical journey through Time and Space we have continually stressed the mystical significance of the number *Seven* which constantly appears in Spanish writings and in folklore. Music was the first among the Seven Arts according to Saint Thomas Aquinas. We have the Seven Guides in Music. We speak of the Seven Mysteries of the Romanichals. Salinas divided his great History of Music into Seven books.   Here we have *The Chariot*, the magic seventh Key of the Gipsy Tarot pack of cards. This represents the Gipsy car in which the tribe wander through the world.

Through Time and Space...

THE LADY OF ELCHE *(Prado Museum)*
dating from the first half of the fifth century B.C., and discovered in 1897.
Possibly the work of an Iberian sculptor, familiar with the Græco-Asiatic art of
his time, and believed to be the portrait of a young priestess. The strange head-
dress resembles that of several Kores of the Acropolis.

a b

c d

(a) Granada: The Alhambra, the Court of Myrtles.   *(b)* The Alcazar of Seville: the fine Ambassadors' Hall decorated under Peter the Cruel.   *(c)* The ancient mosque of Córdoba, now a cathedral, with its 850 columns of precious marble.   *(d)* Granada: The Garden of Daraxa.   A poem encircles the basin of the fountain.

ty of these silver arabesques in stone...

Seville.
The Gardens of the Alcázar which were witness in the Middle Ages of the gallant adventures of King Peter the Cruel, hero of so many dramas of Lope de Vega.

"Music, first among the Seven Arts, noblest among Sciences..."

(SAINT THOMAS AQUINAS)

(a) Saint Isidore, León. In the same church, dating from the XIIth century, in the chapel of Santa Catalina, "Pantheon of Kings," eleven kings, twelve queens and twenty-one princes lay buried. *(b)* Musician angels from the cathedral of Tudela. *(c)* Musician angel from the Pórtico de la Gloria, Santiago de Compostela.

The statue of Saint James in the Pórtico of Glory (**XII**th century).   Supreme masterpiece of sculpture by Maestro Mateo, with Christ and his Apostles surrounded by angels, saints and the orchestra of the twenty-four Ancients of the Apocalypse. — Since the Middle Ages it has been a tradition for pilgrims to sing in the Pórtico of Glory and they often left behind them, as mementos, music of their countries.

Montserrat, Sanctuary of the Holy Grail and Home of religious singing

On the road to Montserrat. The Chapel of Saint Cecilia, patroness of Music (IXth century),
in the Benedictine Monastery. Amidst these mountains studded with hermitages,
according to Catalan tradition Parsifal and the Knights of the Holy Grail built their shrine.

Back of the Church of the Benedictine monastery of Montserrat.   Here the Antics Escolans, one of the most cele-brated religious choirs in the world, have preserved an unbroken tradition of choral singing from the Middle Ages.

Toledo Cathedral...

...XVIth-century reredos of the High Altar of Toledo Cathedral. It represents in its five panels scenes from the life of Christ. This masterpiece dates from the end of the flamboyant Gothic period and was the work of Spanish, Burgundian and Dutch artists.

a   b

c   d

The reredos of the High Altar of Granada Cathedral: *(a)* Isabel the Catholic; *(b)* the Baptism of the Moors; *(c)* Ferdinand of Aragón; *(d)* the Capture of Granada. The two polychrome wooden statues (left), by Felipe de Vigarny († in Toledo 1543), are in the sacristy of the Royal Chapel, where the monarchs are buried.

Three epochs of Spanish architecture: Burgos, Salamanca,

Burgos Cathedral. Sarmental gateway. French influence (XIIIth century). The Portal of the Schools of Salamanca University. A brilliant example of Plateresque style (XVIth century). Here we find medallions of the Catholic Monarchs, the escutcheons of the Emperor Charles V and at the top the Pope seated on the throne of Saint Peter.

Avila . . .

Panorama of Avila with its fortified walls.
Erected in the XIIth century with stones from Roman monuments. It has 88 towers and 8 gateways.

Panorama of Toledo, the most ancient city in the world according to Spanish
legends, some of which attribute its foundation to Hercules or to Tubal-cain. In
the foreground we see the river Tagus, the bridge of Saint Martin (XIIIth and
XIVth century). In the background we see the belltower of San Juan de los
Reyes, erected by the Catholic Monarchs to celebrate the victory of Toro in 1476
which decided that Castille and Aragón would rule Spain. Still farther in the
background we see the Cathedral and the square belltowers of Santo Tome (originally a mosque in the Moorish days), where we find El Greco's celebrated picture
The Burial of the Count of Orgaz.

Two supreme examples of Castilian genius

The Escorial, erected by Philip II in honour of Saint Laurence on whose feast day his armies had won the battle of Saint Quentin, and whose church was shelled in this same day, in 1558. He ordered his architects to give the building the shape of the gridiron on which Saint Laurence had suffered martyrdom. The building was begun in 1563 by Juan Bautista de Toledo and was finished in 1584 by Juan de Herrera. The immense monastic palace of granite, porphyry and marble, noble materials, with its eleven hundred windows, dominates the austere plateau of New Castile.

a

c

b

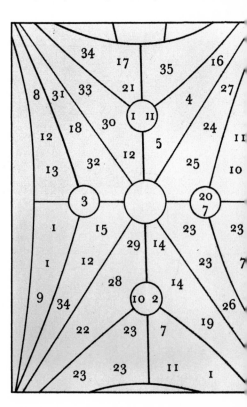

Diagram of the complete ceiling

(a) *Details from the left medallion*
(b) *Details from the right medallion*
(c) *Details from the upper center medallion*

scription of the ceiling; Centre :dallion: The Adoration of the agi.

st of the instruments played by : angels:

) Gothic harp; (2) Portable organ;) Fixed organ; (4) Manichordion, ind of cythara with keyboard, the estor of the clavichord; (5) Stringed trument, shaped like a flattened lute;) Rebeck; (8) Little viol; (9) Rota, mall harp like the welsh one; (10) te; (11) Mandora or italian lute;) Full size psaltery; (13) Half e psaltery; (14) Two reeds; (15) nch variety of bagpipe; (16) nch variety of bagpipe bombard;) Bagpipe; (18) Panpipes; (19) aight alto flute; (20) Straight r flute; (21) Double flute; (22 n; (23) Saracen horns; (24 umpet; (25) Hunting horn; (26) le metal drums; (27) Little al cavalry drums; (28) Tambou- and flageolet; (29) Bells; (30 angle; (31) Square drums; (32) ls mounted on a wooden ring;) Castanets; (34) Cymbals; (35) ee angels singing.

the XVIIIth century this chapel was incorporated in the Baroque Dalmases palace. The ceiling with its orchestra of 56 els dates from 1400 or thereabouts. The anonymous sculptor has combined fantasy with precision in such a delightful way in his trayal of the instruments and the various poses and gestures of the players that this angelic orchestra, in addition to its stic merits, possesses the highest significance for the musicologist.

Owing to its thousands of palm trees and its oriental aspect Elche has been called "the Jerusalem of the West". The palm trees were planted on the eastern coast of Spain by the Phoenicians, centuries before the Christian era. In the church of Santa Maria in Elche the celebrated Mystery Play or "Festa" de Elche takes place on the feast of the Assumption, August 14-15. Its tradition goes back to the fourteenth century.

TABLE OF PICTORIAL AND MUSICAL ILLUSTRATIONS

The musical illustrations are included in the four following records:

1ST RECORD ANCIENT MUSIC—from the VII to XVIII centuries
2ND RECORD SPAIN FROM COAST TO COAST—Folklore and Zarzuelas
3RD RECORD THE GYPSY JOURNEY—Flamenco and Cante Jondo—The Zambra in Madrid
4TH RECORD RECORDED TREASURES—Immortal Spanish Artistes

(The page number of the Pictorial Illustrations is indicated on the right-hand side—that of the comments on the Musical Illustrations is on the left)

PART I

PRELUDE

THE MESETA, coloured photograph by Loygorri, Madrid 13

CHAPTER I

SAINT JAMES, Patron Saint of Spain, popular colour print 19

SAINT JAMES, engraving from "La Légende Dorée" by Jacques de Voragine 23

23...ANTIFONA, VIIth century. Antics Escolans of Montserrat. 1ST RECORD—SIDE I—Nº. I

LIBER ETYMOLOGIARUM, page of a manuscript by St. Isidore. Royal Academy of History, Madrid 25

CHARLEMAGNE, pen-drawing by Albrecht Dürer. Oesterr. Nationalbibliothek, Vienna ... 26

CHAPTER II

THREE BISHOPS (colour). Museum of Catalan Art, Barcelona (photo Oriol Maspons, Barcelona) 29

30...CANTANTIBUS HODIE, XIIth century, Sequence of a Troparium at Vich (anonymous). Antics Escolans of Montserrat. 1ST RECORD—SIDE I—Nº. 2

30...AVE MARIS STELLA, XIIIth century (anonymous). Antics Escolans of Montserrat.
1ST RECORD—SIDE I—Nº. 3

CHAPTER III

THREE MINIATURES from the "Libro de Cantigas de Santa María", edited by Alfonso the Wise (1252-1284). Escorial Library (photo Loygorri, Madrid)

(a) Minstrels playing the cymbals 33

(b) Alfonso the Wise with his court of musicians and poets 37

(c) Christian Minstrel and Moorish Minstrel 39

40...CANTIGA Nº 353 by ALFONSO THE WISE. Antics Escolans of Montserrat and
Barcelona Wind Quintet. 1ST RECORD—SIDE I—Nº. 4

CHAPTER V

48...SA-SIBILLA (XVth-XVIth century version) (anonymous). 1ST RECORD—SIDE I—Nº. 8

CHAPTER VI

KING FERDINAND OF ARAGON AND QUEEN ISABEL OF CASTILLE, ancient engraving. Oesterr. Nationalbibliothek, Vienna 53

55...PASEABASE EL REY MORO, XVIth century. Luís de Narváez.
Sung by Nuria Quer, Eduardo Sainz de la Maza, guitar. 1ST RECORD—SIDE I—Nº. 10

*FERDINAND OF ARAGON, THE CATHOLIC KING, engraving, Oesterr. National-
bibliothek, Vienna* 56

CHAPTER VII

CHRISTOPHER COLUMBUS, anonymous engraving 59

63...RIU RIU CHIU, XVth century—Villancico (anonymous). Adapt. Miguel Querol.
Antics Escolans of Montserrat. IST RECORD—SIDE I—Nº. 5

64...ALTA DANZA, XVth century. Francísco de la Torre. Adapt. Miguel Querol.
Barcelona Wind Quintet. IST RECORD—SIDE I—Nº. 6

64...VIRGEN BENDITA, XVth century. Pedro de Escobar. Adapt. Miguel Querol.
Antics Escolans of Montserrat. IST RECORD—SIDE I—Nº. 7

CHAPTER VIII

*EXTRACT from "DECLARACION DE INSTRUMENTOS" by Juan Bermudo, Ossuna
(1555). Bibliothèque Nationale, Paris* 72

CHAPTER IX

*EL DELFIN DE MUSICA, title page of the Treatise on the Lute. Luís de Narváez. British
Museum, London* 73

*CRISTOBAL DE MORALES (1500-1553), Italian drawing. Real Academia de la
Historia, Madrid* 74

FRANCISCO GUERRERO (1527-1599), engraving. Real Academia de la Historia, Madrid 74

*ORPHEUS PLAYING THE VIHUELA, title-page of "El Maestro" by Luís Milán,
British Museum, London* 79

*THE SEVEN ORDERS OF THE VIHUELA, extract from "DECLARACION DE
INSTRUMENTOS" by Juan Bermudo, Ossuna (1555). Bibliothèque Nationale, Paris* ... 80

81...PASEABASE EL REY MORO, XVIth century. Luís de Narváez.
Sung by Nuria Quer, Eduardo Sainz de la Maza, guitar. IST RECORD—SIDE I—Nº. 10

*DIAGRAM INDICATING POSITIONS FOR MADRIGAL SINGERS, engraving from
the book "DECLARACION DE INSTRUMENTOS" by Juan Bermudo, Ossuna (1555).
Bibliothèque Nationale, Paris* 82

CHAPTER X

QUEEN JOAN THE MAD, anonymous engraving. Oesterr. Nationalbibliothek, Vienna 84

CHARLES V, portrait by Titian. The Prado Museum, Madrid (Photo Loygorri, Madrid) ... 87

*ISABEL OF PORTUGAL, portrait by Titian. The Prado Museum, Madrid (Photo Loygorri-
Jafer, Madrid)* 91

CHAPTER XI

PHILIP II, anonymous engraving. Oesterr. Nationalbibliothek, Vienna 99

101...DIFERENCIAS SOBRE EL CANTO DEL CABALLERO, XVIth century. Antonio de
Cabezón (1510-1566). Esther Nadal de Janés, harpsichord. IST RECORD—SIDE I—Nº. 11

106..MAGNUM MYSTERIUM, Motet. Cristóbal de Morales (1500-1553). Antics Escolans
of Montserrat. IST RECORD—SIDE I—Nº. 12

108...EN EL CAMPO ME METI, XVth century, Villancico. Antics Escolans of Montserrat.
IST RECORD—SIDE I—Nº. 9

108...ESCLARECIDA MADRE, religious madrigal. Francísco Guerrero. Antics Escolans
of Montserrat. IST RECORD—SIDE II—Nº. 1

PHILIP II, drawing by Titian, Chantilly Museum 108

111...O VOS OMNES. 1ST RECORD—SIDE 11—Nº. 2. Tomás Luís de Victoria (1550-1611).
Adapt. Dom David Pujol. Mixed Choir of the Montserrat Monastery
THE ENTOMBMENT OF CHRIST, polychrome sculpture by Juan de Juni (1507-1577).
Museum of Valladolid (Photo Loygorri, Madrid) 113

CHAPTER XII

COMMEDIA DELL'ARTE, Harlequin, Corneto and Pantalon, anonymous engraving. Phot.
Archives, Paris 117
124...CANARIO, XVIIIth-century dance. Gaspar Sánz (1640-1710). Adapt. Germán
Lago. Orquesta Ibérica de Madrid, dir. Germán Lago. 1ST RECORD—SIDE 11—Nº. 5
ADORATION OF THE SHEPHERDS, painting by El Greco. The Prado Museum, Madrid 125
THE FOUNTAIN OF THE TRITONS, painting by Velasquez. The Prado Museum, Madrid 129
QUEEN ISABEL OF BOURBON, painting by Velasquez. The Prado Museum, Madrid 131
(Photos Loygorry-Jafer, Madrid)
135...SON TUS BELLOS OJOS SOLES, XVIIth century. Juan Cererols (1618-1676),
Antics Escolans of Montserrat. 1ST RECORD—SIDE 11—Nº. 3
135...VUELA, PALOMA DIVINA, XVIIth century. Juan Cererols (1618-1676).
Lolita Torrentó and Assunción Serra. Esther Nadal de Janés, harpsichord.
1ST RECORD—SIDE 11—Nº. 4

CHAPTER XIII

BAROQUE XVIIIth-CENTURY STAGE DESIGN by JUVARRA taken from "Denkmäler
des Theaters" by Joseph Gregor. Oesterr. Nationalbibliothek, Vienna (Photo Luc Joubert, Paris) 149
PORPORA (1687-1767), engraving by Biondi. Oesterr. Nationalbibliothek, Vienna 153
MARIA LOUISA OF SAVOY, anonymous engraving. Oesterr. Nationalbibliothek, Vienna... 153
PHILIP V, anonymous engraving. Oesterr. Nationalbibliothek, Vienna 153
METASTASIO, anonymous engraving. Oesterr. Nationalbibliothek, Vienna 153
Carlo Broschi, called FARINELLI (1705-1782), engraving by Wagner (1735). Oesterr.
Nationalbibliothek, Vienna 154
THREE PAGES OF A MANUSCRIPT BY FARINELLI. Oesterr. Nationalbibliothek, Vienna 154
160...ALLEGRO PASTORILE from the QUINTET Nº. 3, XVIIIth century. Fray Antonio
Soler (1729-1783). Agrup. de Música de Cámara de Barcelona. 1ST RECORD—SIDE 11—Nº. 7
160...VILLANCICOS DE NAVIDAD, Francísco Morena. The little singers of the
Capilla Clásica. 1ST RECORD—SIDE 11—Nº. 6

CHAPTER XIV

JOAQUIN COSTILLARES, colour print by Juan de la Cruz... 161
170...ALMA SINTAMOS, XVIIIth-century Tonadilla, Pablo Esteve (1730-1792). Adapt.
Joaquín Nín. Lolita Torrentó, soprano, and Orch. dir. Rafael Ferrer.
1ST RECORD—SIDE 11—Nº. 8
A STEP OF THE SEGUIDILLAS BOLERAS, popular colour print... 173
GOYA, a self-portrait (1746-1828) (Frontispiece of the "Caprices") 179
A SCENE OF SHOOTING from "The Disasters of War", etching by Goya (1810)... ... 179
PAROCHIAL FESTIVAL AT VALENCE in 1862, engraving by A. Rouargue 180

CHAPTER XV

LA MALIBRAN, painting of the English School (Photo Luc Joubert, Paris) 185
A STREET SCENE, early XIXth-century colour print 189
THE "CHARIOT" of the Gypsy Tarot pack of cards 193

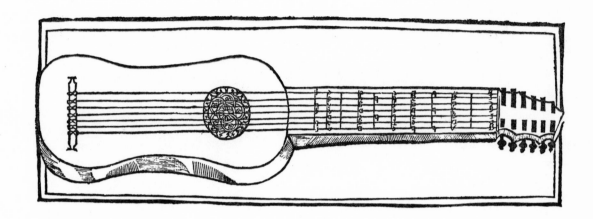

First Part

THE MUSICAL JOURNEY THROUGH TIME

Introduction   5

Preface   11

PRELUDE

    THE BULL'S HIDE   13
        The Central Meseta
        The Coastal Periphery
        Tartessian Spain
        The Phoenicians and the Greeks
        The Romans
        The Visigoths

CHAPTER I

    SAINT ISIDORE OF SEVILLE, THE FIRST SPANISH MUSICIAN   17
        The Mozarabic liturgy
        Córdoba, the sacred city of the Moslems
        The discovery of the tomb of Saint James
        The Ordeal by fire

CHAPTER II

GREGORIAN CHANT—CLUNY AND CHARLEMAGNE ... ... 🐦 27

CHAPTER III

ALFONSO THE WISE—MINSTRELS AND TROUBADOURS ... 🐦 31
Minstrels on the road of Saint James
Alfonso the Wise and the Canticles
A celebrated woman minstrel
The tragedy of Alfonso the Wise

CHAPTER IV

THE GOLDEN TREASURY OF THE MINSTRELS   ... ... 🐦 41

CHAPTER V

THE SONG OF THE SIBYL   ... ... 🐦 47

CHAPTER VI

MUSIC IN THE FIFTEENTH CENTURY ... ... 🐦 51
Ferdinand of Aragon and Isabel the Catholic
The Romancero and the War of Granada
Colophon

CHAPTER VII

MUSIC AT THE COURT OF FERDINAND AND ISABEL ... ... 🐦 57
The Rise of Polyphony in the Isabeline Renaissance
Juan del Encina (1469-1534), Poet, Composer
and Patriarch of the Spanish Theatre

CHAPTER VIII

THE MYSTERY PLAY AT ELCHE   ... ... 🐦 65

CHAPTER IX

VALENCIA IN THE RENAISSANCE   ... ... 🐦 75
The Lutenists of the Spanish Renaissance

CHAPTER X

MUSIC IN THE REIGN OF CHARLES V ... ... 🐦 83

CHAPTER XI

PHILIP II, THE MAECENAS OF SPANISH MUSIC   95
  Philip II's Journey to England
  Music at the English Court in the sixteenth century
  Antonio Cabezón "the Spanish Bach", and his influence
  Shakespeare and Music
  Berruguete, Palestrina and the Counter-Reformation
  Cristóbal de Morales (1500-1553)
  Francisco Guerrero (1527-1599)
  Tomás Luis de Victoria (1540-1611)
  The Spanish Counter-Reformation and Music

CHAPTER XII

MUSIC AND THE THEATRE IN THE SEVENTEENTH
CENTURY IN ITALY AND SPAIN   115
  Music, the Cinderella of the Arts in the Renaissance
  The masked improvised play of the Commedia dell'Arte
  The Spanish Comedia
  Music and Dancing in the Spanish Theatre
  Lope de Vega, portent of nature (1562-1635)
  Velasquez, chronicler of Philip IV
  Philip IV and Isabel, Patrons of the Theatre
  The origin of the Zarzuela
  Calderón and his Autos Sacramentales
  Naples under Spanish domination in the seventeenth century

CHAPTER XIII

THE EIGHTEENTH CENTURY   143
  Philip V and Elizabeth Farnese
  The story of the King, the Minstrel and the Poet
  Domenico Scarlatti (1685-1757)
  Antonio Soler (1729-1783)

CHAPTER XIV

THE SPANISH REVIVAL IN DRAMA AND MUSIC   163
  The Madrid of Ramón de la Cruz
  Goya

CHAPTER XV

THE SPANISH MUSICAL DEMON SPREADS ITS WINGS ...   181
  The musical dynasty of the García Family from 1775 to 1946

Table of pictorial and musical illustrations   213

PRINTED IN SWITZERLAND